Ed Melet

The architectural detail

Dutch architects visualise their concepts

Wiel Arets

Benthem Crouwel

CEPEZED

Erick van Egeraat

Herman Hertzberger

Mecanoo

MVRDV

OMA

Hans Ruijssenaars

UN Studio

Rudy Uytenhaak

Koen van Velsen

NAi Publishers Rotterdam

Contents

The architectural detail

The architectural detail
God is not in the detail

The quest for the architectural meaning of the detail in contemporary Dutch architecture is based on a large number of questions. Is God still in the detail, is the detail a condensation of the architectural concept, or are details something belonging to old-fashioned architecture and should we therefore be aiming for a no-detail architecture? Are details just joints; as small parts of the whole, are they an essential part of the composition, or should details be assigned spatial properties? Can details lack scale? Can, or rather should they assume the form of an ornament again? Where is the border of detail fetishism? How are details experienced? In what way do engineering details differ from architectural details?

The last question is apparently the easiest to answer. Architectural details are designed details, the result of an intensive design process. The final form is more the outcome of a creative than of a technical process, and its creation is therefore comparable to the way in which the form of the building, the ground plan, the composition of the façades or the choice of materials are determined. In each case a number of limiting conditions (urban development criteria, programme of requirements, technical possibilities) form the parameters, but it is the architect's vision that in the last resort determines what the building, the ground plan, the materials and thus also the details will look like within those parameters. So an architectural detail tells us a lot about the architect's philosophy. And since it is a question by definition of the smallest and thus the easiest level of scale to manipulate, the detail is perhaps even the most direct expression of that philosophy.

So in the first instance the technical side plays a subordinate role, and that is perhaps remarkable for something that handles the architectural transition from one surface to another and from one material to another. If something goes wrong (leaks, thermal bridges), it is always at these joints. Since these details at the same time determine the way the building is conceived, it is only after the architectural problems of the different transitions have been resolved that the architectural details are resolved in technical terms. Of course, the by definition non-standard nature of these architecturally important details entails a risk. They are details which require rethinking the joints and layers. The architects deliberately seek this challenge. Sometimes the technical result is hopelessly wrong.

Sometimes a façade turns out to be very maintenance-sensitive or even incapable of being maintained (like the façade of the Technical College by EEA), parts of it fall off (as in the case of UN Studio's De Kolk in Amsterdam), or the roof leaks (the roof of OMA's Kunsthal or of Wiel Arets' police station in Vaals).

It is also certainly the case that the appreciation of a building is partly determined – at any rate in the long term – by the qualities of the details. Nevertheless, this book is not about mistakes of this kind. Without wanting to underestimate the importance of technical perfection – no one wants a building that functions badly or grows ugly with age, and buildings remain functional objects – it is clear that, if architects want to put the ambition of the design into a building without making too many concessions, they will have to walk a tight-rope. The architectural detail is of inestimable importance in how the architecture of a building is experienced. Ben van Berkel and Caroline Bos are right in stating that in the long run architectural idealism is best expressed in the details: 'Long after the idiomatic treatment of the whole has been exhausted, details can provide new insights and surprising discoveries that determine the vitality of a building'.[1]

To give details such a status, new paths of engineering have to be entered, and this naturally entails risks. It is not for nothing that Berlage's municipal museum in The Hague leaked, and the anecdote about one of Frank Lloyd Wright's villas is recounted with relish. Wright was called one night by a furious client who told him that there was a leak right above his place at the dining table. 'Then you'd better sit somewhere else,' Wright replied. This laconic reply makes it clear that the dividing line between what was and what was not technically feasible at that moment had been deliberately or unintentionally overstepped in order to create the architecture that he envisaged, but also that living and/or working in architecturally progressive buildings can entail risks like these. As Wiel Arets once put it: 'Whoever is frightened of architecture and its harshness had better leave it'.[2]

The extent to which architectural details are dangerous in technical terms depends on the architectural ambitions, but also and above all on the technical ability to make the building wind-proof and water-proof without making too many concessions to its architectural look. This book is primarily about how the architectural ambitions are translated in the details, about the architectural story behind a chosen detail strategy.

Of the firms of architects discussed in this book, Benthem Crouwel Architekten is probably the one that comes closest to the current standard and/or bureau details. There is a simple reason for this: these details are completely logical and have proved themselves in the past. Jan Benthem and Mels Crouwel aim to make buildings with rapidly legibly ground plans and explicable materials with clear details. This reduces the risk of confusion during the elaboration of the design and during the construction of the building, and with it the risk of mistakes. Incidentally, mistakes are not always ruled out, as can be seen, for example, from the Malietoren in The Hague, which was surrounded by scaffolding for months because of the risk that sheets of glass might fall to the ground. The fact that their buildings are not standard is partly connected with their feeling for using materials in the right places just slightly differently from what is usual, as well as with the higher appreciation of carefully selected details. This takes place by making the details architectural and in some cases by translating the original technical functions into ornamental elements. As may be expected from architects who were originally regarded as high tech architects, they made and still make aesthetic constructions, as in the Terminal West at Schiphol Airport or the roof construction of the Villa Arena in Amsterdam. However, the roof edges of some Benthem Crouwel buildings are festive canopies, as in the Anne Frank House in Amsterdam → 1, the Malietoren → 2, and the Groningen Provincial Hall. In the 013 pop music centre in Tilburg they used CDs to make the EPDM-façades look like a buttoned façade. → 3 The fact that they can play this game without running into technical problems is because they make a very controlled use of these kinds of 'mutations'. Their great technical knowledge enables Benthem and Crouwel to know how far they can go with their modifications of the standards before these changes lead to completely new details that are difficult to manage. They make clever use of the margins in the building. In addition, the firm has a large number of engineers in its employ to make sure that these architectural details have a solid technical foundation.

The strategy adopted by Benthem Crouwel has led some,

not entirely without justification, to regard their buildings as too 'safe'. Many other firms run more risks in their choice of materials and handling of detail, while some of them at the same time do not want the burden of a large technical apparatus for the elaboration of the designs. These firms confine themselves to concepts or contours for the details, as medieval architects did. The technical implications of the specific details were solved at that time by the different craftsmen on the spot – which was possible in those days because of the low pressure of time, the low labour costs and above all the high quality of the craftsmanship – while in the present-day variant engineering consultancies are brought in to do the job. They have to ensure that the details are (relatively) easy to make, comply with current regulations, without doing violence to the architect's signature, because the ideas about architecture, as we have seen, are legible, among other places, in the details.

The customers of consultancies of this kind include foreign architects with a project in the Netherlands who have to bring the details into line with Dutch regulations, small and/or inexperienced firms of architects who simply do not have the capacity to elaborate larger or more complicated projects completely, and firms that regard themselves primarily as architecture studios and want to keep the more banal aspects of engineering out of the design process as much as possible because this knowledge would frustrate their creativity too much, and because a focus on the technical side would divert attention too much from what matters most: the architectural concept.

MVRDV and Neutelings Riedijk Architecten belong to the latter category of firms of architects. There is an enormous difference between the approaches to detail of the two firms in spite of the similarity in the technical elaboration of the designs and in their background – not only Willem Jan Neutelings, but also Winy Maas and Jacob van Rijs from MVRDV have worked for Rem Koolhaas' Office for Metropolitan Architecture.

Conceptual details

MVRDV makes details that follow naturally from the concept; the details more of less give the concept away. This is almost classical, and the details seem to match the description by the critic Dietmar Steiner: 'Where architecture comes to the point, the work is condensed to become a miniature of itself. Details are like batteries that are charged with the energy of the architectural work, the biography of the architect, his philosophy, and his relationship to things'.[3] The rest of Steiner's article concentrates on the ornamental qualities that details can have by which they detach themselves from the building and can be regarded as independently operating and designed elements. MVRDV, however, concentrates in the concept on a series of sparse and

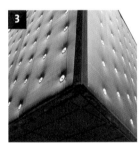

sometimes, if the concept demands it, harsh details. Nevertheless, the details explain the idea behind the design and say a lot about the architectural philosophy of MVRDV. A hollow block like the bright orange studio cum house in Amsterdam → **4, 5** or the design for the Nijmegen Polytechnic is made as nothing more than a hollow block. Windows and doors are sharply cut out elements that are kept as detail-free as possible. Every element (doors, frames, security devices) has the same colour as the synthetic skin. → **4** Even the letter-box is just a slit. A volume which seems to have been cut off arbitrarily like the Villa VPRO in Hilversum was originally intended to show the roughly finished sides of the concrete floor plates where the glass façade ran in front – a detail that the client considered too dangerous. → **6**
The design of the Expo 2000 pavilion contains a very striking example of the detail that gives away the concept. → **7** On the floor with the forest, heavy wooden tree trunks are used for the columns, and this constructional solution fits in perfectly with the image of the forest. However, the steel joints are clearly accentuated at top and bottom. With these details, that seem to feature almost as autonomous elements, MVRDV seems to have made an architectural version of René Magritte's painting *Ceci n'est pas une pipe*. What looked like a forest is actually an artificial forest. This reinforces the impact of the building and of the forest on the fourth floor, and unambiguously gets across MVRDV's idea that nature is something that has to be constructed.
The concept for Villa VPRO betrayed the large influence of Herman Hertzberger's Centraal Beheer building in Apeldoorn. Hertzberger also seems to have influenced MVRDV to some extent at the level of the detail. As Hertzberger did with buildings like Centraal Beheer, MVRDV makes the structure of the building legible in the façades and in the programme of details. Moreover, in elaborating the design Hertzberger followed the idea of the architectural order, in which the smallest part is a logical consequence of the whole, just as the whole is a

logical consequence of the smallest part. Such a direct translation of the concept in the detail is also visible in most of MVRDV's buildings. In the case of MVRDV, however, the traffic is in one direction only: the detail is derived from the concept, but vice versa the detail is certainly not allowed to exert any influence on the concept. Finally, both firms use details to influence the behaviour of the users. MVRDV expected that the original façade detail of the Villa VPRO, with glass running in front of the concrete, would generate extra maintenance because everyone wants to avoid its getting dirty; Hertzberger deliberately left some parts of his buildings incomplete so that the users could take possession of them. → **8**
The main difference between these two firms lies in the use of the quantity of details. MVRDV is satisfied with just a few details, while Hertzberger tried to control the building down to the tiniest details.
In a certain sense Hertzberger's original treatment of details, in which the detail was directly derived from the total form, is reasonably close to the notion of the fractal detail introduced by the French mathematician Benoît Mandelbrot. (Mandelbrot's theory of fractals was first published in 1975.) → **9** Mandelbrot has carried out intensive research on mathematical fractals and on the side he has also looked into the possibility of architectural fractals. A property of fractals is that the total form consists of a large number of fractals with the same (or virtually the same) shape as the total form. A number of baroque buildings can be called more or less fractal (at least the ground plan), but it is hardly applicable to present-day buildings. Daniel Libeskinds Victoria and Albert Museum (London, 1996-) has façades that consist of fractals. → **10** The relation between the tiniest detail and the form of the building in the buildings of Hertzberger mentioned above is strong enough for them to be called fractal-like, even if they cannot really be considered fractals.
Incidentally, Hertzberger has abandoned this specific and exhausting approach to the detail by now. He has also given up the strict rules of structuralism to satisfy his demand for greater architectural freedom. That the detail has acquired a larger scale is above all connected with the changing position of power of the architect. Without the backing of the client, who has scant regard for the importance of the detail, instead of making spaces dominated by the series of details, the architect now makes mainly spatial areas with the corresponding big details. Zooming in is only done at strategic points such as the recurrent walkways, steel steps and balustrades. The controlled retreat of the architect is also visible in the detailing of the façade. Instead of façades in which the structure can be read off and which have a refined programme of details, Hertzberger is making more sculptural, even more chaotic forms in which the

9

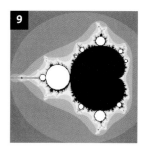

contours of the functionality of the building are only dimly visible.

Sculptural details

Like MVRDV, the firm of Neutelings Riedijk avoids the traditional architectural details as far as possible. However, they do not use the façade to illustrate the concept of the building as MVRDV does, but treat it as a more or less autonomous thing that is laid over the building. The casing envelops the technical elements. 'Normal' technical details that place too much emphasis on the different elements, on the traditional composition of the façade, are avoided in this way. The spray concrete façade of the Minnaert building (Utrecht, 1997) → **11**, for example, is extended just beyond the frames, and it was the intention to make this spray concrete façade curl over the edge of the roof too; the ventilation grilles of the Maastricht fire station (1999) are placed behind the zip-like seams between the prefab elements; and the windows of the Veenman press in Ede (1997) are situated behind sheets of glass printed with letters. The many incisions that are required to turn a building into a sculpture are sharply detailed, while the overhangs that were just as necessary are genuine overhangs as a result of the materials that have been applied everywhere. Neutelings Riedijk has no qualms about making use of ornaments to achieve the effect of a single sculptural body. In fact, in his column 'Tattoo, decoration and taboo', Neutelings delivers a passionate plea for the reintro-duction of the ornament boycotted by the Modernists: 'Since the eighties the division between public and private has once more become stricter, but more ambiguous and versatile too [...]. Accordingly, the façade is once again the mediator between public and private, the elevation of public space rather than the extension of privatised internal space. It is a ground in the chaos of urban space that can be charged with meaning using iconographic appliqué or decorative pattern. [...] Appliqué provides an extra compositional layer,

liberating façade design from this one-dimensionality, and impacts on the scale of the entire building as well as that of public space. Moreover, building technology has turned the façade into a distinct "apron", permanently separating interior and exterior with its air cavity and insulation blanket. These days the façade is an ornamental membrane [...].'[4]

Neutelings uses the ornament to emphasise the unity of the sculptural skin. The 'creasing' in the skin of the Minnaert building, the wooden panels that conceal the vertical joints between the Eternit plates of the tower block in Amsterdam ('IJ-toren', 1998) → **12**, and the profile of a Michelin tyre in the prefab plates of the Maastricht fire station all stress the whole, the monolithic instead of the separate elements. They are thus completely different ornaments from those of the artists of the Viennese Sezession referred to by Adolf Loos in his famous *Ornament und Verbrechen* [Ornament and Crime]. Those ornaments were above all an illustration of the craftsmanship of the designer, and especially of the sculptor. Loos considered making ornament to be a waste of material and labour power, and besides he regarded ornaments as too élitist a decoration. In the buildings of architects like Josef Maria Olbrich, Josef Hoffmann and Otto Wagner, the ornaments are isolated, non-functional decorations that have no connection with the architectural concept. → **13** They were used purely for their beauty. (J.M. Olbrich, Wiener Sezession, Vienna, 1898)

Beauty – if such a concept can be defined – is not the principle of the treatment of detail of Neutelings Riedijk (nor of MVRDV). This approach to the detail also marks a break with the traditional approach to detail that is still followed by most firms of architects today. The detail was and is not just the illustration of what the architect wanted, but it is also a demonstration of his technical capacity. The architects who focus on the concept – on the inner structure of the buildings – see little point in showing off their technical skill. That is not where their strength lies. Willem Jan Neutelings actually finds the technical aspect of his details so uninteresting – he is interested in what they look like, not how they are made – that he was not prepared to lend his detail drawings for this book. That is why his work does not appear in this volume, in spite of his unmistakably interesting approach to detail from an architectural point of view.

Ornamental details

Many other Dutch architects also use ornamental elements to enrich their façades. This is not very surprising, for in spite of the rejection of the ornament by Louis Sullivan and Loos and their call for pure architecture, the Modernists like Le Corbusier, Mies van der Rohe, Alvar Aalto and Louis Kahn made use of the ornament to give their buildings the look they were

after. In an article in a special issue of *l'Architecture d'Aujourd'hui* on ornament, Norman Foster defends this approach by claiming that it is difficult to indicate the difference between ornament and detail in Aalto's work, but that it is ridiculous to label ornaments of this kind as criminal: 'They are pure poetry'.[5] That is why a number of Dutch firms of architects deploy ornaments too. They want to use the ornament to achieve a prewar richness, though of course this takes place now in a different way from in Aalto's buildings. First of all, the details are simpler and 'more functional'. Moreover, they are less independent elements. They are primarily used to accentuate the way in which the surface of the façade or the concept of the building has been conceived on the outside.

Although Hans Ruijssenaars calls himself an illegitimate child of Johannes Duiker and Louis Kahn, the merging of these two great Modernist architects has led to a series of ornamental elements that make his buildings both recognisable and completely non-Modern. They seem to be more inspired by Italian architecture of the seventeenth and eighteenth centuries. He applies arcades of extremely slender columns to his buildings, and these arcades regularly grip the timber roof frame that supports the overhanging roof by means of circular steel elements. → **14, 15** Yet the columns are not required by the construction. The irregular surfaces of his façades are decorated with glass eaves or a variation on them. → **16** The bricks are never just stacked. The bricks are whitewashed – never plastered, because the materiality must remain in sight – or he applies special bonds to make an entity of the façade while continuing it around the corner. Finally, towers stand independently next to the building, or canopies float above the volume. They both serve as an extra landmark. However strange it may sound, the final result is the incredible mixture of Duiker and Kahn. The materiality of Kahn (achieved by means of the whitewashed brickwork façades, as well as by the use of glass bricks) is alleviated by the use of ornaments; the

arcades, the glass elements and the overhanging roofs soften the transition between the building and its surroundings. (Yale University Art Gallery, New Haven, Connecticut, 1953) → **17**

Rudy Uytenhaak also uses the ornament as a weapon to give his façades three-dimensionality. Where Neutelings and Riedijk use ornaments as a means of emphasising the building as a sculptural entity, Ruijssenaars tries to find it in a literal layeredness by means of separate elements, and their autonomy is confirmed in the detail, Uytenhaak searches for it in a deepening of the surface of the façade itself. As he puts it himself, he wants to give the façade a nap and thereby to give the façades a nineteenth-century richness using present-day materials and techniques. He wants to compose unusual textures. To a large extent he achieves this by manipulating the material. His bricks are wavy, cut short or have a trapezoid shape, enabling the creation of different reliefs by means of different bonds → **18**; his prefabricated concrete elements are placed like roof tiles and tilt slightly forwards, which gives the flat façade depth. Moreover, the material of each façade is treated in a different way, simply because the context of that specific façade is different. The meeting of the different façades with or more or less different materials is accentuated with details in which the materials are kept as detached from one another as possible.

Uytenhaak's fascination with a rich use of material closely resembles that of the Italian architect Carlo Scarpa. The balustrades in the House of the Arts in Apeldoorn have a large number of different handrails, so that it is almost possible to feel your way through the complex building, and he also turns the connections between the different surfaces into something ornamental. The composition of his façades, however clearly betrays the influence of Mies van der Rohe. The wooden jambs on which thin sheets of glass are fixed, the concrete jambs in the housing complex in the Weesperstraat → **19**, are Uytenhaak's translations of Mies' façades enriched with I-profiles.

Details without scale

Mies and Scarpa are the most admired detailers of the twentieth century. Scarpa adopted a fragmentary approach to material and detail. He thought much more in materials than in spaces. His details were the ultimate illustration of the rich material compositions and not of the perfect façade composition or a graphically brilliant ground plan, as was the case with Mies. Each space was materialised in a different way, every corridor, transition, corner and ledge was singled out by Scarpa to emphasise the 'materiality of the materials'. → **20** Unlike Mies, who regarded his buildings as an inviolable work of art, Scarpa chose materials that weathered and looked better under the influence of the sun, wind and rain.

→ **21** He was not looking for the cool perfection that Mies was after. Scarpa did not mind if a straight line with handmade tiles wobbled a little. He allowed parts of his buildings to become overgrown with greenery. His buildings are alive. (20, 21, 25: Brion cemetery, S. Vito d'Altivole, Treviso, 1969)

All the same, the critique of Scarpa is harsh. He constructed series of interesting details, not buildings. His buildings are not spatially interesting. In their article 'Het ideale detail: thema en motief' [The ideal detail: theme and motif], Ben van Berkel and Caroline Bos from UN Studio try to give Scarpa's approach to detail an architectural charge: '[in the work of Scarpa] the detail assumes the form of the Leitmotiv. The fact that Scarpa confers such independence on the detail has sometimes led to his work being interpreted as fragmented, lacking in harmony, and de-compositional. This is because people vainly persist in believing that the detail should occupy a subordinate position, and become confused if they are confronted with the work of an architect who examined the details of his buildings by night with a torch to get them better into focus. By daylight it would be impossible to isolate the detail from its surroundings in such a way.'[6] That is precisely the criticism that has always been levelled at Scarpa: the details are brilliant when seen in isolation, but they have much less significance as an underlining of the architectural concept or expression of the structure or use of the building.

Although the work of UN Studio pays considerable attention to the design of the individual detail (leading its critics to compare it with a cabinetmaker, especially in connection with the earliest projects), unlike the details of Scarpa, this detail does not stand by itself. UN Studio sees the façade as a whole and uses the details to reinforce that impression of a single entity.

Sometimes the details serve as a kind of vague illustration of the horizontal structure of the building, as in the IJsselstein municipal office or the Het Valkhof Museum in Nijmegen. → **22** It is equally common for the façade to appear as an autonomous entity that has been folded around the building (the REMU building, Karbouw, NMR laboratory and the bridgemaster's house in Purmerend → **23**). The precision in the detailing of the skin ensures continuous lines and accentuates the sculptural form of the building. It confers structure on the façade; it gives the skin a contour, without its becoming a direct translation of the building. The use of the building is not a direct starting point for the design, let alone for the detail. Van Berkel and Bos design parametrically: various parameters are fed into the computer, and the computer then takes charge of a large part of the design on the basis of these limiting conditions. UN Studio also chooses fascinating natural phenomena (the magnetic field for the laboratory for Nuclear Magnetic Resonance in Utrecht), (mathematical) shapes (the Moebius strip for the villa in Het Gooi), or a Chinese character → **24** (the IJsselstein municipal office) as the basis for the form. The detail is used by UN Studio to accentuate the structures generated by these forms. In his text 'Storing the Detail', Van Berkel describes strategies to get the details to take on this function.[7] They are partly abstracted, and partly made lacking in scale. The details in Scarpa's work are 'subject' and are purely orientated towards pleasing, while in the UN Studio buildings they are at most 'indirect object' because they are structural and thus often lacking in scale, but also because they can be abstracted.

Desirable details

The sensitive treatment of detail with precisely combined and often contrasting materials that are primarily out to please, as Scarpa practised it, is now most clearly followed by Mecanoo and by EEA (Erick van Egeraat Associated architects). Van Egeraat was a member of the Mecanoo collective for several years. Their strategy of 'upgrading banal materials through their context' is not very different from Scarpa's.[8] Scarpa combined rough concrete cast on site, in which the formwork seams remains visible, with expensive natural stone and gilt frames. → **25** Mecanoo combined teak with concrete for the studio cum house in Rotterdam. → **26** What is at stake is the beauty, creating an atmosphere that appeals to everyone. Mecanoo and Van Egeraat are primarily out to please, or as Van Egeraat puts is: 'Architects should simply make tasteful buildings'.[9] By tasteful he means above all plenty of a new, impulsive baroque that is not based on any mathematical foundations. 'The critic Hans van Dijk recently wrote that Rem Koolhaas is the only innovative Dutch architect and that all the others are merely concerned with putting together nice materials. I think that's utter rubbish. The advantage of good contemporary architecture is precisely that there's space for those things that are not strictly necessary, that extra bit is what makes life interesting.' And 'On the one hand you have this reverence for modernism with its flirtation with the virginity of white walls and large boxes; every architect gets a kick out of making a detail where there's nothing further to experience. And on the other, there's a strange need for designs like those in The Hague where Rob Krier is trying to create a more friendly, humane architecture using postmodern classicism. It's thought, quite wrongly, that these two poles are mutually exclusive. It is assumed that contemporary and humane can never go hand in hand. [...] What concerns me [...] is how to use contemporary means to produce emotional architecture.'[10]

So Van Egeraat applies screened glass façades, sets glass in front of closed concrete walls or a banal material like rockwool. → **27** He designs bizarre shapes like a conference room suspended in the glass roof in the shape of a whale → **28**, the protruding glass entrance in his design for the new NOS building, or a misshapen copper body as a pop venue, Mezz, in Breda. His details add to the richness he is striving for and he is usually successful in his aim of creating layered and exciting buildings. Scarpa is under fire because his materials were chosen purely for their beauty and tactile qualities. The work of Mecanoo has been criticised on similar lines. In the article 'On stagnation and innovation' to which Van Egeraat referred, critic Hans van Dijk introduced the term 'aesthetic pragmatism'.[11] Instead of concerning themselves with essential questions about architecture and the content of the profession, Van Dijk argued that the majority of architects incorporate the programme as pragmatically as possible in a building envelope, which is then covered with tasteful, often tactile materials. In his view, the cladding no longer has any meaning except that it is used to please the users of the building. In an earlier article, critic Roemer van Toorn had already claimed that firms like Mecanoo make architecture purely for architecture's sake and that the ideological

component of the heroic Modernists has been levelled out.[12] The detail, according to these critics, is too design-like, too detached from what the architecture ought to be saying. However, Wiel Arets argues that it is precisely the severing of modern architecture from the ideology of the heroic Modernists that has created an enormous freedom that makes it possible to combine new forms, precisely because they have lost their ideological freedom and are thus open to new interpretations.[13] Janny Rodermond writes in a reaction to the introduction of aesthetic pragmatism that 'prettifying is directly linked to the empty-headedness of the architect. Aesthetics and pragmatism, however, are not terms that can be used by themselves to distinguish "good" from "bad" architecture. Pragmatic architecture is almost a tautology, since there is no building that cannot be experienced. If this property is taken into account in any way during the design stage, that seems to me an important quality [...] Actual pragmatic architecture focuses not only on the budget, but also on the spatiality and tactile quality of an object'.[14] Indeed, there seems little wrong with buildings that are not only practical and spatially interesting, but are also fitted with materials and details that are considered simply 'beautiful' by the majority.

Incidentally, since the departure of Van Egeraat from Mecanoo and perhaps also in reaction to the criticism of their architecture, Mecanoo's work does display a change of direction. The forms are still attractive and the choice of materials is still primarily intended to be found attractive, but the detail fetishism has also partly gone. This can be seen, for example, from the St Mary of the Angels Chapel in Rotterdam, whose detailing is much less precise and perhaps less sterile than in the earlier Mecanoo buildings. → **29** So both firms try in their own way – Van Egeraat by using unusual shapes, layeredness and unexpected materials, Mecanoo by admitting a degree of roughness – to heighten the tension. As in the case of Ruijssenaars and Uytenhaak, the choice of materials and the handling of detail, however, display a non-Modernist exuberance.

Minimal details

Although Van Dijk's article cites Koen van Velsen as *the* example of an aesthetic pragmatist, he is in fact the opposite. Van Velsen discusses his work in an incredibly down to earth way – in this sense he can be called a pragmatist – but ever since the public library in Zeewolde his choice of materials and his handling of detail have certainly not been aimed at pleasure alone. His buildings are not by definition beautiful or examples of a sensitive approach to materials. On the contrary, they are surly, closed. They are primarily urban planning objects used to create squares and city walls. → **30** An approach of this kind calls much less for a festive skin

that appeals to the senses than for a façade that can stand the ravages of time. There is no trendiness in the choice of materials, no social criticism in the handling of detail. Although he still considers his cinema in Rotterdam to be a very interesting building, Van Velsen would perhaps handle the materials of the façade in a different way with material that stays beautiful, in the sense of intact, for decades instead of plastic corrugated sheeting. Bricks, concrete, metal and glass are now Van Velsen's main façade materials. Van Velsen's buildings are no longer built up from different volumes in which almost every element is detailed separately and often very specifically. They now have relatively simply geometric forms that are covered all over with the same materials or combinations of materials. His treatment of detail shows the same calmness. The extrovert character of his early buildings with their many unusual details has given way to introversion. Whereas its artificiality used to be central – Van Velsen enthusiastically revealed how the different elements were constructed, and in the case of the cinema the bolts with which the corrugated sheets are fixed to the steel construction are an important architectural detail – details of this kind have disappeared from his latest buildings, such as the town hall in Terneuzen or the building for the media commission in Hilversum. The windows have no frames, the façade plates look as though they have been hung up without any support, and the roof edges have been camouflaged. Van Velsen is satisfied with little, such as the subtle difference between the matt and the slightly glossy bricks in the extension of the town hall in Terneuzen. Only in the interior of the Media Commissioner's Office (2001) have the wooden frames been enriched by steel profiles (though they are only rarely fully visible). → 31

Although the buildings cannot be compared with one another, a similar development can be traced in the development of the oeuvre of CEPEZED. While Van Velsen opts for reticence because he is convinced that it

enhances the durability of his buildings, Jan Pesman of CEPEZED calls this strategy 'dosing information'. Pesman assumes that people are so bombarded with images that there is a need for quiet buildings. This firm used to give its buildings, budget permitting, extrovert exo-skeletons; all attention was on the carefully detailed joints in the construction, while the boxes that were supported by this construction played a subordinate role. Now the construction has been brought inside too and the handling of detail has generally become more introvert. Referring to the Minimalist architecture of John Pawson and others, Herman Hertzberger once used the term architectural anorexia,[15] accusing this type of building of not having enough life, of offering too little to experience. There seems to be a danger of this in the CEPEZED architecture too, especially because Pesman opts for the simplest possible forms and rigid, cool materials. But that there is no question of a tedious, one-dimensional beauty is before all else due to the treatment of detail. In specific cases, it used as a sort of lubricant to fit the building into its surroundings, like the pronounced roof edge of the CEPEZED office in Delft. → 32 If the buildings are autonomous volumes in a nondescript setting, the handling of detail is flat, rigorous and calm. However, at least one element is singled out – often the staircase or the lift. Completely packaged in glass and moved slightly outside the actual volume, it attracts attention because of the 'nothingness' created by the completely glass skin; not only the element itself, but also the movements that take place within these elements, are striking. finally, most of the buildings have unusual layered façades created by CEPEZED's introducing an extra layer of more or less transparent material in front of the actual façade. Besides being functional – the screens enable light buildings without installations and act as noise barriers – they are also architecturally interesting. first of all, they function as a compositional element, secondly they give the buildings an air of mystery because they are semi-transparent, and finally they largely hide the genuine façade with all its necessary details from view. → 33 The building is visually stripped of disruptive technical details and is abstracted without its becoming an icy object. → 34 Strikingly enough – or perhaps not – the office façade of the CEPEZED building in Graz looks exactly like that of the AZL building by Wiel Arets. Both of them are fitted with remote-controlled, perforated steel plates. When this façade is closed, the result is a perfectly abstract surface. → 35 While Pesman talks about dosing information, Arets refers to the autonomy of the architecture. The calm in the CEPEZED buildings is the result of a protracted intellectual and engineering process by which increasingly more is achieved with increasingly less – a direct striving for the *beinah nichts* of Mies van der Rohe, with the different screens taking the place of Mies' ornamental I-profiles to enhance the

façade. Arets has been convinced ever since his first building that everything is at the service of architecture. Every visual technical element, and thus every detail, disturbs the illusion of an unassailable building. In fact, Arets' buildings are compositions of more or less independent surfaces, or rather volumes. The volume may be the size of a complete building or of a façade, but it can also be a step on the staircase or a window. → **36** The different volumes are combined in such a way that perfect compositions are achieved each time. The reason for this is that Arets is convinced that people regard buildings in a fairly fragmentary way. At any rate, that is how he views most buildings. He takes his slides from a moving taxi, so the buildings are not seen and assessed as a whole, but image for image. And each individual image taken from his building has to be an autonomous, interesting, exciting and perfect composition. That is how his buildings are always photographed, usually by Kim Zwarts.

By making the divisions very hard and thus stripping the details of their technicality, Arets creates the requisite hard lines. 'Normal' details in which often a third material (the frame, for example) acts as an intermediary between two other materials (the façade cladding and glass) produce untidy transitions with overdrawn lines. The autonomy of the surfaces and volumes is not only achieved by reducing the visual details to zero or to a single taut line, but also, for example, by allowing the volumes to overhang enormously and by integrating large spans in his buildings. This introduces a new, apparently floating line, as well as suggesting that the buildings challenge gravity, just as their lack of detail seems to ignore the elements (wind and rain).

NO-Detail = ornament?

'For years, we have concentrated on NO-Detail. Sometimes we succeed – it's gone, abstracted; sometimes we fail – it's still there. Details should disappear – they are old architecture.'[16] This plea by Rem Koolhaas for the abstraction of details follows from his desire to give priority to the concept in his buildings instead of trying to give them an inviolable, perfect look as Arets tries to do. Perfection does not interest Koolhaas. It is too sterile for him, so he prefers to leave room for the unexpected. On the one hand, he looks for danger by thinking up increasingly daring building concepts and by using unusual materials, some of which are alien to the world

of building; on the other hand, he does so by opting for 'NO-Details'. Where Benthem and Crouwel stay on the safe side and try to rule risks out as far as possible, Koolhaas flirts with danger. At the same time, however, Koolhaas has a portfolio with such ambitious projects that genuine constructional errors have to be ruled out as much as possible. This paradox immediately brings out the ornamental nature of NO-Details.

Of course, 'NO-Details' do not exist. The connection between one surface and another, and between one material and another, still has to be made, no matter how much the architect tries to avoid the detail for architectural reasons. At a certain point in the design process the architectural detail has to become a waterproof, windproof and soundproof technical detail. The client demands it. The purest form of NO-Detail is the detail at which the materials seem to be juxtaposed without any interventions. Koolhaas' villa in Bordeaux → **37, 38** and his Casa da Música in Porto (but also Wiel Arets' Academy in Maastricht) have such exciting NO-Details. These are the most difficult details to design and to make. Any impurity, impairs the fully abstracted details and the intended visual absence of the NO-Detail, making them more rather than less present. These details are therefore a part of the danger that Koolhaas deliberately integrates in his buildings. That something will go wrong during building is accepted to a certain extent because it sometimes leads to new experiences in the building which could not have been anticipated in advance. But if things go wrong at crucial moments in the building, undoing it and starting all over again becomes inevitable, as was the case in the Casa da Música.

Less ambitious, less dangerous and in some cases just as inevitable are those NO-Details in which the banal, functional connection is simply hidden from sight – hidden behind continuous façade surfaces, behind upright roof edges, in hollowed walls or behind sheeting material. Not only Koolhaas but also Van Velsen → **39**, Arets → **40**, CEPEZED → **41**, Neutelings Riedijk and MVRDV → **42** make considerable use of details of this kind. Of course, this NO-Detail has nothing to do with purity or honesty. It is a visually orientated detail, as all architectural details are. These NO-Details are derived from the 'pure' lack of detail at which Mies aimed in his *beinah nichts*.

Mies strove for compositions of perfect surfaces and sharp lines. Visualising how the different elements were linked together would have impaired the compositional purity that he wanted to achieve, and so most of the details disappeared behind finishing material. His buildings had no truck with the Modernist principle of efficiency and sobriety – although his buildings were generally inexpensive because of the consistent repetition of elements; they concealed more than they

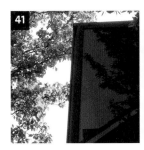

displayed. In this environment of flat, abstracted surfaces that were virtually without detail, the ornaments chosen with an incredible sense of proportion (usually in the shape of I-profiles) provided the poetic, the shimmering, God in the detail. Although this motto was not devised by Mies and it fails to do justice to the geometric qualities of both his façades and his ground plans, Mies managed to bring his buildings to life with just a few details. The dangers of trusting the quality of that single extra detail in an otherwise geometrically perfect, sterile setting of steel, glass, plaster and natural stone can be seen from the dull glass buildings of Mies' epigones like Skidmore, Owings and Merrill. In striving for a lack of detail, the Dutch architects do not usually fall into the trap that Mies created with his *beinah nichts*. They do not put their trust in the divine effect of the single detail. They exorcise the danger, using unusual building concepts and new materials that determine the look of the building. Ornaments are primarily deployed to reinforce the conception of the building further. The distinction between detail and ornament has virtually disappeared in the case of those architects who go for buildings with little or no detail. The materials that are required to hide technical details from sight are just as much a non-functional addition as the original ornaments were. They have nothing to do with a non-ornamental authenticity. Generally speaking, the significance of the detail thus transcends that of a pure connecting element. However, the vitality of the building does not depend on the vitality of the programme of details, but much more on the strength of the concept, the choice of materials and the way in which the detail is deployed to reinforce the concept of the building. God is no longer in the detail, but the detail (and the ornament as supplement) is the adult illustration of the architectural concept and in that capacity it may assume any shape and scale.

1. B. van Berkel and C. Bos, 'Het ideale detail: thema en motief', *Forum*, 1987, no. 4.
2. W. Arets, *Een albasten huid*, Rotterdam 1991.
3. D. Steiner, 'Jedes Detail eine Geschichte', *Archithese*, 1983, no. 4.
4. W.J. Neutelings, 'Tattoo, decoration and taboo', *Archis*, 2000, no. 4.
5. N. Foster, 'Ornament ou detail', *l'Architecture d'Aujourd'hui*, 2001.
6. B. van Berkel and C. Bos, 'Het ideale detail: thema en motief', *Forum*, 1987, no. 4.
7. B. van Berkel and C. Bos, 'Storing the detail', in: *Mobile Forces*, Berlin 1994.
8. E. Koster, 'De aaibaarheidsfactor van architectuur', *Architectuur/Bouwen*, 1992, no. 9.
9. C. Koole, '"Architects should just get on and make tasteful buildings." Interview with Erick van Egeraat', *Archis*, 1997, no. 11.
10. Ibid.
11. H. van Dijk, 'On stagnation and innovation. Commentary on a selection', in: Ruud Brouwers et al. (eds.), *Architecture in the Netherlands. Yearbook 1994-1995*, Rotterdam 1995.
12. R. van Toorn, 'Architectuur om de architectuur. Modernisme als ornament in het recente werk van Mecanoo', *Archis*, 1992, no. 11.
13. G. Hansen, *Arkiteturtidsskrift*, 1991, no. 47/48.
14. J. Rodermond, 'Mooi Nederland', *de Architect*, 1995, no. 10.
15. H. Hertzberger, lecture in the series 'Een haast onmerkbaar lichte tinteling – het architectonische detail' [An almost imperceptible light tingling – the architectural detail], Academy of Architecture, Amsterdam 1996.
16. OMA, R. Koolhaas, B. Mau, *SMLXL*, Rotterdam 1995.

Wiel Arets
Pure architecture

Wiel Arets regards himself as somebody who makes things, but his buildings bear few traces of the activity of making itself. Where there are visible traces, such as the seams between the concrete plates, the form spacer holes in the concrete, or the imprint of bamboo that is used in the cathedral in Ghana as formwork, they are stylized traces. → **1** The detail, the construction and the installation show little or nothing of their intrinsic ingenuity; they are completely at the service of the architectural image. If the thesis in his text 'Een albasten huid' [An alabaster skin] that architecture is a longing for purity and a striving for perfection is interpreted architecturally as well as philosophically, then is this striving for an unobtrusive engineering, or at any rate for an engineering without a pronounced aesthetics of its own, explained.[1]

Incidentally, the use of building engineering in this way and with this end in view is not at odds with the fact that Arets sees himself as someone who makes things. After all, it is necessary to go through extremely intensive designing and constructing processes before such a purely architectural work can be achieved. During these processes he is fully capable of stimulating his clients, his advisers, the manufacturers and eventually the subcontractors in such a way that he gets exactly what he wants. Consultation is the key word here. 'I take the very earliest opportunity to get together with all my advisers (...). This is when I work out the systems. I reach agreements and conclude contracts that everybody is bound to honour throughout the building process. We've got to think in systems with the other parties because they think in systems, too. And it's something that had to be done at an early stage. Clients who are only interested in their profit margins are not about to listen to high-falutin architectural arguments at a later stage of the process. The building process consists of an overlapping of several fields, each with its own way of doing things. The management field is differently structured from the architectural field. That is why we are at pains to reach explicit agreements that give every field its due. (...) None of these agreements relates to the form of the building.'[2] The last sentence is telling. Arets implicitly makes it clear that the shape of the building is not a matter for discussion. The design is already determined to a large degree, and the task of all the advisers is to construct the buildings with the perfection and purity he has in mind. There are no technical impossibilities here, and Arets is

not prepared to make any concessions to such down-to-earth factors as gravity, building physics, or even the convenience of the user. A citation from 'An alabaster skin' gives this away: 'Anyone who is frightened of architecture and its harshness is advised to give it up.'[3] The challenge to the advisers lies in solving all of the technical difficulties inherent in the concept within the strict parameters laid down by Arets. Every solution is developed to serve the concept. This results in an intertwining of the different parts. Architecture and technology become an indissoluble whole. This process, and where it leads to, are clearly visible in the development of the perforated stainless steel façade of the office building of the AZL insurance company in Heerlen (1995). It is not for nothing that Arets himself sees this façade as *the* architectural detail of this building. → **2**

The client wanted exterior awnings to ward off the heat of the sun effectively. Awnings, however, are intrusions that mar Arets' façades. Besides, not only do awnings introduce an extra material – and Arets wants his volumes to be made of the absolute minimum of different materials – but they also form an element on which Arets himself exerts little control. In the long run they certainly fall outside the field of influence of the architect. Arets therefore wants to resolve additions of this kind in an architectural/constructional and thus more or less permanent manner. He sees that as an intellectual challenge.

Together with his building physics adviser from Cauberg-Huygen, Arets designed for this office wing a double skin façade with an outer sheath of perforated stainless steel panels that can be operated by the user by remote control.[4] The close collaboration between architect and adviser results in what is in every respect a typical Arets skin. In terms of introversion and abstraction, this double skin façade can be compared with the glass brick façades in Arets' Academy of arts and architecture in Maastricht (1993) → **3**, or with the completely glass Reglit façades of his police stations in Cuijk → **4** and Boxtel (1997). This is particularly striking because double skin façades are usually deployed to achieve a large degree of transparency. However, when the steel screens are closed, the façade gives away nothing of what goes on in this office wing. The seams between the panels ensure a strict division of the surface, though a special device was needed to produce it: genuine seams alternate with artificial seams between the steel panels of the AZL office to produce the ideal geometry. Arets is concerned not with a constructional authenticity, but with an architectural purity. When the panels are opened, a strange effect takes place because the screens open in pairs while the panels in front of the spandrel remain closed. → **5** As a result, the panels that seemed to be very uniform turn out to have different meanings. This façade clearly shows that the architecture encapsul-

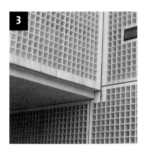

ates the technology. This is also revealed in the way in which the end of the façade is detailed. Just before the steel plates meet the austere concrete wing, the façade is swung back. → **6** Not only does this keep the façade away from the concrete wing, but since the depth of the part that is swung back is the same as the height of the movable parts of the steel façade, the uncontrollable movements have been framed, as it were. The shadows of the screens when they are open do not reach the concrete wing and leave it unimpaired. The two surfaces that are perpendicular to one another maintain their independence.

Holes in the façades

Although Arets applies the detail tactic to obtain unimpaired surfaces and volumes in all his buildings, he applied it the most rigorously and took it the furthest in his first large building, the Academy of Art in Maastricht. Inspired by the Japanese architect Tadao Ando, Arets covered the simple concrete skeleton of the Academy with glass bricks. The building does not really have any other visible details. Aluminium roof edging has been omitted because it would mar the geometry of the volume. → **7** In its place, a detail as simple as it is clever has been applied: the actual join between the façade and the roof is set slightly further back, and is thus out of sight. Just as the roof edging has been smoothed away, the doors of the Academy were not allowed to disturb the surface either. They must not be allowed to behave like holes. The doors leading to the new building and to the roof terrace on the fourth floor look as though they are made entirely of concrete, except for a simple steel border painted black. The characteristic grid of spacer holes and the seams of formwork panels are even continued on the doors, making them not a way of filling a hole, but pure extensions of the wall. → **8** The other swing doors in the building are made of glass in black steel frames. This is consistent too, because these doors form part of a glass wall or are at right angles to the spaces. Their transparency guarantees the visual continuity of the walls, and thereby of the spaces. The doors are camouflaged in this manner, and this explains why Arets usually opts for swing doors or sliding doors. After all, 'ordinary hinges' give away the presence of the door, while the pivots of the swing door or the rails of the sliding door are incorporated in the surface of the door itself and are thus out of sight.

The encapsulation of the entrance by the mass of the building is another device that Arets uses to keep doors out of sight. The entrance to the AZL office, for instance, is a dark hole beneath the overhanging meeting rooms, the entrance to the balcony access flats in Maastricht is hidden behind a perforated steel screen, and the main entrance of the Lensvelt company premises (Breda, 1999) is accessed via a patio that is situated behind a floating box. Not only does this make entering the building more ceremonial, but it also leaves the different surfaces apparently intact.

This tactic is not always desirable or feasible. A police station, for example, calls for an explicit entrance. This has been solved in Cuijk by turning the entrance into an almost independent element. It is covered with steel strips which are distorted as though the insertion of this volume in the glass main volume of the police station was done too violently. → **9** Moreover, by making the attachment of this steel element to the construction behind the Reglit visible, Arets accentuates the impression of two separate volumes. The many doors required in the production area of the Lensvelt building are similarly cut out of the architectural volume. The steel plate frame which holds the Reglit in place has been wrapped around these openings, as it were. Within the framework lies the strictly designed architectural volume; outside it the architect's influence is inevitably less. Both the glass and the steel frame remain intact. In that sense it is symptomatic that the essential ventilation ducts have been introduced beneath the raised steel frames and have thus been removed from sight. → **10**

It is more difficult to maintain the autonomy of the surface when it comes to window openings. Nevertheless, Arets applies similar tactics to the ones used with the doors in order to minimise any interference with the surfaces. In this sense it is understandable that Arets sees the perforated steel façade of the AZL building as the architectural detail. When the offices are not in use and the screens are closed, the holes disappear and the façade becomes a single, tight unity. The office wings of the AZL building and of the Lensvelt building are adjacent to a patio, so that employees look out onto the environment designed by the architect. The usual rows of office windows are absent from the façades on the street side. Arets also often uses sky lights to avoid windows. This is how light enters the staircase of the Academy and the entrance of the AZL building. If none of these alternatives is possible, then Arets makes the windows holes in the skin with as few details as possible. One material (the skin) seems to merge imperceptibly with the other material (the glass). Window frames are regarded as intermediaries that only create noise. The window is a precise incision in the body of the building. Arets created an equally precise hole in the walkway of

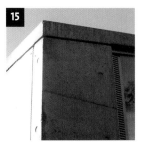

the Academy in Maastricht. In the building itself, he used concrete frames around the windows and deep black steel window frames in order to produce sharply incised openings. Through the use of black the vertical and horizontal elements of the window frames disappear in the black surface of the glass. → **11** As he did with the doors, Arets also turns the windows into separate elements if he is unable or unwilling to win the 'battle'. The latter can be seen, for instance, in the case of the window opening in the conference room of the AZL building, where Arets certainly could have chosen to detail the window 'merely' as a dark hole. Instead of that, he turned it into a new element that completes the composition of the overhanging block and whose protruding frame forces the attention of the users of the conference room even more in the direction that Arets wants it to follow. → **12** In the Cuijk police station Arets turned both the windows and the doors into separate, almost self-sufficient elements. Here too he left the attachments visible behind the Reglit, and accentuated their plasticity, and thereby their independence, by means of the steel protruding edges and the bolts by which the window frames are attached. → **13** Finally, leaving the surfaces intact also plays an important role in the detailing of the stairs. While in the Academy the horizontal surfaces intersected the sloping gradients in an abrupt way, in his later buildings Arets seems to be no longer willing to accept such an intrusion on the play of vertical and horizontal lines. In the AZL office and in the office building on the Céramique site in Maastricht (1995), the staircases consist of concrete stairs that stop just before the point at which they join the floor. → **14** And as there are no risers, the staircase miraculously comprises only very fragile, floating, horizontal surfaces. Moreover, the floor is allowed to continue beneath the staircase without any interruption. These staircases seem to be exemplary for the way in which Arets deals with construction, not only because the different surfaces continue without disturbance, but

above all because they are mute elements whose ingenuity and all the strength that is required to give the staircase its supportive function have been rendered anonymous. The staircase has become primarily architectural instead of purely functional. That is why there are many different staircases to be seen in Arets' buildings, each with its own character. After all, each space calls for its own unique elements.

Volumes and surfaces

As can be seen from these details, but above all from the corner details, Arets treats the façades and walls as intact, separate surfaces, which, incidentally, in turn combine to form unmistakable volumes thanks to the uniform choice and deployment of materials. The corner detail of the concrete main volume of the AZL building, for instance, clearly shows that the two façades collide at this point. The use of continuous corner elements would have made the building much more of a single volume. A similar detail is used in the Hedge House (Wijlre, 2001), making it possible to distinguish the front, side and roof plates from one another despite the fact that they are made of the same material. → **15** Other parts of the AZL building contains even clearer instances of the composition in surfaces. Arets has slid a new concrete plate into place in front of the masonry façade of the existing building. This detail leaves both surfaces (the masonry and the concrete) intact. In addition, of course, it is also a way for Arets to avoid the difficult join that is often done with irregular fitting pieces. → **16**
In the Lensvelt building and the two Reglit police stations in Cuijk and Boxtel, the different façades are detached from one another at the corners by using stainless steel corner profiles. → **17** Although these details all clearly make the different surfaces recognisable, Arets gives these surfaces mass by the specific use of detail for the corners, the roof edgings (as in the Academy) or the window openings. In this way façades become three-dimensional, and thus separate volumes too.
In the police station in Vaals (1995), the surfaces have been stretched into three genuine volumes, separated from one another by sky lights. → **18** Incisions have been made in the vertical surface too, the façade, but they are too shallow to have any effect. These incisions were not architecturally necessary – in constructional terms they facilitate the joins – because the autonomy has been achieved by covering each volume with its own material. Although the architectural premise is completely different – not every function is allocated its own material, but every volume – there was a risk that the building would be too Mecanoo-like. The danger was averted precisely by making as few details visible as possible.
According to critic Hans van Dijk, the details in Arets'

work are not invisible, but the buildings are composed of them. 'His architectural repertoire consists of details', and 'Arets' work can be summed up in a single phrase (...): "a swarm of details".'[5] This is true in so far as almost every millimetre has been thought, designed and then made the way it is. However, the details are not developed for the sake of the details themselves; the details do not have an identity of their own, unlike the details in, say, the work of Mecanoo; the details cannot be recognised as such. Every surplus visible detail is a threat to the idea of an autonomous and unapproachable body. → **19** That is why Arets puts an unbelievable amount of time into removing the technical details from sight. The roof of the wooden volume in Vaals, for example, is stripped of all its characteristic details. It looks like a closed surface, and it is unclear what happens with rain water. However, the visible surface turns out to be a fake. The real roof lies beneath the Western red cedar. The rain water falls onto it through slits and is then drained away. In this way, the idea of a body without detail remains unimpaired.

An even more attractive example of Arets' strategy of concealing constructional elements is the Hedge House. This exhibition space appears to consist of nothing but concrete and glass. Even the sloping roof surfaces are made of concrete. Instead of opting for lack of detail, as in the concrete volume in Vaals, Arets uses stylized concealed gutters for drainage, but the gutters have been produced and applied in such a way that they function primarily as a beautiful lining to the uninterrupted roof surface. → **20**

Heavy, floating volumes

Arets often uses his constructions as a second layer that is just visible behind the first layer – the skin: the concrete skeleton of the Academy; the clearly visible steel construction behind the Reglit in the Lensvelt building; but especially the concrete constructional wedges that pop up behind the skin of the KNSM tower in Amsterdam (1999) and the double tower derived from it in Rotterdam (2000). The construction becomes an almost independent, new layer. Moreover, in most of his buildings the way in which the skin is attached to the construction reveals the relative thinness of that skin – negating the apparent weight that is evoked by the other details in order to elicit new contradictions – while at the same time revealing how the building is support-

ed. The counterpart to this form of constructional honesty can be found in Arets' attempts to use the construction to resist gravity. The KNSM and Rotterdam towers are covered with special prefab elements of deep grey concrete. → **21** The colour and structure of the concrete resemble blocks of basalt, an effect that is obtained by using a rubber mat for a mould. The jointing between the 'blocks of coal' is the same width (16 mm) as that between the prefab elements. Unfortunately the work was not carried out perfectly, resulting in differences of tone between the panels, and the pigmentation is faulty too so that the panels grow lighter and lighter. This all frustrates the illusion that Arets was trying to achieve of towers built up of stacked blocks. As in the majority of his buildings, Arets tried to immediately negate the weight that is created. He does so most subtly in the KNSM tower, where the skin ends ten centimetres above the covered car park, which functions as a sort of socle. The heavy, solid tower seems to be floating. → **22** Arets does not always use the construction as a means of interpreting the building. It is just as common to find anonymous wedges that give an imperturbable rhythm of its own to the building. A good example of this is provided by the concrete wedges in the central hall of the AZL building. These wedges create the impression that the building, although made up of heavy volumes, is floating. The two stacked conference rooms jut out considerably above the staircase leading to the entrance, in the middle of the building there is a twenty-metre long clear span that makes the inner garden accessible and in which a conference room is suspended, and at the back the glass box of the canteen seems to rest just above ground level. → **23** Similarly, the Lensvelt building floats above the ground that has been removed, and the front of the police station in Cuijk is just above the level of the grass.

Architectural installations

Arets' design for the new Utrecht University Library (2001) represents a new peak in his striving for a pure and unimpaired architecture. → **24** The skin is mainly of glass but, as in all his buildings, it is not transparent but silk-screened with an unusual pattern. From a distance the glass has a floral print, but at close quarters only the pixels are visible. This gives the façades an enormous, typically Arets abstraction. Moreover, the glass – that alternates with closed concrete façade panels with a 'fossil branch' impress – will probably give the building an introverted character in the same way as the use of Reglit or glass bricks does elsewhere. → **25** The exceptional nature of the glass can be seen in the covered car park of the tower blocks in Rotterdam, where the glass has been printed with the basalt stones that decorate the prefab concrete façade elements. This produces the surprising effect that from a distance the glass seems to

be solid and closed, while it becomes more transparent as you approach it. Another interesting detail of the double skin façade in the library, where the silk-screened glass forms the outer layer, is that, instead of small ducts to let fresh air into the building, as is often the case with façades of this kind, complete glass panels are opened. As in the double skin of the AZL office, this guarantees the unbroken surface of the façade.

Inside, it is above all the enormous depots that are striking because they have not been hidden underground, as they usually are, but they 'float like clouds in the sky'. Daylight enters through the gaps between the depots, and the view upwards is maintained too. → **26** The constructional problem was that the walls must be fire-resistant for no less than four hours. This entailed concrete walls and floors forty centimetres thick. This thickness is used to create forty-metre spans, and these elements also ensure the stability of the rest of the building. In fact, the depots are pure construction, but by suspending them in the volume they become architectural and their constructional nature is concealed. The tops of the depots are used as the floor of the reading room. The other floors in the library can also be regarded as floating fields. A building of this kind with such a large open space cannot be air conditioned with a single central air conditioning installation. Besides being environment-unfriendly – too many cubic metres would not be heated or cooled – it cannot guarantee a comfortable climate in every part of the building. Instead, a large number of decentralised units have been applied, which will be integrated in all kinds of furniture to be designed by Arets. The installations are absorbed by the building. This tactic – designing the engineering in such a way that it becomes an important part of the architecture – resembles the tactic that Louis Kahn applied and which derived from his dislike of all kinds of piping. Kahn once said: 'I do not like ducts. I do not like pipes. I hate them really thoroughly, but because I hate them so thoroughly I feel they have to be given their place. If I just hated them and took no care, I think they would invade the building and completely destroy it.'[6] At first, in his striving for perfection, Arets did not apply any installations in the Academy in Maastricht. This guaranteed the severity of the design and preserved its spatiality, but at the expense of functionality. In the meantime coolers have been installed here and there. Afterwards, mainly because high demands are made on

a comfortable indoor climate, Arets integrated the installations more and more in his buildings. The double skin façades, the machines disguised as furniture, the concealing of the diffusers and piping in the floor (AZL office) show how cleverly Arets handles this. The only exception is formed by the glass halls of the Lensvelt building, where the installation and even the rainwater drainage are still visible, but in such a controlled fashion that their presence is beautiful and calm. → **27, 28** Unlike Kahn, Arets does not hate engineering of any kind. He finds it intriguing, not an independent entity, because thanks to his own technical knowledge and a number of very good advisers with many of whom he has been working together for years, he is able to make the pure architecture that he wants to make. In this architecture is little or no distinction between the architectural premise and the completed building. The details, the construction and the installations in Arets' work are pure architecture too.

1. W. Arets, *Een albasten huid*, Rotterdam 1991.
2. H. van Dijk, 'Conjugal cunning. Recent work by Wiel Arets', *Archis*, 1996, no. 4.
3. See note 1.
4. E. Melet, 'Dubbele bodems van Wiel Arets', *de Architect*, 1995, no. 11.
5. See note 2.
6. R.S. Wurman and E. Feldman, *The notebooks and drawings of Louis I. Kahn*, Cambridge Ma 1973.

Detail of junction of glass brick façade and pivoted steel door

1 concrete floor with monolithic finish
2 reinforced concrete
3 acoustic ceiling
4 190 x 190 x 10 mm glass bricks
5 stainless steel L-section
6 anchor
7 non-shrink mortar
8 anchor bushing
9 tape
10 80 x 40 x 5 mm L-section
11 12-6-12 glazing
12 80 x 160 x 6 mm steel duct
13 59 x 66 mm steel section
14 56 x 2 mm steel plate

Detail of roof edge and bottom of glass brick façade

1 50 mm gravel
2 asphalt roofing
3 30 mm dimensionally stable mineral wool
4 rainwater drain
5 reinforced concrete
6 acoustic ceiling
7 water spout
8 stainless steel L-section
9 anchor for fixing precast concrete unit to glass bricks
10 190 x 190 x 10 mm glass bricks
11 insulation
12 concrete column

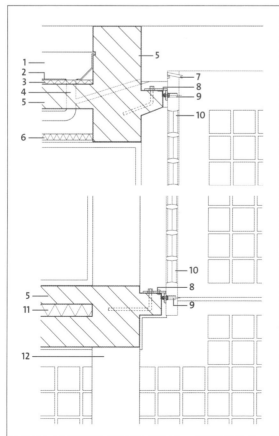

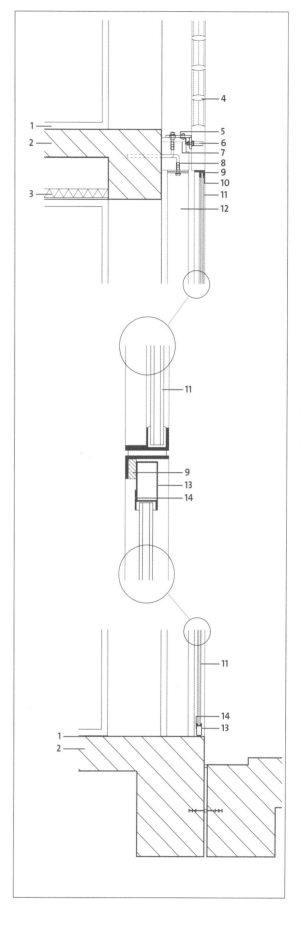

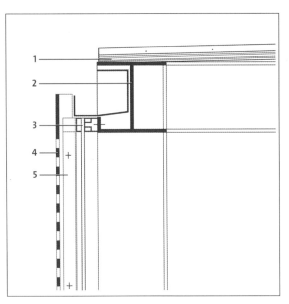

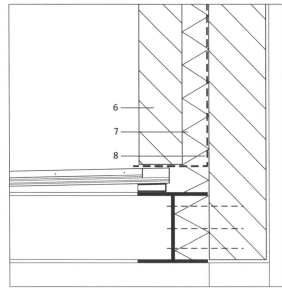

1 solar glass
2 steel construction
3 steel curtain wall with insulating glazing
4 1800 x 3600 mm stainless steel façade panels, 30% perforation
5 steel profiles for fixing façade panels
6 1220 x 2440 mm reinforced concrete panels
7 80 mm insulation
8 waterproof breather membrane

Wiel Arets AZL insurance company head office Heerlen 1995

Horizontal details of façade with stainless steel screen
1 80 mm insulation
2 steel sections for fixing façade panels
3 render
4 1800 x 3600 mm stainless steel façade panels, 30% perforation
5 double glazing in steel frames
6 100 mm steel sandwich panel
7 reinforced concrete

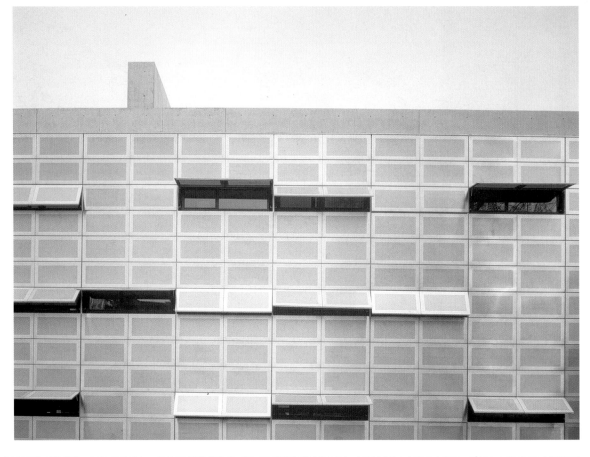

24

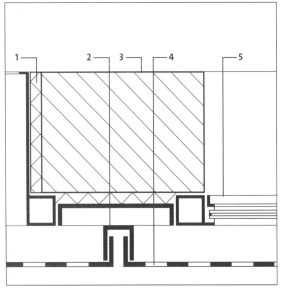

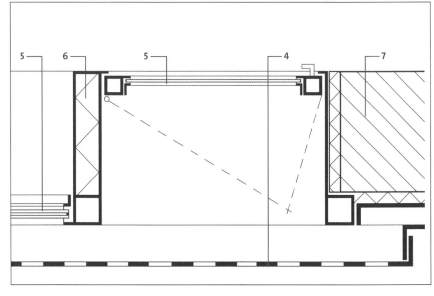

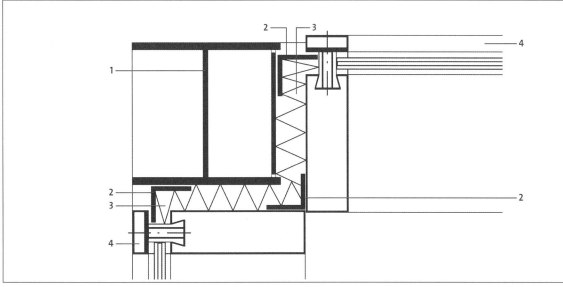

Roof edge

Details of 'glazed' canteen extension
1 HE 200 A
2 50 x 50 x 4 mm L-section
3 80 mm insulation
4 steel curtain wall with insulating glazing
5 insulation
6 steel U-section (260 x 80 x 5 mm composite)
7 steel section
8 compression layer
9 insulation
10 concrete panels
11 steel plate

25

Detail at HE-section

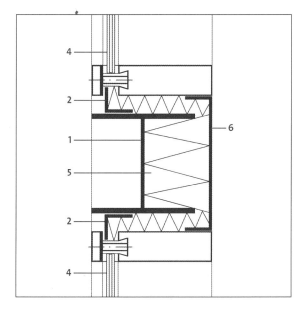

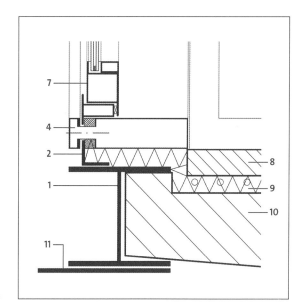

Lower junction glass façade/concrete structure

Roof edge of concrete volume

1 80 mm gravel pea concrete, pigmented black, mechanically polished
2 saw cuts with mastic
3 two layers of PE membrane + roofing
4 80 mm styrofoam and vapour check
5 levelling course
6 260 mm hollow-core slab
7 joint filler
8 sealant on backup strip
9 slip membrane
10 50 mm Foamglas®
11 50 mm mineral wool
12 200 mm fair-face concrete, pigmented black
13 metal stud facing wall
14 metal stud false ceiling
15 3 mm white spray plaster

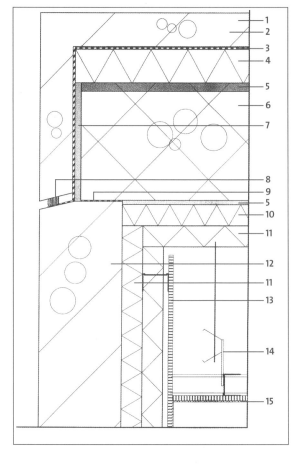

Roof edge of wooden volume

1 western red cedar planks glued in frame
2 western red cedar edge beam
3 plywood board
4 pinewood top rail
5 battening
6 rock wool slab
7 asphalt roofing
8 gutter below fall line
9 UNP 280
10 100 mm rock wool
11 PE membrane
12 hollow-core slab
13 80 mm rock wool
14 framework
15 western red cedar battens
16 15 mm floated coat on levelling course
17 15 mm floated coat on plasterboard

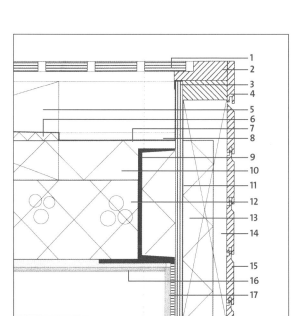

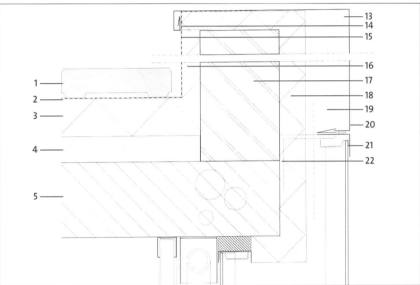

Detail of roof edge

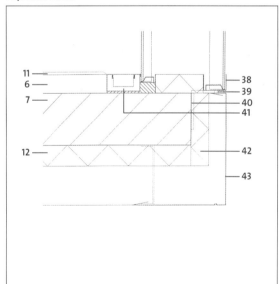

Façade at window

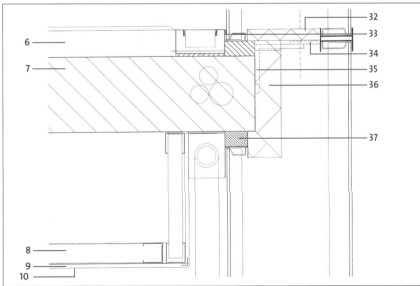

27

Façade at intermediate floor

1 300 x 300 x 5 mm concrete tiles
2 plastic roofing
3 100 mm insulation
4 70 mm cement floor laid to falls
5 200 mm wide-slab floor
6 70 mm cement finish floor
7 200 mm hollow-core floor
8 false ceiling

9 9.5 mm Gyproc
10 3 mm spray plaster
11 carpet
12 Foamglas
13 pre-formed aluminium sheet fixed in snap-on profile
14 fixing of aluminium sheeting
15 synthetic edging strips of roofing membrane coated on both sides
16 50 mm mineral wool

17 214 mm lime sandstone
18 70 mm insulation
19 cavity
20 aluminium cladding
21 aluminium Reglit profile
22 300 x 300 x 50 mm L-section
23 Reglit SP 25
24 cavity
25 Reglit Plus
26 solar shading
27 aluminium sheathing

Façade at projection above ground level

28 steel Reglit profile
29 aluminium window frame
30 sub-sill ends below frame
31 local connection between steel Reglit profiles
32 30 mm insulation
33 mastic filler
34 80 x 40 x 8 mm L-section
35 130x130x12 mm L-section
36 70 mm insulation

37 wooden cleat for fixing Reglit profile
38 aluminium profile
39 Compriband
40 150 x 150 x 10 mm L-section
41 cable duct
42 80 mm insulation
43 pre-formed aluminium sheet fixed in snap-on profile

Upper and lower junction steel volume and large window in lobby

1 pre-formed steel plate
2 mineral wool
3 HEA 140
4 DPC
5 plasterboard
6 UNP 140
7 sill
8 sliding door fixing
9 insulated steel frame
10 toughened double glazing
11 compression layer
12 260 mm hollow-core slab floor
13 pre-formed steel plate
14 Foamglas®
15 UNP 260
16 neoprene
17 200 x 10 mm sheet steel

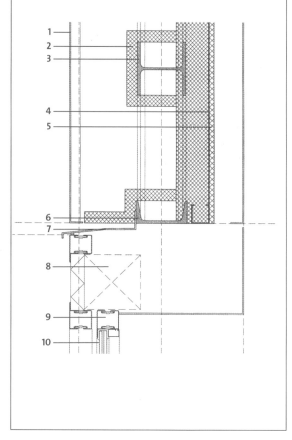

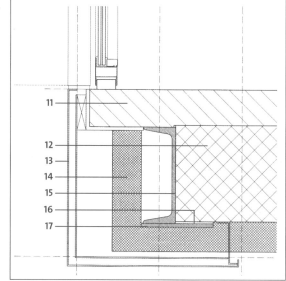

Wiel Arets Lensvelt company premises Breda 1999

Junction glass façade and steel frame, 'floating' above ground level

1 glass plank
2 aluminium bottom profile with integrated condensation drain
3 steel cladding
4 UNP 240
5 mineral wool with coating
6 steel bracket
7 perforation for cavity ventilation
8 ground plane
9 120 x 80 x 8 mm L-section
10 precast concrete crash barrier
11 in situ floor on subgrade
12 60 mm polystyrene
13 edge beam (cast in situ)

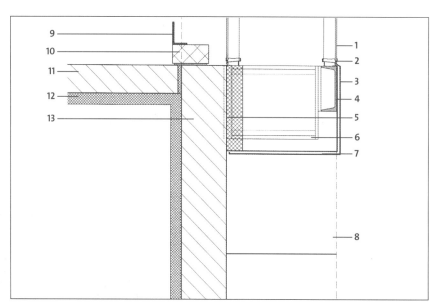

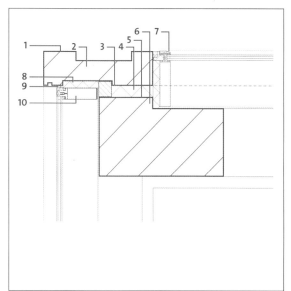

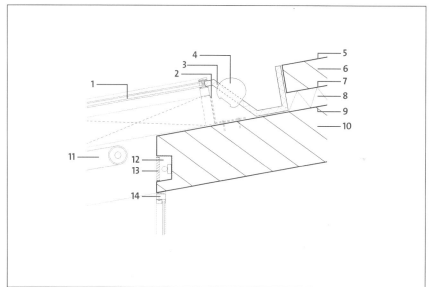

Junction curtain wall and glazed roof

1 Tremco coating
2 150 mm concrete outer leaf
3 plastic roofing
4 polystyrene foam
5 vapour barrier of bituminous glass fleece
6 300 mm concrete inner leaf
7 aluminium glazed roof
8 high-performance insulation
9 sealant on backup strip
10 Schuco curtain wall

Junction glass roof and concrete roof

1 aluminium glazed roof
2 fixing of glazed roof aluminium profiles
3 insulated gutter
4 mechanical ventilation
5 Tremco coating
6 150 mm concrete outer leaf
7 plastic roofing
8 polystyrene foam
9 vapour barrier of bituminous glass fleece
10 300 mm concrete inner leaf
11 solar shading mechanism
12 recess for lighting
13 grid
14 aluminium front

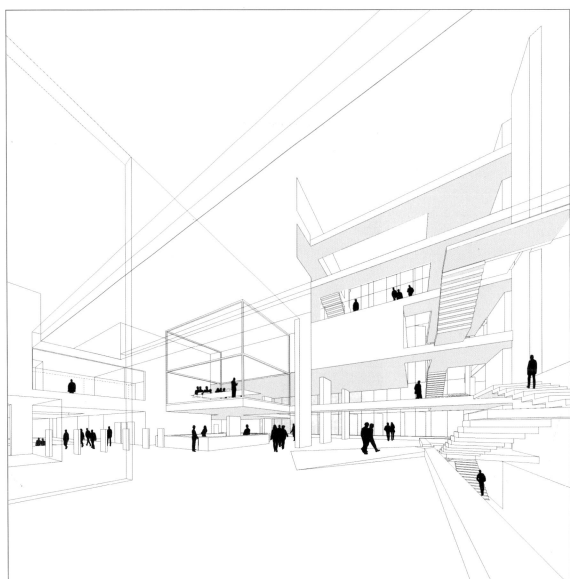

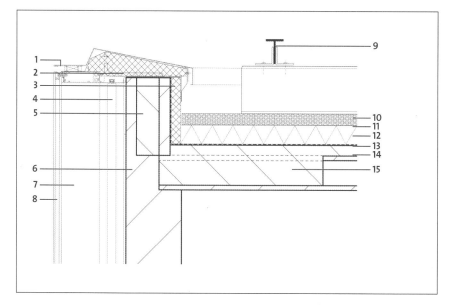

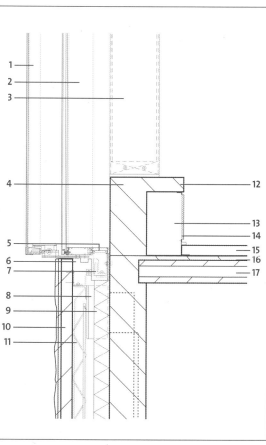

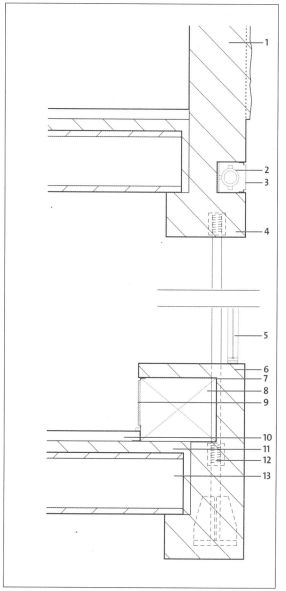

Junction of glass façade and roof
1 pre-formed aluminium roof edge
2 insulation
3 40 mm Foamglas®
4 anti-glare shading
5 Alvon wall with black coating
6 precast concrete beam with black coating
7 aluminium frame
8 structurally bonded glazing
9 double rail track for window cleaning system
10 roof ballast, black split-face block
11 PVC roofing
12 min. 50 mm insulation
13 vapour barrier
14 compression layer
15 150 mm hollow-core slab

Junction of glass façade and façade clad with precast concrete panel with special relief
1 automatically operated glazed leaf
2 aluminium frame with structurally bonded glazing
3 composite profile for façade
4 250 mm in situ concrete, with black coating
5 ventilation grille
6 waterproof membrane
7 pre-formed steel substructure
8 fixing of concrete panel
9 100 mm insulation
10 80 mm textured concrete panel with black coating
11 lightning conductor
12 in situ concrete coping
13 services zone
14 four-sided pre-formed perforated steel plate
15 monolithic floor with epoxy coating
16 compression layer
17 hollow-core slab

Detail of floor suspended from concrete structure
1 in situ concrete with added texture
2 200 x 200 mm recess for sprinkler pipe
3 perforated covering plate
4 HE600 B and threaded bush (cast-in)
5 frame composed of steel strips, 70 x 15 mm and 30 x 10 mm
6 in situ fair face concrete
7 recess for steel cable
8 services zone
9 four-sided pre-formed perforated steel plate
10 monolithic floor with epoxy coating
11 compression layer
12 threaded bush and anchor
13 hollow-core slab

31

Benthem Crouwel
Functional buildings, details to match

In 2000 the firm of Benthem Crouwel Architekten moved into the Benthem Crouwel Lab building. The addition of the word 'lab' does not stand for experiment. After all, Jan Benthem and Mels Crouwel do not have a reputation for the urge to experiment. The name seems rather to refer to the almost scientific approach of the two architects, in which inspiration seems less important than the meticulous dissection of the programme and the reasoning of every stage in the design process. The aim is a logical and functional building with materials derived from the functions and details to match. The architect Bruno Taut (1880-1938) might almost have had them in mind when he remarked: 'The purpose of architecture is to create perfect and thus also beautiful efficiency. The most important objective must be the attainment of optimal utility. The materials and constructions used must be attuned to that goal.'[1] The success of this design strategy can be seen from the enormous number and from the size of the assignments on which the Benthem Crouwel Architekten is engaged at the moment and which it has completed in the recent past.

Being the clients' favourites does not necessarily mean that the architecture is exciting – certainly not, in fact. After all, many clients want attractive but at the same time risk-free buildings. The Benthem Crouwel buildings are risk-free in a sense, but primarily because the architects themselves are not looking for trouble. Benthem Crouwel wants to solve every problem as simply as possible. There is no room here for the danger of the unknown. Experimenting with new materials, that is often – wrongly – associated by many young firms in particular with the introduction of risk, raises problems. That is why materials will seldom or never be used improperly in their buildings. The use of a material follows from the combination of the function and the image of a building (the location), on the one hand, and from the characteristics of the material, on the other hand.

The only exceptions seem to be the 013 pop music centre (Tilburg, 1998) and Villa Arena (2001) in Amsterdam. The façades of 013 are cushioned with EPDM roof foil with CDs as buttons. → **1** This façade rests on a robust socle of profiled prefab concrete elements and stainless steel grilles. → **2** The roof of the Villa Arena is covered with transparent air cushions, a material that until then had mainly been used in halls.

In both buildings, however, the materials are also above all logical. The soft façades of 013 covered with rubber foil provide sound insulation from the music, and the concrete plinth of the pop centre had to be vandal-resistant. The ground plan of the Villa Arena has somewhat strange angular rotations and the transparent roof was supposed to follow these rotations as far as possible. → **3** This would have been virtually impossible and in any case extremely expensive with glass. The air cushions, on the other hand, can be cut into any shape, have a simple detailing, are very light, and are available in large sizes. In this sense this use of material is also typical of Benthem Crouwel because it is purely functional and also demonstrates that function, especially in 013, but the material, whose choice is understandable in itself, is deployed in an unusual way to give these buildings a remarkable vitality. In many other buildings this bringing to life takes place on a smaller scale than the choice of materials.

Architectural standard details

Benthem Crouwel façades are usually made of glass, stainless steel, untreated aluminium or, rarely, brick. They are all materials that have proved their worth in the past, are durable, and become more attractive as they age. Besides, the treatment of detail has already been elaborated to a large extent. There are many standard details available which are then made more architectural by the firm. At first sight there sometimes seems to be little to the façades of Benthem Crouwel buildings; they sometimes look too standard and perhaps not architectural enough. Or as the critic Vincent van Rossem has said: 'The architecture of Benthem Crouwel is so businesslike that the question of whether something is beautiful is marginalised'.[2] Genuine beauty at the level of the detail, however, sometimes turns out to be situated inside, as in the façade of the World Trade Centre at Schiphol Airport (1996). This strip of offices with the almost standard planning grid dimensions of 14.4 metres stands on top of roofed car parks with grid dimensions that are more than 3 metres larger. The problem was how to 'fit' the construction of the offices onto that of the car park. It has been done in a typical Benthem Crouwel way. The office blocks have been simply raised a storey; placing the concrete columns at an angle beneath the support façades resolves the difference in dimensions in a simple manner. → **4** The slender Y-shaped columns are elements that help to create an image in the otherwise fairly neutral office façades. At the level of the entrance, however, a curved volume continues under the office blocks, which prevents this trick from being applied here. This volume is naturally given the same dimensions as the car park. The difference in size between the upper and the lower building is then used to achieve the

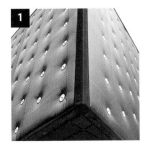

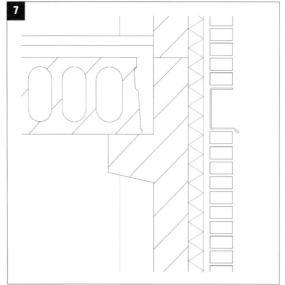

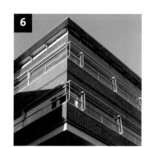

difficult connection between the rectangular office blocks and the rounded roof of the central hall. A 1-metre wide gutter had been introduced here, which serves to detach the two volumes more or less from one another. → 5

The avoidance of troublesome details in this way is one of the characteristics of the Benthem Crouwel approach to detail. By just preventing materials from touching, so that the air forms the connections between the surfaces, or by means of this kind of easily controllable bridging details, the architects enhance their grip on the building process. There is therefore no need to work out all the details precisely to the millimetre, because corrections can be made during the building process. Finally, fitting pieces were still needed in the façade of the entrance volume of the WTC to fit the grid dimension into the modular system. The roof drainage has been hidden behind these 20-centimetre wide strips. So the details ensure in the first instance that the façades are smooth and reasonably anonymous. An office complex on this site does not call for attention-catching façades and details, but for quietness and rhythm. The architects derive satisfaction from solving differences in dimensions in this way within the parameters that they have laid down themselves. At the same time, Benthem Crouwel introduces accents and layers into the façades with small but significant details. The aluminium curtain wall of the office blocks of the World Trade Centre, for example, is enriched by horizontal profiles that have not been applied over the whole length of the façade, but only start at the transition from square to rectangular windows. Besides, the profiles have been continued slightly around the corner. This prevents the façade that is singled out by the two window formats from falling apart, while it also confers a new rhythm on the façade. What is more, it links the front and the side together.

The brick façade of the Provincial hall in Groningen (1996) also contains a number of details that bring the façade to life. First of all, the solid façades are broken up by simple frames with C-profiles. → 6 These profiles are both an aesthetic and a functional detail. These details have been used in the Provincial hall to give the façade a new rhythm, but above all to negate the solidity of the façades. → 7 Normally speaking, steel shoes are attached to the inner cavity wall plates to prevent the external cavity wall plates from buckling under their own weight, and the masonry is supported by them. A putty joint conceals the steel construction, so that the façade looks like a heavy whole. Making the steel profiles on which the bricks rest visible brings out both the thinness and the weakness of this brickwork skin.

→ 8 In other words, this skin is no more 'genuine' than the metal curtain façades that are used elsewhere. An interesting feature of this building is the transition from the façade to the almost classical eaves, where wooden frames, a strip of extended metal and brick meet. This combination of very different materials could have led to the collapse of the façade in compositional terms, but its unity is preserved because the jambs of the frames continue via the seams of the metal plates into the stiffening profiles that support the overhanging eaves.

In a similar way to the Provincial hall, the entrance of the Anne Frank House in Amsterdam (1999), another Benthem Crouwel design, reveals the vulnerability of the brickwork façade vis-à-vis the stone walls of the canal houses. The columns rise up here behind the brickwork façade. The masonry is not self-supporting, but is visibly dependent on a steel profile. The brickwork façade beside the Prinsengracht also contains details that negate its solidity → 9: the masonry is supported by sturdy steel profiles that, like the eaves of the Provincial hall, bring about a transition to the glass substructure with the metal louvres.

The rhythmically distributed windows in this façade, like the enormous expanse of glass on the first two floors, has a slightly recessed metal frame beside the window

frame, thereby casting shadows over the ventilation grilles. → **10** This frame gives the windows an independent character and the façade acquires a second tempo. Moreover, the transoms of the metal window frames are accentuated with elements that look like handles, but above all the overhanging, sculpturally designed steel elements on the roof can be seen as modern ornaments. Benthem Crouwel therefore attempts to fit in with the seventeenth-century canal houses, though it does so using strikingly up-to-date resources, so that the façade becomes much more than just a present-day copy.

Detail systems

Benthem Crouwel manages to make what are in themselves neutral façades more layered with relatively small gestures and the use of detail and ornament. The reverse – silencing potentially eye-catching façades – applies to many of the large glass walls that form the entrance of large public buildings. Benthem Crouwel does not succumb to the temptation to try every trick in the detail and constructional box here. It wants to prevent the crowdedness of many façades with structural glazing by means of fine tension cables, somewhat heavier compression rods and beautifully made, preferably cast gussets. Such a plethora of details, Benthem and Crouwel believe, would disturb the balance that it is out to achieve in the buildings and in the use of detail. The architects follow the principle that every detail must be good and clear but unobtrusive. That leads to a balanced detail system and instead of being drawn to a single well-designed detail, attention is focused on what Benthem Crouwel considers really important, such as the functionality of the building, the clarity of the ground plans, and its spatiality. For the details of these glass walls the architects follow the same strategy as in the rest of the building. Instead of getting lost in a maze of details, Benthem Crouwel tries to find overarching systems in which the details follow logically from the façade concept. These systems are easy to handle, not only for the architect but also for the subcontractors. Despite what might be expected, Benthem Crouwel elaborates by no means all of the details. Given the scale of the projects, this would be practically impossible anyway. The carefully thought out detail systems give the subcontractors a large amount of freedom to devise their own solutions, provided they fit

into the framework of the architecture.

The glass façade of Schiphol Plaza, for example, is crowded (1995). → **11** There are a number of entrances, the walkway to the garages and the WTC intersects the façade in a rather unfortunate manner, the escalators and slopes leading to the underground NS station poke through the façade, the façade has a remarkable sculptural construction, and the construction of the roof of the hall is continued to the outside. A complicated glass façade would have made the picture even more chaotic. That is why Schiphol Plaza has a simple construction consisting of rectangular profiles against which the glass wall leans. A striking, almost banal rear construction complete with grille floors provides the requisite support. → **12** The profiles and details of the glass wall can hardly be called refined, but it is neutral enough to absorb the irregularities caused by all the penetrations, almost without its being conspicuous and without heavy damage being inflicted on the system. The same is true of the glass wall of Terminal West (1993) on the airport side. → **13** Because of the view of the planes taking off and landing, the busy shops and bars, and the large volume of passengers, this façade had to be made even more neutral. All the same, a little more effort on the part of the designer could have made this façade a bit calmer. The problem was that the façade had to be suspended, as it were, because the supporting construction is not on the same site as the foundations. A stable trestle made of sloping columns and vertical tensile bars had to be used to guarantee the stability of this façade. These bars are placed in front of the already heavy façade jambs, and the constructional packet is too conspicuously present as a result. The tensile bars could have been integrated in the façade jambs to produce a calmer result, although this would have been at the expense of the differentiation between the different building components that Benthem Crouwel appreciates so much.[3]

Subtle glass details

That Benthem Crouwel can also produce subtle glass details is shown above all by the older and smaller projects like the Sonsbeek pavilion (1986) in Arnhem → **14**, Benthem House in Almere (1984) → **15, 17** and Crouwel's house in Tienhoven (1992). → **16** The Sonsbeek pavilion consists almost entirely of glass. The security glass roof is supported by simple steel truss girders, which in turn are attached to the glass via the corner lines and which partly rest on glass fins. Synthetic discs have been introduced between the glass and the steel to prevent the glass from cracking from unexpected tension. The roof of Benthem's home is supported on glass too, though in this case the roof is of light steel – a material so light that extra precautionary measures had to be taken to prevent it from flying off. Benthem

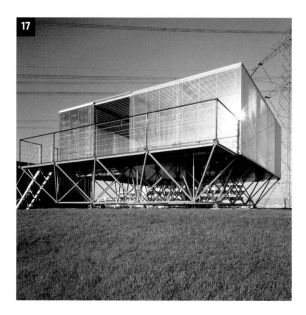

Crouwel devised an ingenious but simple detail. Two corner lines support the roof and the wedging together of the glass fins ensures that the roof remains fixed to the façade construction. This detail automatically creates space between the corner lines for the extra steel construction that was required to keep the roof in place. This extra construction consists of a number of compression members and traction cables that are attached to the floor by means of two traction cables. This solution means that a relatively large space is only interrupted by the two slender cables.

Crouwel's house shows clearly how thinking about detail and construction has changed over the years. It was designed eight years later than Benthem's, though it should be mentioned that the conditions were very different. Almere was nothing but meadow, and the house was built in connection with the Unusual Homes competition, which meant that it did not have to comply with building regulations and was only to stand for five years. In the meantime a permanent permit has been issued for the house. The glass extension of Crouwel's house, on the other hand, is next to a house designed by Jan Rietveld in 1951. The choice of materials results in a fairly harsh confrontation between new and old. At the same time, though, everything has been done to turn the two volumes into one. The dark brickwork of the existing north façade has also been applied in the extension, and the architects followed the same modular dimensions in the construction, while expanding it to twice the original size.

35 The construction of the glass façade of Crouwel's house is modest. No glass fins but ordinary steel profiles support both the glass and the roof. The roof construction is hidden behind blinds – proof of increasing reticence in showing off the technical aspects. The steel profiles are, remarkably enough, less conspicuous than the fairly deep glass fins of Benthem's house, and the desired transparency in Tienhoven is unexpectedly greater as a result, above all because the

steel construction enabled one of the corners to remain entirely construction-free. The disappearance of the construction behind the lowered ceiling arouses curiosity – as in Terminal West, the viewer wonders how the roof is supported – and enhances the visual calm. Not the details but the surroundings attract attention.

The fact that Benthem's house has a totally different look is not just the result of the glass façade. The house is situated on an enormous green space structure. → 17 The design of the supporting construction, incidentally, was not by Benthem Crouwel but by Mick Eekhout, while Jan Benthem thought of integrating the flat joints of the Octatube constructional system in the floor. The result was a fusion of infrastructure and superstructure that also made it possible to scrap an extra detail, thus making the design somewhat more efficient.

Benthem and Crouwel owe their reputation as high tech architects to this construction, the elegant roof construction of the Hazeldonk Customs Building (1984) → 18, the exoskeleton of the MORS building (1988) and to a lesser extent the construction of the entrance of the De Pont foundation for contemporary art, where a space structure is covered with perforated steel plates to mark the entrance. To a lesser extent than famous British architects like Norman Foster, Richard Rogers, Michael Hopkins and Nicolas Grimshaw, who emphasised the aesthetic quality of the constructions and installations at that time, Benthem Crouwel adduced primarily functional motivations for its eye-catching constructions. According to Benthem and Crouwel, it is logical for such buildings to have large span constructions, and it is simply easiest to make span constructions with steel lattice constructions. Even the bright green colour of the Customs Building has its reason: green is a durable colour, unlike red, which turns brown, or white, which turns yellow. Green darkens slightly over the years, but it stays green.

Logical construction

As Crouwel's house shows, the role of the construction has grown less conspicuous in the course of time. In this respect the work and development of Benthem Crouwel can be compared to that of Norman Foster. Foster used exhibitionist constructions in his early buildings, such as the Renault plant in Swindon (1983) and the Hong Kong and Shanghai Bank (Hong Kong, 1986) → 19, but afterwards he came to place more and more emphasis on the perfect skin, while the construction came to play a secondary role in determining the look of the building. Moreover, his constructions became increasingly functional. The exuberance of Swindon or Hong Kong caused eyebrows to be raised, but the later constructions, such as the Stansted Terminal (London, 1991), the Carré d'Art (Nîmes, 1993), Chek Lap Kok Airport (Hong Kong, 1998), or even the designs that consist

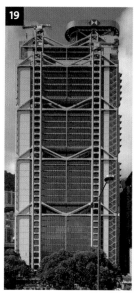

almost entirely of construction like the communications tower in Barcelona (1992) can be explained in terms of the simple rules of mechanics.

Benthem Crouwel seeks to explain the constructions using the same rules, plus – like Foster – functional requirements. In their view, every stage in the design process has to be explained. Beauty, like the treatment of detail, must be a logical result. The construction of Terminal West at Schiphol Airport, for example, is one of the most beautiful in their oeuvre. → **20** By setting the columns at an angle and making use of increasingly fragile branches in the construction, whereby the span of 12.6 metres is reduced via 6.3 metres at floor level to 3.15 metres in the roof, the hall acquires an exciting spatiality. The joints between the columns and the foundation blocks, and between the columns and the space structure, underline the spatiality of the constructional design.

The inclined angle of the columns, however, was not conceived in advance. To shorten the time required for building, the foundation was laid on the basis of a provisional design. While it was being elaborated, however, it transpired that the full programme did not fit inside the building volume. The architects created extra space by tilting the originally upright columns at an angle. The form of the joints follows from the fact that they link constructional elements that are at different angles. A sphere is therefore the logical solution, but it is difficult to effect joints on a closed sphere, so joints have been constructed from circular discs.

All constructions and in fact all details, however attractive they may sometimes be, are thus reduced by Benthem Crouwel to a fully logical whole in which aesthetics is almost a byproduct. 'The rhetoric-free matter-of-factness with which the two architects talk about their work suggests that they are the last representatives of nineteenth-century structural rationalism,' the critic Hans van Dijk wrote with reference to the Malietoren in The Hague in 1996. At the same time he tore off their disguise: 'But in reality Benthem & Crouwel are refined aesthetes'.[4] The construction of this tower and of other buildings certainly is aesthetic to a degree. The tower was built in The Hague above the motorway to Utrecht and the surrounding buildings left only an area next to the tunnel free for the foundations. Two heavy concrete discs rise from it. Stability is provided by the shores that are

prominently displayed on the front and rear façades. → **21** Benthem Crouwel bent the glass façade inwards to free the construction of the skin and vice versa. The design and details of the stability braces give away the fact that the architects were primarily out to achieve an attractive construction that would determine the look of the building. The shore constructions are three storeys high and give the building the articulation that is missing in the side walls. The depth that the building was supposed to acquire through the application of patterned glass is limited. The connection between the stability braces and the concrete side walls is attractively done and looks like another Benthem Crouwel ornament. → **22** It has been hidden behind streamlined stainless steel roofs that emphasise both the smoothness of the tower and, through the contrast between the grey and the indeterminate greyish-green background, the two directions of the constructions. Benthem's explanation that otherwise the required fire-resistant covering would have been visible is not convincing enough. Particularly in the rear façade, the construction produces a fascinating building where the wind braces pass via a system of V-columns into the spiral that winds its way up around the outside of the building to the garage. But it is not exactly logical. → **23** Schiphol Airport also has some aesthetic details in the construction. Some columns of Schiphol Plaza, for example, are wedged in place. This means that they require reinforcement at the base. Simple reinforcement ribs applied to the shaft of the column are actually all that is needed, but Benthem Crouwel replaced the bottom of the shaft with a cropped steel cone and welded V-shaped reinforcements on to it. → **24** The play of forces is more sculpturally visualised in this way. The columns in the Plaza that are not fixed and can only absorb vertical forces have a different detail at the base. → **25** It is a subtle touch that only insiders will be able to grasp. In this way Benthem Crouwel plays with the rules of mechanics to create constructions that are both functional and aesthetic at the same time, and that conceal the play of forces to a greater or lesser degree and thereby provoke curiosity. Perhaps the clearest example of this is the Freight Station 8 at Schiphol Airport (1997). The spans of 32 by 36 metres consist of Vierendeel girders that have acquired a V-shape on top of the square columns to distribute the forces more evenly over the column. Vierendeel girders are by definition heavier than triangulated girders because they are primarily designed to absorb horizontal forces. In this hall the Vierendeel girders are made of IPE girders that have been sawn in half and UNP profiles. The tubular wind bracing is suspended below these girders. It might have seemed natural to integrate the two systems, but the result now is a thick package of construction that matches the function of the freight

hall. Especially when seen from the gangway, the building seems to be made of nothing but constructions. The skylights and semi-transparent corrugated sheets produce intriguing light effects. The roof of the Villa Arena has a completely different look. Here Benthem Crouwel opted for thin lattice girders so that the strange shape of the roof could be made without its transparency becoming cluttered by the construction. The ingenuity of the work in the Benthem Crouwel Lab lies in the fact that it largely minimises the risk of building, which generally results in well-made buildings, but that it still always manages to create exciting buildings. The construction is an important resource to this end. It is not given the opportunity to be too prominent, it is true, but in almost every case it introduces an extra layer to the enjoyment of the building and the spaces. Benthem Crouwel achieves the same effect with its handling of detail. The smoothness is not everywhere. Small mouldings and ornamental details applied at the right points provide enough accents. Without allowing details of this kind to become too dominant, the architects prevent boredom from setting in. Moreover, the handling of detail is not perfect because of the liberty that is left up to the subcontractors. Occasionally this goes wrong, as in the case of the details of the Wagon Lits office in Amsterdam (1992), where the round form of the façade is rather awkwardly done, but generally speaking the treatment of detail livens up the buildings. → **26** As a result, unlike some of Foster's buildings, such as the ITN building (1990) in London and the Kop van Zuid office block (2000) in Rotterdam, which consist of nothing but a smoothly detailed skin, the buildings of Benthem Crouwel are never boring or overplanned.

1. H. Moscoviter, 'Als het maar functioneel is, Benthem Crouwel architecten', *Items*, 1993, no. 2.
2. V. van Rossem, *Benthem Crouwel Architecten*, Rotterdam 1992.
3. E. Melet, 'De ingetogen machine, Terminal-West van Benthem Crouwel NACO architecten', *de Architect*, 1993, no. 9.
4. H. van Dijk, 'Tall bridge. Benthem and Crouwel's office building in The Hague', *Archis*, 1997, no. 4.

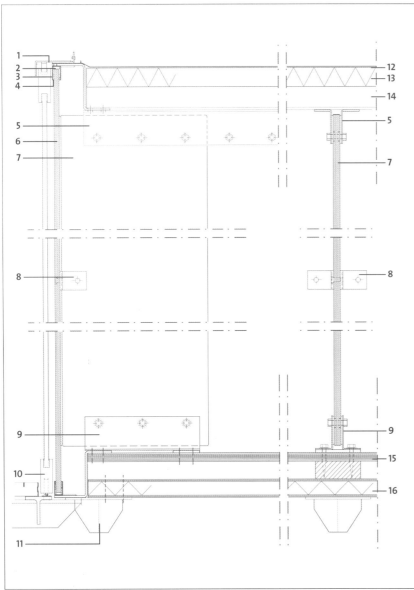

Glass façade (left), section through glass stabilizer (right)

1 sill with track for sliding door
2 neoprene
3 30 x 20 x 30 x 2 mm UNP
4 sealed joint
5 two 75 x 40 x 3 mm L-sections (roof truss)
6 12 mm toughened glass panel
7 5 mm toughened glass stabilizer
8 60 x 60 x 6 mm stabilizer clamp, 40 mm high; mounted using countersunk bolts
9 75 x 40 x 3 mm L-section for anchoring stabilizer
10 bottom of sliding door with rollers and lock
11 connection with space frame girder
12 roofing
13 insulation
14 roof slab
15 plywood floor
16 insulated composite floor panel

Junction between roof light and standing seam roof

1 roof light
2 aluminium profile
3 water bar
4 insulation
5 insulation
6 PE film
7 roof light support
8 pre-formed steel plate
9 standing seam roof
10 insulation
11 insulation
12 PE film
13 steel roof sheet
14 trapezium-shaped steel roof sheet
15 IPE 100

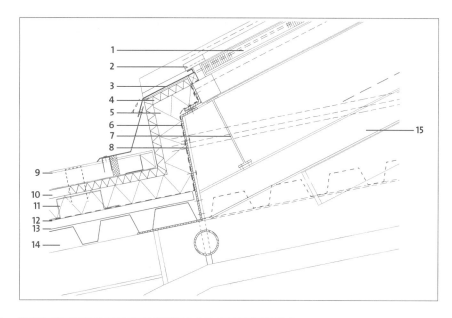

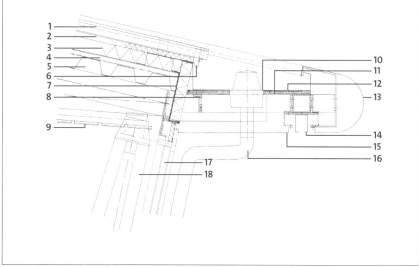

Roof edge at canted glass façade (airport side)

1 standing seam roofing
2 30 mm mineral wool
3 80 mm mineral wool
4 steel roof sheet
5 trapezium-shaped steel roof sheet
6 EPDM flashing
7 steel plate
8 50 x 100 x 6 mm L-section
9 aluminium strip ceiling
10 bituminous adhesive strip
11 plywood
12 aluminium gutter
13 3 mm-thick aluminium sheet
14 window cleaner's rail
15 2 mm-thick aluminium sheet
16 75 mm dia downpipe
17 glass façade
18 steel structure
19 stainless steel plinth with plywood glued to L-section
20 hot-galvanized grating

21 neoprene tape
22 pre-formed steel plate
23 mullion tied to bracket
24 convector well
25 insulation
26 mullion
27 façade system
28 pre-formed steel plate
29 rainwater discharge
30 woodwool cement slab + insulation
31 steel pipe for crash barrier
32 steel tube with anchor strips

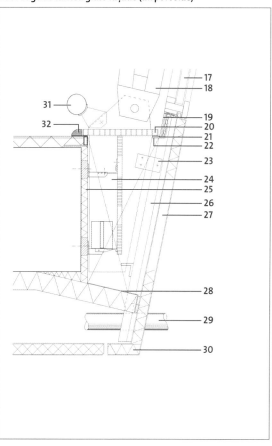

Lower detail of canted glass façade

**Junction office façade and
semicircular underpass**
1 window wall
2 aluminium drip
3 EPDM flashing + groove for
façade condensate
4 glass wool
5 120 x 80 x 12 mm angle
6 felt
7 aluminium gutter
8 3 mm-thick sendzimir
galvanized sheet
9 50 mm glass wool
10 sandwich panel
11 pre-formed steel sheet
12 aluminium sill
13 steel profile for roof light
14 glass roof light
15 170 x 80 mm box section
16 rubber profile (x2)
17 insulation
18 aluminium cladding void
19 DPC
20 profiled steel sheeting
21 UNP 240
22 wooden cleats
23 possibility for installing
new internal wall
24 2 mm-thick sendzimir
galvanized sheet
25 fair-face concrete

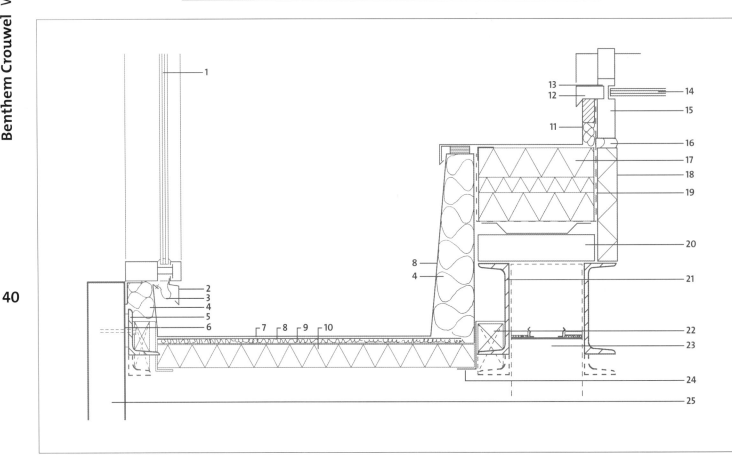

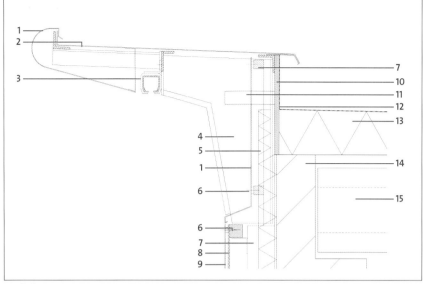

Roof edge

1 stainless steel cladding
2 white anodized aluminium
3 window cleaner's rails, hot galvanized
4 galvanized steel bracket
5 70 mm mineral wool, coated on one side
6 stainless steel screw, countersunk head with nylon washer
7 Wolmanized wooden battening
8 6 mm Eterspan, painted black; joints sealed
9 3 mm-thick stainless steel perforated sheeting
10 plywood
11 stainless steel water spout
12 bitumen roofing
13 mineral wool laid to falls
14 precast concrete inner leaf
15 hollow-core slab floor
16 60 x 60 x 4 mm angle bar, hot dip galvanized
17 aluminium cover strip
18 aluminium front
19 aluminium profile
20 concrete column
21 PVC-IP flashing
22 10 x 50 mm notches at 400 mm centres, for ventilation
23 15 mm pine sub-frame with pine slat
24 80 x 40 x 4 mm duct glued to middle rail
25 middle rail

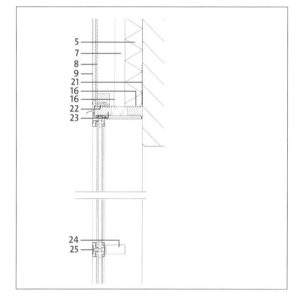

Junction frame and stainless steel façade

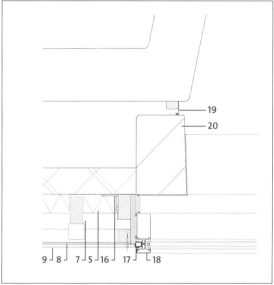

Horizontal junction frame and stainless steel façade

Roof edge
1 pre-formed aluminium roof edge
2 pre-formed aluminium panel
3 aluminium vanes in steel supporting structure
4 construction
5 metal ceiling
6 HE 140A column
7 figured glass
8 aluminium curtain wall with clear single-strength glazing
9 insulation
10 clear figured glass
11 precast concrete unit
12 ceiling lined with mineral fibreboard panels
13 insulating glazing with top-hung window, structural sealant, figured glass
14 clamped insulating glazing (clear)
15 aluminium window ledge
16 spray rendering
17 open joint

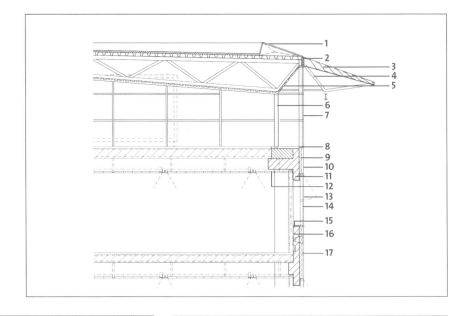

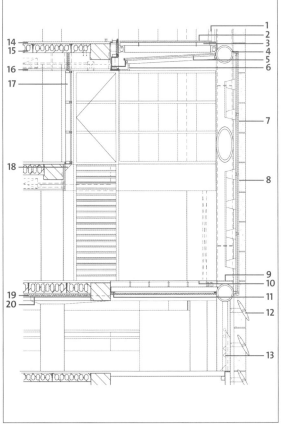

Section through façade at frame girder
1 balustrade
2 floor gratings
3 1/2 IPE 270
4 stability bracing made up of 460 mm round pipe + insulating sheath
5 metal ceiling
6 insulated gutter structure
7 insulating glass + screen printing
8 clear laminated glass
9 convector gratings
10 computer floor
11 angle
12 aluminium fins on steel structure
13 steel guard rail
14 compression layer
15 hollow-core slab floor
16 ceiling lined with mineral fibreboard panels
17 fire-resistant façade panel (60 min.)
18 spandrel panel support frame
19 insulation
20 woodwool cement slab

42

Roof edge

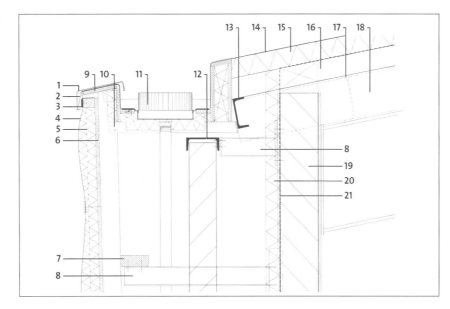

1 2 mm pre-formed steel section, hot dip galvanized and finished with EPDM
2 hot galvanized steel tingle
3 aluminium clamping strip
4 EPDM film, fixed with studs (CDs)
5 2 x 50 mm insulation
6 19 mm underlay on background structure
7 wooden beam
8 IPE 100
9 19 mm underlay with angle iron
10 50 x 50 x 5 mm hot dip galvanized angle to support gutter
11 Pluvia chute
12 curved UNP 180
13 curved UNP 160
14 EPDM roofing
15 100 mm insulation
16 profiled steel roof sheet
17 IPE 240
18 IPE 550
19 214 mm glued calcium silicate brickwork
20 80 mm insulation
21 vapour check
22 59 x 156 mm horizontal beam
23 cavity closed off with underlay on vertical beams
24 HE 140 A
25 precast concrete panel
26 3 mm finishing layer
27 10 mm Veka floor finish
28 90 x 250 x 10 mm hot dip galvanized angle

Corner EPDM façade

Junction EPDM façade and precast concrete panels

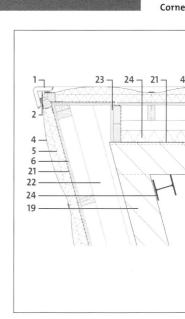

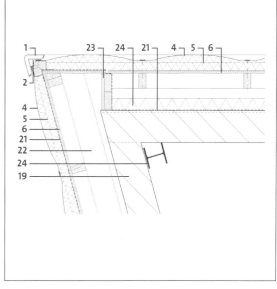

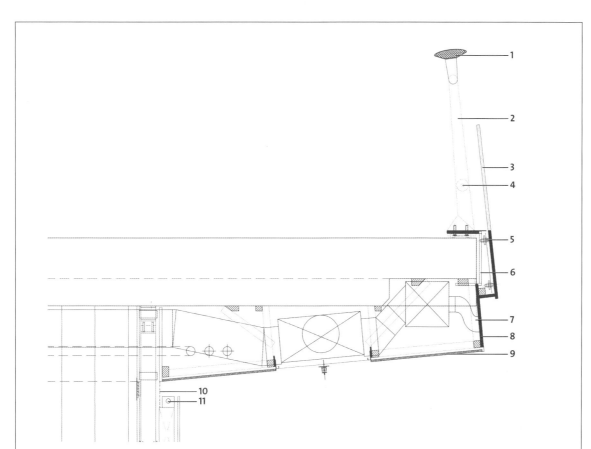

Detail of gallery
1 hardwood rail
2 cast aluminium baluster, barrel polished
3 sheet of glass; obscured and frosted in places
4 glass fibre lighting
5 glass fixing
6 continuous steel section
7 outlet grating
8 aluminium sheet
9 perforated plasterboard
10 ventilation grille
11 light fitting

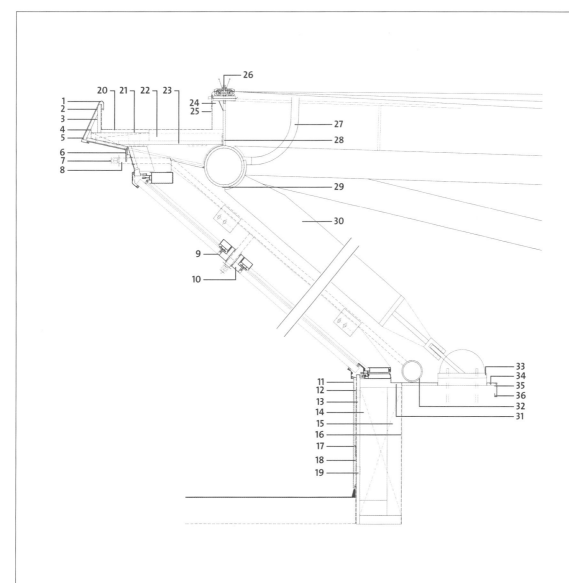

Junction façade and air-cushion roof
1 aluminium tingle
2 extra damp barrier, EPDM foil
3 cleat
4 waterproof plywood
5 aluminium sheet
6 movement-tolerant connection
7 side-wall sprinkler
8 heat coil to prevent pipes from freezing
9 aluminium curtain wall with glued glass structure
10 insulated sandwich panel
11 aluminium sheet
12 plywood strips
13 plywood
14 wooden framing
15 insulation
16 moisture barrier
17 clamp profile
18 damp proof course
19 ventilation grille
20 PVC gutter
21 plywood
22 60 mm insulating sheet
23 damp proof course
24 40 mm insulating sheet
25 PVC flashing
26 aluminium clamping profile for air-cushion roof
27 compressed air pipe for air cushions
28 continuous steel T-section
29 219 mm dia steel tubular section; also main air pipe
30 steel pipe
31 steel base plate
32 aluminium sheet
33 plywood
34 tingle
35 ring main for sprinkler
36 aluminium sheet

CEPEZED
More intelligence leads to more neutrality

During a lecture to the Steel Engineering Association, Jan Pesman introduced a new unit of measure: intelligence per kilo of building. More intelligence is needed in designing buildings. The time of monofunctional building elements, he believes, is over. A construction that merely supports is dumb; so is a façade that only resists rain, wind, heat and cold. Besides, the dimensioning of the building elements needs tightening up. Every kilo and every detail too many is waste. Pesman sees the search for more efficient ways of making buildings as an ongoing intellectual process. The buildings of his firm CEPEZED, that he set up in 1975 with Michiel Cohen and Rob Zee – who left the firm soon after its establishment – can therefore not be regarded as pure unica and thus as prototypes. They are rather one of a series, in which the next design embroiders (to some extent) on its predecessor in order to improve the engineering applied and to enrich the aesthetic effect achieved.

CEPEZED wants to achieve this goal by prefabricating the building components. The use of prefab elements makes it easier to draw on the experience acquired in earlier projects and thus to arrive at qualitatively better components, and moreover these elements are manufactured under regulated conditions in the factory. This makes them less susceptible to error. All that has to be done on the building site is to screw or bolt the elements together. Building becomes assembling. The final quality of the building is thereby less dependent on weather conditions and on the involvement of the builders. Nevertheless, the first project – four homes in Naarden (1981) – was not exactly an engineering success in spite of the application of prefab wooden sandwich panels. The subcontractor assembled the elements traditionally, which resulted in serious dimensioning errors. The many cover fillets that this required, which impaired the smoothness that CEPEZED was aiming for, the often poorly made details, and the long building period, partly due to the bankruptcy of the first subcontractor, made it clear to Pesman and Cohen that not only the building process but also the design process would have to be changed in order to derive optimal benefit from prefabrication.

Since then CEPEZED has been unravelling its designs in building elements that in principle correspond to the different building stages: foundation and ground floor (often constructed traditionally, i.e. in concrete, the main supporting construction, the casing (façade and roof),

the installations and the interior. The firm then designs each of these components, breaking the more complex elements down into smaller parts. This anatomy of the design and its individual components enhances insight into the functions of the parts, making it possible to scrap redundant components while at the same time enabling the improvement of the individual elements on the basis of their specific function. Since all of the components and their functions are clearly defined, CEPEZED knows what it wants when it is looking for the most suitable manufacturer. The manufacturer need not necessarily be in the building trade, since it is not experience but just the product that counts. For instance, each component of the staircase in the 'two without a roof' house (1989) in Delft – the steps, newel, handrail, balusters and stainless steel cables – came from a different supplier; the cables, for example, were supplied by a sailmaker. → 1, 2

When these products have been purchased and applied without any alterations, in a number of cases the combination of the engineering requirements or CEPEZED's architectural demands with the manufacturer's specific knowledge results in new products with intelligent details. The best-known example is the self-supporting steel sandwich façade panels that CEPEZED applies in virtually all its buildings. → 3 They are made by what used to be a refrigerator car manufacturer. The fact that Pesman and Cohen ended up at the door of this manufacturer is connected with the reluctance of traditional façade manufacturers who were not very keen on this product and with the fact that the requirements that refrigerator cars have to meet correspond more or less to those of homes: they have to be stable, strong, well insulated, waterproof and durable. The panels for the trucks consisted of two steel plates with a layer of PUR foam between them. The factory coating on the steel plates removes the need for inside or outside coating, and also makes them low maintenance. In short, the elements were highly suitable for application in the building trade, except that the handling of details naturally had to be adapted. After working for years with an aluminium-coloured or black coating with concealed attachment that contributed to the abstract quality of the façade, CEPEZED has made the sandwich panels more aesthetic for the halls of the German car manufacturer Porsche (2001), where glass has replaced the steel outer sheet. This gives the façade more depth. → 4

The development of the CEPEZED floor displays even more of an engineering evolution than the façade. Over the years the floor has acquired a more minimalist look and has become more intelligent at the same time. The first, more primitive versions of the floor were applied in the 'two without a roof' house and in the house in the Schutterstraat in Delft (1996). In both cases the profiled

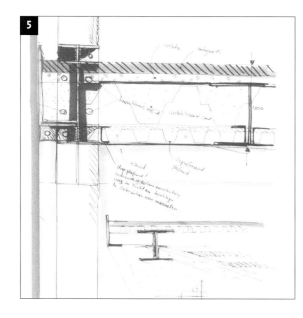

steel plate is covered with a layer of stabilising sand with insulating material on top, and finished with an anhydride floor. → **5** By much more deliberately adapting the materials used to their specific function (support, partition, fireproofing and sound insulation), it became possible to make this floor lighter than a traditional concrete floor, and thus easier to put into position using less heavy material. But the floor was still unintelligent. In the preliminary definitive version, as applied in the CEPEZED office (1999) in Delft, steel U-shaped cassettes form the basis. → **6** The floor is lacking in any kind of mass. Sealed insulation blankets are laid in these cassettes for sound insulation and fireproofing. Moreover, the shape of the cassettes enables them to be used as a plenum to guide fresh ventilation air to floor grids in the offices. Finally, all cables are incorporated in the floor. While the moulded plate was visible on the underneath of the early versions, providing information about how the floor was constructed, the smoothly coated undersides of the steel cassettes now form the ceiling. The floor has become more anonymous.

Restructuring of the building process

The development of products of this kind calls for close consultation with the suppliers. This is difficult in the building process that is usually followed in the Netherlands, where the general contractor acts as coordinator. This means that he is responsible for the contacts with the subcontractors, and as a result of the principle of equality he can look for other, often cheaper manufacturers who produce more or less the same products with similar detailing. CEPEZED wants the manufacturers who collaborated on the development of the various components to receive the final brief as well. Of course, this guarantee is attractive for the manufacturer too, since he puts a lot of time and money into the development of these new products. Because CEPEZED wanted to build using prefabricated components, it also assumed many of the tasks that are

usually carried out by the traditional general contractor. The longer manufacturing time of the building components, for example, requires the details to be completely elaborated at an early stage of the design process. Moreover, all the dimensions must be exact, because it is not possible to make corrections on site when prefab elements are used. In addition, CEPEZED also arranged the planning of the different stages of building. The firm was not paid for all this extra work, so it was a logical step for Cohen and Pesman to assume the place of the general contractor and to set up the sister company Bouwteam bv. Since then, this firm makes the initial contacts with subcontractors, coordinates on site, and contracts work out to the different suppliers. Splitting the building up into different parts also makes it easier to contract out part by part. Finally, Bouwteam monitors the budget. Incidentally, CEPEZED does make use of a general contractor for large and/or complex projects, such as the renovation of the enormous Entrepot building (1998) in Rotterdam, or the projects abroad.

Legible details

Prefabricated building naturally has consequences for the detailing of the buildings, though it is not clear which came first – the chicken or the egg. Details of prefab buildings – at least if no finishing materials have been applied – are clearly legible, and that is exactly how Pesman wanted his buildings and details. Every building component and its function had to be recognisable. This attitude to design has changed somewhat. After all, the different components have become less eloquent. For example, while it was clear to see how the floors had been constructed in the older buildings – since the steel profile plate and the concrete remained in view – and the installation and construction were separate elements, now the floor is much smoother and abstracter, as well more multifunctional. This development is rather similar to that of many domestic appliances, whose complexity cannot be read off at all from the abstract skin. Pesman calls this dosing information. He investigates very precisely at every level what his buildings are supposed to communicate. This proves to be less and less. This is evident, for example, in the ways in which CEPEZED deploys the constructions. Pesman used to share the predilection of the English high tech architects to ostentatiously show off the skill of the constructions in particular. Hence the industrial complexes in Haarlem (1986) → **7, 8** and Nieuwegein (1987) and the porter's lodge in Rotterdam (1985) were equipped with modest exo-skeletons. These constructions were well detailed, but by no means as spectacular as Norman Foster's Renault Centre in Swindon (1983) or as subtle as Renzo Piano's travelling IBM pavilion (1984). → **9** To some extent this will have been connected with the fact that

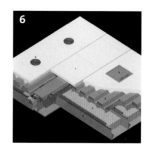

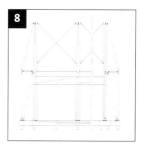

CEPEZED only disposed of limited budgets. Now that CEPEZED has carried out projects with generous budgets, especially outside the Netherlands – the new Porsche head office in Stuttgart and the ÖAW Forschungsgebäude [Research Centre] in Graz (2000) – Pesman has lost the urge to profile buildings by means of exhibitionist constructions. The insides and outsides of CEPEZED buildings are no longer concerned with eye-catching details of this kind. Now that the design has become reticent, the experience of the building has become greater.

Pesman illustrates how CEPEZED wants to deploy details by bringing out the differences between Norman Foster's Stansted Airport (1991) → 10 and Nicolas Grimshaw's Waterloo Station (1993) → 11, both in London. 'I find Foster's Stansted one of the most beautiful buildings there is. It is calm and logical. Nicolas Grimshaw, on the other hand, seizes upon every possible extension to turn it into a detail. This makes the detail almost a caricature of the genuine detail. You must not give a detail the attention that it does not deserve. Foster's quiet method of detailing is much harder to achieve.'[1]

The constructions in the CEPEZED buildings have also become quieter, and it is tempting to compare them no longer with those of the high tech architects, but with those of Mies van der Rohe. This comparison certainly holds for the constructions of the Woeste Willem crèche in Rotterdam (1994) → 12, although this is by no means CEPEZED's best building, and for the house in Boskoop (1997). The tubular constructions of these buildings have been placed outside the building envelope, but certainly not as in the other CEPEZED buildings as a sort of exo-skeleton to show off its ingenuity. Their detailing is modest and simple. For the crèche, the initial idea was to join the vertical and horizontal tubes with a cast-iron joint, but this proved to be beyond the budget. In retrospect, the building is none the worse for that. The connection between the different parts is now effected almost without detail, so that the construction seems to consist of a single whole. This makes it more abstract. Instead of being simply a support, the construction has now become a structure that tempers the transition from inside to outside because it continues horizontally outside the functional building. → 13 In the case of Woeste Willem, this idea is reinforced by the fact that the profiled roof plates are also suspended in the outdoor area framed by the construction, where they function as awnings.

However, the differences between CEPEZED and Mies van der Rohe are still great. According to his succinct texts, Mies strove for 'simple and logical building (Bauen) that was susceptible to further refinement (Baukunst) and that in principle was open to the optimal utilisation of industrial techniques'.[2] Seen in this light, the CEPEZED ideas seem to stem directly from Mies. According to critic Edward Ford, there is, however, a big difference between the theoretical Mies and his buildings. Mies wanted quiet, perfect details. Ford argues that Mies 'demanded seamless perfection. He hated visible joints and exposed fasteners. [...] The Constructivist desire for maintaining the visual identity of the individual member, although common in his formal vocabulary, is absent from his detailing [...]. By cladding the structure in simply seamless envelopes he was able to hide the crude structural joints, minimise the number of joints exposed and execute these exposed joints with the required precision. [...] The cladding must emphasise certain aspects of the structure it clads while concealing others. Mies expressed the columns in the strongest way possible while hiding the girders and beams above a flat plaster ceiling.'[3]

As this quotation shows, and as can be seen, for example, from the unusual construction that Mies designed for the enormous Convention Hall (1954; model, interior) in Chicago, he was primarily concerned with making the construction aesthetic. → 14 With an unequalled sense of proportion, he created wonderful images in which the final functionality remained subordinate to the image. CEPEZED also makes architectural constructions, but distils the aesthetic much more from the functional. The constructions are logical and often legible. In the postwar period Mies displayed a great predilection for I-profiles. CEPEZED is more pragmatic in the choice of profiles, although it seems to have a preference for tubes or rectangular profiles because they are less prominent. Both I-profiles and H-profiles have a clear direction and depth, and are therefore more conspicuously present. They ensure scaling. This is what Mies was after. A tube, on the other hand, only has a perimeter. It is rather mute. It is the same from all sides and has no face of its own. Besides, by adapting the thickness of the tube to the requirements with regard to strength, the diameter can be kept relatively small, so that it can be accommodated more easily into its surroundings and obstructs the view less. Finally, joints at the beams are simpler and less contrived. This is important because CEPEZED details the construction in a different way to that used by Mies. Mies polished every joint away and created primarily open, quiet spaces in which the construction consisted of abstract columns without head or foot. CEPEZED, on the other hand, often keeps the joints in sight, and since CEPEZED wants to make beautiful buildings as well, this means that the connections must be logical. → 15 Only then do they exude enough calm and match the firm's aesthetics. Incidentally, where desirable the joint between beam and column is – following Mies – increasingly out of sight (as in the CEPEZED office building) → **16** or stylised (Forschungsgebäude Graz). CEPEZED uses the roof construction to emphasise the visual axes in the building, by which the eye is directed from the inside to the outside, as it were. The red braced beams in the library and the crèche in Delft (1992) accentuate the sloping line of the roof of the building and lead the eye towards the pieces of glass above and below in the triangle. At first sight the main supporting construction of the 'two without a roof' house which is perpendicular to the diagonal and thus perpendicular to the main visual axis, is an exception, but in fact it made it possible to lay the profiles of the floor plates in the optimal direction to guide the eye towards the meadow. → **17** The positioning and detailing of the construction are thus done to involve the outside with the inside as far as possible. The opposite direction, unlike in the work of Mies, is much less common.

The relation between inside and outside
Of course, the relation between inside and outside is not only determined by the design of the construction, but above all by the choice of materials for the façade. In his essay 'CEPEZED, architecten', architect and critic Piet Vollaard distinguishes clearly between the use of the façade by CEPEZED and its use in Mies' Farnsworth house (Plano, Illinois, 1950). → **18** 'The outside is involved in the interior, but vice versa – unlike in the case of Mies or the flowing spatial concept of De Stijl – a more or less demarcated border [...]. The aim is not to increase the presence of the building, but to bring about its absence.'[4]
While Mies' buildings are often completely open, the street side of CEPEZED buildings is regularly closed. The 'two without a roof' house → **19**, the house in the Schutterstraat in Delft → **20**, and the villa Beckius (2000) have closed sandwich panel façades that have been opened up at strategic points for the user. The 'two without a roof' house and villa Beckius, that is modelled entirely on the 'two without a roof' house, only have a striking glass strip at the entrance, and the side walls of the house in the Schutterstraat have ceiling-high narrow windows which give these façades an exciting surface composition. The closed parts correspond to utilities.

Where the orientation, location and function call for glass façades on the street side, Pesman regulates the relation between looking in and looking out. He makes the large quantities of glass introvert – usually by placing different screens in front of the glass – so that the building retires. That is why aluminium profiles were used for the glass wall of the house on the Rietveld in Delft (1996) → **21**, and a screen of thermal zinc-coated grilles was used for the pavilion in the Nieuwe Waterweg in the Hook of Holland (1994). To arrive at a non-building in the Hook of Holland, Pesman simply continued the line of the natural slope of the embankment. → **22** The resulting triangular building houses a restaurant, an exhibition hall and a dockside office. Given the location and function, the view was important, but large expanses of glass would have led to an unregulated heating up of the building. That accounts for the fairly banal, thermal zinc-coated grilles, although they do fit in with the industrial environment of the Nieuwe Water-weg and the dock. They keep (some of) the warmth out-side, as well as hiding the activities in the building from sight.
Pesman placed black perforated steel plates in front of the Centre for Human Drugs Research (CHDR, 1995) in Leiden. → **23** Like the grilles in the Hook of Holland, the screens give the building a somewhat mysterious air, especially because the building is not as wide as the screens. Sometimes the building is visible, sometimes not. While the screens thus regulate looking in, the screen – surprisingly enough – hardly blocks the view from inside at all. The building is remarkably light. → **24** For these reasons Pesman considers the hole in the screen – the precisely determined dimension that generates all these qualities – as the detail of this building. Besides, the screens prove to be extremely important for regulating the indoor climate, and CEPEZED wants to make light, clear buildings without too many installations. This seems to be a paradoxical ambition. Light buildings heat up from sunlight and internal heat more rapidly than solid buildings do, but on the other hand they retain the heat for a shorter period and can therefore be ventilated more efficiently. The building reacts more directly to the weather. If the outside cools down, the theory goes, the inside cools down immediately.
In practice, however, this idea proved not to function so well, above all because of the lack of opportunities to ventilate properly in a natural way. The fact that the wind is almost always blowing in the Netherlands makes it uncomfortable to open windows. That is why the Nan orthodontic practice in Voorburg (1989) was later fitted with cooling machines, whose design and integration, as is usually the case with such additions, are not exactly in harmony with the architecture. → **25** The perforated screens in front of the buildings, however, turn out to

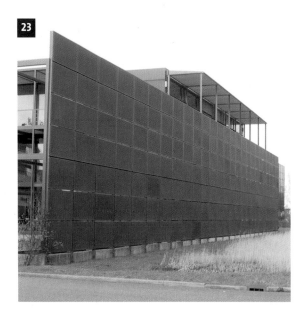

level the effect of the wind. The wind is converted into small turbulences behind the holes, creating a wind-free zone between the screen and the window that makes it possible to open the ceiling-high sliding doors for a large part of the year. This is sufficient to ventilate most of the rooms without installations.

The positive version of the black screen with light holes was applied in an office building in Delft (1999). → **26** Thanks to the new floor system, this is an even lighter building than the CHDR, where traditional channel plates were used for the floors, and so ventilation had to be provided in some way. Thin, perforated steel plates like those used in Leiden were out of the question here because the noise from trams, trains and cars demanded a heavier material. CEPEZED chose a glass screen that is not perforated, of course, but has been printed with a pattern identical to the perforated steel plates in Leiden. An identical effect is therefore obtained in terms of view and natural lighting.

Accommodating details

The dimensions of the glass screen are unusual. By only starting the glass at the first floor and leaving the aisle open, the screen has become a square. This gives the building an attractive division of surfaces. The glass plates are glued to specially developed rotulae, which are themselves attached to zinc-coated steel HE 120A profiles that also support the grilles of the balconies. The screen does not have a detail too many. → **27**

The same applies superficially to the real eye-catcher of this building, the glass lift on the corner. → **28** In collaboration with lift manufacturer Schindler, CEPEZED reduced the lift to essentials. The stainless steel safety device and the control panel are attached to the immaterial glass. In spite of, or because of this immateriality, the lift attracts all attention. CEPEZED made the rest of the building retire discreetly to achieve this effect.

The glass screen and the aisle covered with sandwich

panels are neutral, calm and lacking in detail. The façade of the offices is otherwise almost traditional. The aluminium facing of the front and rear façades is pretty hefty and has a detailing that somewhat resembles that of wooden window frames, and the roof edge is heavily accentuated. → **29** In spite of the unusual elements and its completely different character due to the large quantities of glass and metal panels, the building fits into its surroundings on the edge of the historic centre of Delft. The use of detail makes the façade, and with it the building, comprehensible. And thus with every detail Pesman weighs up which information the detail must convey in order to make the building intelligible and pleasant.

Intelligence by the kilo

CEPEZED works in a very different way with buildings without an immediate environment, with buildings that are much more of a pure object. The orthodontic practice in Voorburg is detached from its surroundings by the triangular shape, the use of material (only glass), and because it floats sixty centimetres above ground level – a very pragmatic detail, making it possible to place all of the connections beneath the practice without the need for a foundation pit. → **25** The details underline the abstraction of the volume; particularly striking is the detail of the almost absent roof edge. → **30** A similar object is the Bullewijk thermal transmission station, Amsterdam (2000). Like the building in Voorburg, the content of the station is hidden in the daytime. It does no more than being quietly present. To achieve this, CEPEZED glued opal glass sheets to a steel construction, resulting in the small box without any details.

While the comparison with Mies did not apply completely in the case of the constructions, the principle of the detailing of these objects – less is more – is directly inspired by Mies' views. Pesman shows himself to be a pure aesthete too, who tries to achieve a purely architectural object with as few visible details as possible, even in those cases where the function almost demands a façade with a restless look. The Research Centre in Graz, for example, contains a large number of relatively small offices. The shape of the building – two office wings which form two crosses at angles to one another – made it illogical to use a screen to render the building abstract. The rhythm of the office windows produced a fragmented and troubled picture. The windows have therefore been fitted with panels that are closed at night to hide the holes from sight. → **31** The office wings then become completely closed; detail-free blocks that give away nothing about their function. Even in the daytime when the panels are opened, the details temper the information about the window openings. While CEPEZED accentuated the frames in its own office building, here the frames have disappeared behind the steel panels.

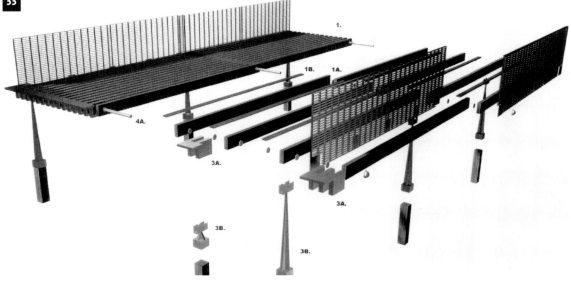

The windows become black holes.

Despite this striving for less and less, there is no question of the architectural anorexia that often occurs in connection with an increasingly minimalist architecture, to the horror of Herman Hertzberger.[5] There is always a balance between what is left out and what remains in sight. Not only the striking ground plan of the Research Centre, but also the completely glass staircases and the remarkable glass heads of the different wings prevent the building from becoming deaf and dumb. → **32**

CEPEZED designs all its buildings in a similar way and with the same design philosophy the series of wooden bridges consisting of nothing but wooden beams held together by steel cables. → **33** The dimensions can be adapted to suit the span and the expected heaviness of the traffic. The combination of wood with stainless steel and the refined, silent details bring the bridge to life. This bridge, but above all the building elements developed by the firm like the self-supporting sandwich façade elements, the multifunctional floor and the perforated screens, are evidence that experience and knowledge of materials are important to be able to make things more intelligently and thereby to make them more neutral and less 'technically burdened', if the intelligence per kilo of building is to go up. In addition, however, they show that the intelligent use of resources is at least as important. In this respect Pesman seems to be more and more prepared to retreat as a designer in order to regain ground immediately as an architect. The effect of a minimal, quietly detailed and thereby neutral building at a time when we are constantly bombarded by screaming images is so striking that in the end it manages to attract more rather than less attention.

1. E. Melet, 'Het doseren van informatie', *de Architect*, 1994, no. 6.
2. F. Schulz, *Mies van der Rohe, a critical biography*, Chicago 1995.
3. E.R. Ford, *Details of Modern Architecture*, Cambridge Ma/ London 1990.
4. P. Vollaard, *CEPEZED, architecten*, Rotterdam 1993.
5. H. Hertzberger, lecture in the series 'Een haast onmerkbaar lichte tinteling – het architectonische detail' [An almost imperceptible light tingling – the architectural detail], Academy of Architecture, Amsterdam 1996.

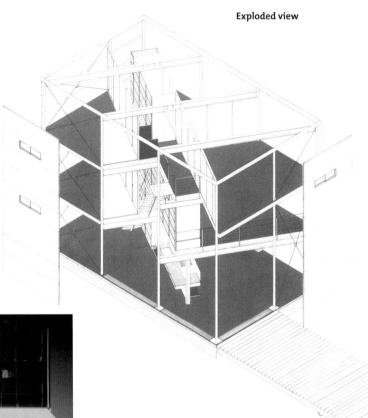

Roof edge of south façade with aluminium louvres on upper floor and junction between intermediate floor and façade

1 pre-formed stainless steel roof edge section
2 PVC roofing, bonded
3 polystyrene insulating plate
4 profiled sheet metal for sheet pile wall
5 angle
6 aluminium curtain wall with silicone rubber terminal strips
7 Sunshield aluminium louvres
8 anhydrite screed
9 mineral wool
10 sand
11 profiled sheet metal for sheet pile wall
12 sun shade

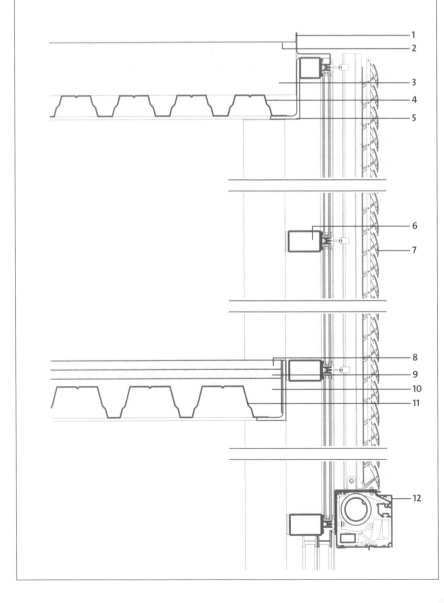

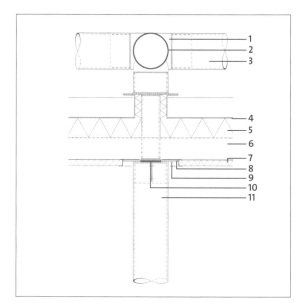

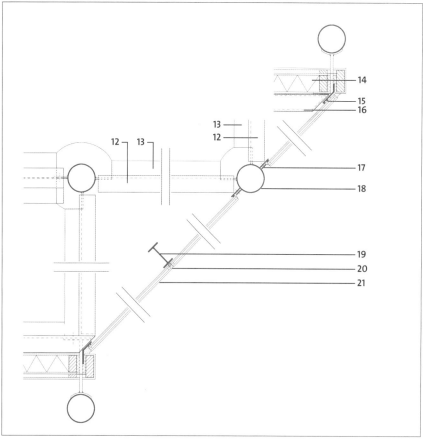

Connection of frame to roof

1 joint
2 168.3 x 5.6 mm tube
3 168.3 x 4 mm tube
4 PVC film
5 steel plate
6 profiled steel for
106 mm-high sheet piling
7 sound absorbing ceiling
8 support tape
9 bearing plate
10 1/2 IPE 200
11 168.3 x 7.1 mm tube (fill
columns with concrete at
intermediate floor)
12 200 x 100 x 15 mm angle
13 200 x 15 mm steel sheet,
welded to column
14 sandwich panel
15 pre-formed steel plate
16 200 x 100 x 5 mm tube
17 nylon strip with nylon bolts
18 168.3 x 7.1 mm 1/2 tube
19 PE 140

20 Norton band; structural
silicone sealant
21 clear float glass; 12 mm
cavity, laminated security
glass

Section through canted glass façade (entrance)

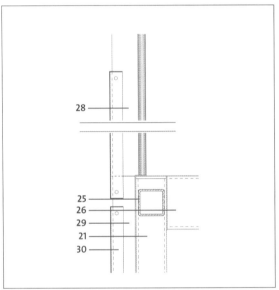

Perforated steel screen

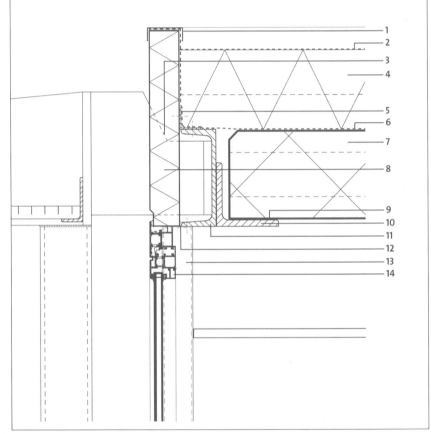

1 edging strip
2 PVC film
3 thermal break, saw cut
4 polystyrene sloping board
5 50 x 50 x 3 mm L-section
6 vapour resistant film
7 200 mm hollow-core slab
8 sandwich panel
9 support strip
10 150 x 15 mm L-section
11 UNP 220
12 sealant
13 70 mm box section
14 frame
15 50 x 60 x 4 mm Z-profile
16 screed
17 250 mm hollow-core slab
18 support strip
19 L-section 150 x 14 mm
20 UNP 280
21 box section 120 mm
22 200 x 400 mm plate for
fixing screen to façade
23 grille
24 rubber bearing pad
25 100 mm box section
26 200 x 120 mm box section
27 70 mm box section
28 composite section:
100 x 10 mm ms strip;
30 mm dia
29 90 x 10 mm ms strip
30 1.5 mm thick perforated
steel plate, taken over edges

Roof edge with junction
façade and perforated steel
screen

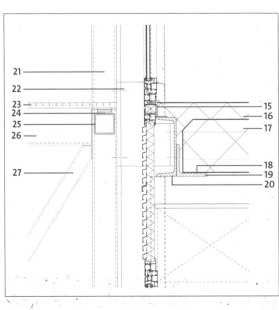

Façade at intermediate floor

54

Roof edge
1 pre-formed aluminium roof edge
2 fixing of rim
3 EPDM membrane
4 steel plate
5 groove filler
6 200 x 100 x 10 mm angle, coated
7 sealing tape
8 sliding patio door
9 120 x 60 mm steel façade column
10 200 x 6.3 mm duct / chute
11 PVC roofing
12 PS insulating board laid to falls
13 106 mm steel floor
14 support strip
15 HE 120 A

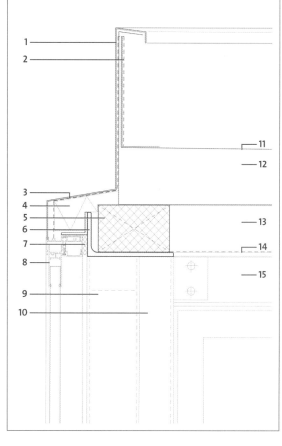

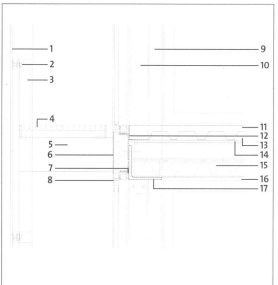

Glass screen and office façade at intermediate floor
1 screen-printed and toughened glass
2 articulated bolt (rotule)
3 80 x 20 mm strip
4 30 mm grille, hot-galvanized
5 steel strip at HE 120 A
6 aluminium cover plate
7 sealing tape
8 sliding patio door
9 200 x 200 mm column
10 120 x 60 mm duct
11 35 mm anhydrite
12 steel formwork for anhydrite
13 steel plate floor
14 rubber strip for acoustic damping
15 sealed rock wool blanket
16 200 x 200 x 16 mm angle
17 steel waffle slab

55

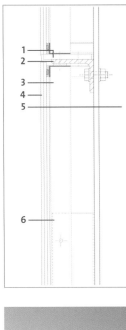

Typical façade detail at support
1 100 x 90 x 10 mm teflon strip to support glass
2 80 x 60 mm L-section
3 40 x 20 x 2 mm aluminium L-section to be attached to glass
4 5-5-4 laminated glass with opaque film
5 HE 200 A corner column
6 433 x 80 x 7 mm welded, hot-galvanized strip

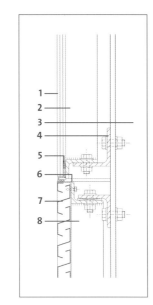

Junction glazed façade and ventilation grille
1 5-5-4 laminated glass with opaque film
2 3000 x 2000 mm welded steel frame for hanging glass
3 hot-galvanized IPE 240
4 80 x 60 mm L-section
5 thermal tape for fixing glass to background structure
6 100 x 14 x 3 mm welded strip to support glass
7 anodized aluminium ventilation grille
8 steel frame for hanging grille

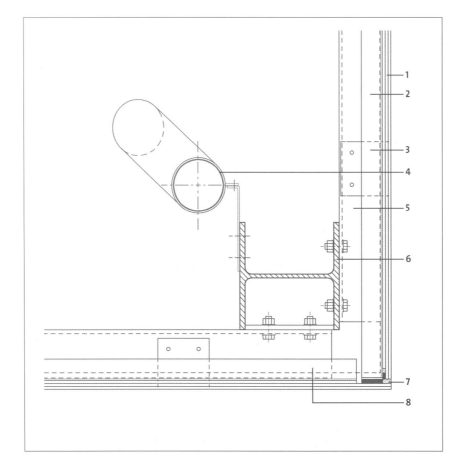

Horizontal corner detail of glazed façade
1 5-5-4 laminated glass with opaque film
2 40 x 20 x 2 mm aluminium L-section to be attached to glass
3 100 x 90 x 10 mm teflon strip to support glass
4 100 mm rainwater drain
5 80 x 60 mm L-section
6 HE 200 A corner column
7 silicone sealed joint
8 90 x 60 mm L-section

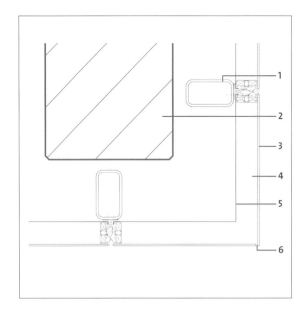

**Corner junction of glass
sandwich panels**
1 220 x 120 x 10 mm box
section
2 concrete column
3 8 mm glass front sheet of
sandwich panel
4 100 mm rock wool
5 0.75 mm steel rear sheet of
sandwich panel
6 8 mm grey sealed joint

57

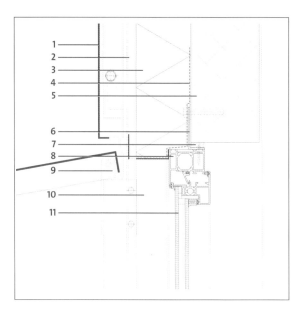

Façade detail at window with movable aluminium panels
1 aluminium panel
2 air cavity
3 steel plate
4 vapour resistant film
5 precast concrete panel
6 angle
7 sealed joint
8 aluminium frame
9 fixing of pivoting aluminium panels
10 view of aluminium box section
11 insulating glass

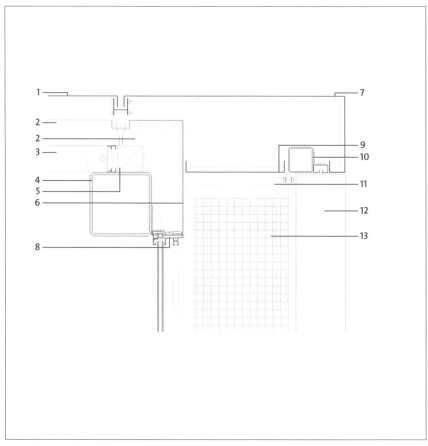

CEPEZED ÖAW Forschungsgebäude Graz 2000

Horizontal junction aluminium façade and glazed end façade
1 aluminium panel
2 insulation
3 view of concrete panel
4 250 x 250 mm steel column
5 shaft for power cables
6 aluminium plate
7 aluminium plate
8 aluminium sliding door
9 aluminium panel
10 box section
11 100 x 50 x 4 mm box section
12 aluminium vane
13 grid floor

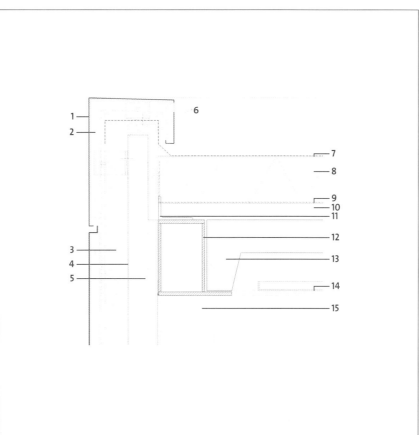

Roof edge
1 aluminium roof edge section
2 air cavity
3 steel plate
4 breather membrane
5 precast concrete panel
6 ventilation
7 roofing
8 steel plate
9 vapour barrier
10 concrete laid to falls
11 angle
12 320 x 200 mm edge beam with welded-on steel plate
13 reinforced concrete floor
14 hot/cold ceiling with acoustic membrane
15 250 x 250 mm steel column

Erick van Egeraat
Uncommonly beautiful

To describe the excitement that he wants his buildings to arouse, Erick van Egeraat likes to refer to one of the most horrific scenes in the film *Apocalypse Now* by Francis Ford Coppola, in which the protagonist is killed by the Vietcong. The killing itself is largely out of the picture. Sometimes you can see the face twisted in pain, alternating with almost romantic shots of cows grazing, for example. In the meantime the soundtrack is a cheerful tune. The director expertly increases the impact of the killing by not showing it and by incorporating contrasting images into the scene. It haunts your mind for days.

Erick van Egeraat's buildings are certainly not as appalling as the film, but he does know how to excite a fascinating tension beneath the skin in all his buildings. They arouse and appeal to the emotions. In this respect it is worth referring to the article 'The Eternal Youth of Mecanoo', in which critic Bart Lootsma analysed the significance of the logo of the collective to which Van Egeraat belonged until 1996. 'The attitude of the [floating] man is distinctly elegant [...] Floating expresses the absence of cares, just as the swimming gear refers to holiday and leisure.'[1] → **1** When Van Egeraat left Mecanoo, he chose a logo for his new firm, EEA, that at first sight looked a lot like that of Mecanoo. It too shows a man falling, but the absence of cares is gone. Instead of an abstract figure, we see a face contorted (in pain?); the arms and legs are not in the position of a smooth glide and the fall is less controlled. → **2** The same change can be seen in his work. While the critic Roemer van Toorn could still write that Mecanoo 'wages a war for quality by the rules, without expressing any discrepancy or ambiguity in the project', Van Egeraat manages – without any social critique, by the way – to elicit a sense that something is not quite right in his buildings.[2]

This tension is produced through contrasts. 'The conviction that architecture is best understood as a complex, multi-layered ambiguity, lies behind Van Egeraat's refusal to be categorised. He insists on the simultaneous use of different architectural codes. He will put chaste structural steel work side by side with richly patinated gold finishes. He can revel in the chilly austerity of metal at the same time as the sensual deployment of timber. He is ready to put swelling curves next to orthogonal geometry.'[3] Van Egeraat's buildings continue to intrigue because he proceeds to successfully fuse the contrasting elements completely in a logical whole. Otherwise some of his buildings would have been simply strange.

For example, take the bizarre Mezz Poppodium in Breda (2002) → **3**, where a copper shell-shaped form containing the auditorium and the foyer has been juxtaposed with an officers' mess dating from 1899, or the even more extreme case of the hanging conference room of the office of the ING Bank and Nationale Nederlanden in Budapest (1994). → **4** It is a zinc object that has landed on the fully glass roof and seems to have fallen through it partly because of its own weight. The volume hangs from the glass of the atrium like a zinc drop. At first it is reminiscent of the designs by US architect Lebbeus Woods (1940), but Woods sketched real intruders, objects that conquer a place for themselves in a world of destruction or parasites that have dug into the soil and try to make a new form of life possible there. (Underground Berlin, 1988) → **5** They are dangerous in a tainted world. Van Egeraat's intruder has landed on a monumental nineteenth-century eclectic building in the Andrassy Ut, or next to an old barracks in Breda the contrast could have caused an unbearable tension or even rejection. But that is further than Van Egeraat wants to go; what he wants to do is to bring things that are inherently deviant together. That is why he has made the aliens so beautiful that they can blend with their surroundings. There is a striking difference in the application of detail between Van Egeraat's Poppodium and Lars Spuybroek's water pavilion Neeltje Jans (1997). In terms of shape and construction the two buildings resemble one another to some extent, but whereas the body of Spuybroek's building is dented to match the Woods designs better, Van Egeraat achieves an enormous perfection with sprayed concrete and a copper skin.

The misshapen wooden ribs of the Budapest conference room have been made as precisely as they were drawn on the computer and then wrapped in a tight skin of zinc. → **6** The accentuated double-lock welts give the skin – and with it the body – more volume. Woods' figures are made from scrap and have a long and painful life behind them; Van Egeraat's alien becomes lovable through the perfection and the kneading of the metal into the precise shape. In the book that was published in connection with the completion of the project, the alien was tenderly called a whale, and the part hanging inside the building its belly.[4]

The whale hangs in the glass roof that covers this atrium. The glass is actually just as odd as the whale itself, it is taut, smooth and, because it rests on glass beams – a constructional application of glass as exciting as it is forward-looking – very transparent.

While Van Egeraat accentuated the joints of the zinc plates of the whale to suggest more volume, the lower side of the beams are polished to camouflage the layered nature of the glass, because in his view a visible layered

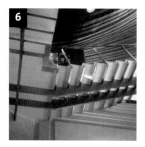

structure of the glass would have caused just too much noise. → **7** Van Egeraat considered that the roof construction with the steel mouldings, the stainless steel stanchions in which the glass beams are fixed, and the glass roof with the black kit joints was already too full. However pedantic this may sound and may even be, it is precisely by paying a lot of attention to these kinds of very small details that he succeeds in allowing the alien to combine with the rest of the building. An equal amount of care has gone into the design of both the new and modern-looking elements and the imitation Neo-Renaissance elements – the building was first stripped completely before the original details were restored in a slightly modernised style–, which enabled them to blend in a single multi-layered whole that is rich in contrasts. The building does not break down into parts.

Modern Baroque

It is striking that Van Egeraat used the more or less original details of the building to create the desired atmosphere. After all, Mecanoo was seen as one of the Dutch firms that adhered strictly to the idiom of the Modernists. They loathed the architecture of the nineteenth century with all its ornaments. Van Egeraat's original idea was not to restore all those details in the interior in their original state. He discovered the potential of monumental buildings like this during a walk in Dresden. 'I looked up to see the buildings that surrounded me. And instead of the compassionate disbelief I usually felt for eighteenth-century gold leaf and angels as well as for the considerably older decorative murals and graffiti, I suddenly realised that these walls appeared more silent than all the contemporary architectural muttering I knew of. The façades of these buildings were not loud, but instead clear and clean. They were not wasteful, but actually very effective and efficient. The architecture provided solace. Built to impress and lavish, they actually provided a pillow for the tired traveller to lay his head to rest.'[5] Van Egeraat went on to introduce the notion of Modern Baroque. The term 'Baroque' is not entirely right, because Baroque is characterised not only by a visual wealth, but also by a very strict, mathematical division of surfaces. Van Egeraat, on the other hand, designs intuitively and the tension that he tries to bring about in his buildings – Baroque was primarily grandiose and celebratory, lacking genuine depth – is closer to Romanticism than

Baroque. However, more important than the exact term is the fact that Van Egeraat tries to combine the austerity of Modernism with the richness of the buildings of the eighteenth and nineteenth century. 'I attempt to get away from the present symmetry and order and instead introduce asymmetry and disharmony disassociated from their obvious negative connotations. For me, it is the excitement which you can feel whenever encountering something unknown and undefinable, to deploy alternative design techniques which enable you to portray the unpresentable and undefinable.'[6] Van Egeraat creates tension in the ING building in Budapest and in the Mezz Poppodium through the combination of more or less historical details with the use of modern materials and above all by the embedding of the aliens. Two completely heterogeneous elements are fused. In fact the same process takes place in his design for the NOS building in Hilversum (1996), where the bizarre protruding glass volume of the entrance is merged with the solid brick volume. → **8** The minimal pointing of the glued masonry gives it a heavier appearance than ordinary masonry. It is a reassuring element here – we are familiar with brickwork. The strangely shaped glass sphere emerges from that brickwork. At first sight this strange volume seems to be supported by slender, apparently too slender steel cables. The impression of a weak construction is reinforced because the stretched glass volume already seems to be sinking. In fact, of course, this is not the case. The cables have been pre-tensioned to absorb both pressure and traction forces. But the idea of an unstable construction is certainly evoked. Confidence is won back – when all is said and done, Van Egeraat tries to undermine certainties, but he does not want the separate parts to reject one another – by the use of detail. First of all there are the details of the construction. The steel cables are linked with sturdy steel girders inlaid in the masonry which remain visible. The ponderous brickwork container is thus merged with the fragile glass volume.

This also ensures that the construction of the glass entrance and the presence of this glass volume itself are made tangible in the rest of the building. It serves as a kind of forerunner of the spectacular hall. In addition, the glass wall has not been made completely smooth, but the sheets of glass have been laid like roofing tiles. The application of details, by which the topmost sheet of glass protrudes slightly above the lower one (a detail that was also necessary to make the wall waterproof) gives the glass wall an almost artisanal look. These details strengthen confidence in the glass wall.

Rough details

The rougher details of the Crawford Municipal Art Gallery in Cork (2000) bring about the fusion of the strange-looking new building with the old, practically worn out building. The brickwork 'bowls' that elegantly effect the transition from the wall to the roof are the incongruous elements here. The two buildings are linked to one another by allowing these 'bowls' to continue for a way in front of the façade of the old building. They have a rougher finish than, for instance, the whale in Van Egeraat's ING building. The lines are not tight and the shape is not smooth or streamlined. Moreover, the transition from the old to the new façade is not perfect. → 9 The detail of the empty space in the glass wall betrays that this lack of perfection is at least to some extent intentional. The concrete of the floor at this point has been hacked away, as it were, between the steel reinforcements. The rusty steel of the reinforcement has been left behind. There are other imperfect details in the building too. For instance, the handrail rests nonchalantly on rough stones protruding from the wall, and the holes in the walls are not properly aligned. As the old building was in a sorry state, there was no budget to finish everything perfectly, and the street where the museum is situated is pretty grim, to say the least, the brickwork 'bowls' in particular – in spite of their remarkable appearance – fall into place thanks to the imperfect finish of the details. The tension created by the strange bowls remains intact, but by adapting the details of the strange elements to the surroundings, Van Egeraat turns the street into a sort of precursor of the museum. The street becomes permeated by the tension of the building. This tension is more subcutaneous, which makes its effect last longer. In the case of the Poppodium in Breda, it is not completely visible from the

homes on the site, but is concealed by the sloping roof of the officers' mess. This hazy presence arouses curiosity. Van Egeraat regards the application of looser details in Cork as a way of making a move as an architect. He wants things to happen more or less by themselves in his buildings, though that turns out to be less simple than striving for perfection. Organising chaos at the level of the detail often leads to rather finicky details, while abandoning control altogether simply leads to bad details, and that is going too far for him. Both kinds of details can be found in the Cork building. The steel reinforcement in the empty space, an intrinsically exciting and visual element, has been cleanly pruned near the exterior wall piers. There is thus no genuine confrontation between the two components, which could have been very exciting. The doors too have been coated very smoothly and their precise finish is out of place in what is supposed to be a rough environment. Traditional painting would have been more appropriate here. The chaos is too tightly reined. On the other hand, the safety lintel of the curving masonry has been facetted because a curved lintel would have been too expensive. The gaps between the masonry and the frame were very irregular. Van Egeraat corrected this detail because it entails too much chaos, and – worse than that – an 'undirected' chaos. → 10

The Ichthus Hogeschool [College] in Rotterdam (2000) also shows clear signs of organised chaos. → 11 The footbridges in the atrium, which also function as a work area, look very industrial. The steel construction is robust and very conspicuous. This gave the building more or less the industrial look that Van Egeraat was aiming for. But not only is the steel construction highly stylized; the sprinkler installations – which are necessary for fire safety – have been incorporated in the hollow steel sections. Making them visible – which could have led to a genuinely raw industrial building – was going too far for Van Egeraat. → 12

Stacking

In order to be able to build in a somewhat more casual way without losing the finished look requires simpler details. It is important that the different materials do not come into contact and enter into a relation with one another in the joints, but that cold joints are made in which the different materials are stacked, as it were. In this way the confrontation between different materials becomes harder, more pronounced, and often more exciting. Details of this kind were developed for the complex of apartments, Stuivesantplein, in Tilburg (1999). → 13 The surfaces have been set behind one another as much as possible to avoid tricky joints. The natural stone side walls of the flats are set starkly between the concrete upper and lower borders. The same is true of the lower façades of the access balconies

made of rough Western red cedar planks. → **14** There is no contact between the wood and the natural stone at the corners. The different materials are juxtaposed on the entrance side of the family units too. Wood, glass, natural stone and even the concrete partitions are independent surfaces. The confrontation of these materials – each of which produces a different visual effect – is one of the unusual and exciting facets of this building. Van Egeraat shows here that avoiding minute details need not be detrimental to the visual richness of a building.

The same approach to detail, in which the different elements do not meet in a joint, but where the materials are simply placed on top of one another, is used in the three blocks of flats, Haus 13 IGA, in Stuttgart (1993), but for a different purpose. → **15** Van Egeraat seems to use this technique in Germany to negate the 'ordinariness' of the various elements. Rough I-profiles jut out of the smoothly plastered walls of the tower block like broken bones sticking out of a body. → **16** The independent volume of the walkways seems to have landed on this system of profiles. The idea of chance is reinforced because the profiles are irregular in length. Moreover, the walkways appear to simply lie on top of the profiles (unlike the balconies, which also lie on top of the profiles that protrude from the volume of the building, but where the wooden beams of the floor overhang the profiles, thereby creating more of a unity). The access balcony looks like a fortunate accident, by which elements that are familiar in themselves (block of flats, lift and walkway) are linked to one another. The components themselves are not new, but first detaching them and then connecting them again with one another makes these familiar elements unfamiliar. What is normal becomes strange, or at any rate more unusual.

Profile glass façades and layered glass

The glass façades of the three tower blocks are not new either, but they are certainly unusual. Van Egeraat has given them extra relief by turning the glass façades

inside out. As a result, the relatively shallow snap-on frames have ended up inside the flats, while the deeper buttress profiles are on the outside. This brings life to what would otherwise have been a dull and slick glass façade. At the same time, this façade very implicitly suggests that there is something wrong. → **17** The profiling of the glass façade in the Ichthus college in Rotterdam assumes almost bizarre forms. The large sheets of glass, placed horizontally like the steel plates of a ship, are kept in place by equally large aluminium wings. This exaggerated construction gives the glass building a rougher exterior and is also intended to inspire confidence. However, the aluminium profiles have not been applied to every sheet of glass. → **18** They are distributed arhythmically across the façade. The result is a graphic image, but at the same time this calls their usefulness into question. What at first looked like a very solid façade because of the profiles now looks like an unstable whole because of the way that some profiles have been left out. What was supposed to inspire confidence is destabilised. What appeared to be functional now looks ornamental.

Besides the detailing of the glass façades, Van Egeraat also manipulates the glass itself to create an exciting tension. Glass is an important material in his work. In the book *Cool Hot Medium*, Deyan Sudjic attributes to Van Egeraat a palette of materials that lies 'very much at the glossy end of the spectrum'.[7] He does use a lot of glass in his buildings, but the glass is rarely used for transparency alone.[8] Van Egeraat tries to strip the glass in his buildings of its natural lack of materiality. The first instance of this can be seen in the extension of the ING main office (1997). This building, which adjoins the monumental building with the alien in a side street of the Andrássy Út, has at first sight a natural stone façade, so it looks as though Van Egeraat has tried to match the other historic buildings in this street. In fact, however, the façades are made of silk-screened glass. → **19** By moving the silk-screening slightly each time, each sheet of glass has a slightly different pattern that comes close to the capriciousness of natural stone. Moreover, the two sheets of glass of the mechanically ventilated façade are silk-screened too, giving the glass even more depth than natural stone would have. The nature of the material gives itself away because the silk-screened impression has been applied in such a way that the façade is blank when you view it from an angle, but transparent when you stand in front of it. This glass also has the special property of filtering the daylight that enters the building.

The glass is glued, so the detailing of the façade is completely flat. This detailing is like a natural stone façade in appearance, giving the façade a certain inaccessibility. Unlike the heavily profiled façades with 'ordinary transparent glass' in Stuttgart and the Ichthus

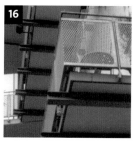

school, the screened glass façades do not require any special profiling. The silk-screening is enough to give the façade a fascinating depth and three-dimensionality. Van Egeraat deploys a different strategy in the Technical School (VLC) in Utrecht (1997) and in the Museum of Natural History in Rotterdam (1996) to give glass a strange third dimension. For the Technical School he was asked to give the school, that had already been designed, the progressive look it needed. The floor plans and the division of the façades had already been determined. In fact, he did no more than he was asked. The original exterior cavity wall has been removed and replaced by a glass veil. Such a simple intervention has produced an optimal effect, especially in the case of the façades where only rockwool can be seen behind the glass. The glass casing suddenly turns this inexpensive material into something sumptuous. The reverse process applies as well. The glass is not really anything, it is not material, but by being set in front of the rockwool it acquires colour, depth and meaning. → **20** By continuing the glass above the volume of the building, Van Egeraat links the sky and the building in which the sky is reflected. They merge. Although the same is true of the glass façades placed in the other wings of the school in front of the wooden and red painted limestone walls, the effect there is considerably less: the glass is just strangely apparently redundant and hardly at home. The glass veil is very simple. The glass is set between aluminium profiles. A gap of 1 cm has been left between each sheet of glass to ventilate the building and the cavity wall. Its position in front of opaque material gives the glass depth, while the aluminium profiles and gaps give the façade rhythm.[9] The banality of this façade is underlined where it meets the ground; grilles have been placed here with almost the same detailing to make the façade less vulnerable. → **21** The contrasts between the different materials – glass, rockwool, grilles – ensure a surprising richness, although that richness is somewhat spoiled by the fact that the rockwool turns out to get very dirty.

The north and east walls of the Museum of Natural History are similar to the façades of the Technical School. → **22** This time Van Egeraat placed a glass box around largely closed concrete walls. On the park side the concrete wall floats 1.5 metres above the floor. This is visually exciting, but it is specially in the exhibition area enclosed in this concrete volume that the value of leaving this strip open becomes clear. On the one hand, it allows indirect light into the space, and on the other hand it offers a glimpse of the Museum Park, without either of them being obtrusively present. → **23** The concrete is further inside in the east wall, where the glass casing forms an enormous showcase in which the skeleton of a whale hangs.

The glass box is confined on top by a pronounced roof edge, that is set slightly inside the glass. These details also make it clear that the glass is not used here to produce a light and transparent building. The glass 'merely' adds a layer to the outer wall, creating depth and arousing curiosity.

Unlike the glued façades with silk-screened glass, the detailing of the glass façades of the Museum of the Natural History and the Technical School is not completely flat. Although glued glass might have been appropriate in the museum, the glass is held in place by simple snap-on frames.

Moments of doubt

The constructions have a disruptive character. This can be seen most clearly in the case of the thick brick wall that 'hovers' above the ground level thanks to a narrow strip of glass. The construction of the glass façade is less logical than appears at first sight too. The slender tubes are fitted with narrow arms that grip the glass profiles. The arms look fragile, but apart from that the construction looks attractive. Upon closer inspection, however, the minuscule tension wires connecting the tube with the horizontal profiles stand out. Apparently Van Egeraat wanted this detail to show how the casing is supported and how the forces exerted on it are absorbed. The wires absorb the vertical forces, while the arms absorb the horizontal forces. The skeleton becomes easier to understand, but it is still not a practical or constructionally effective skeleton, which would have absorbed both forces at the same time. As a result, this construction raises questions too. In this way, much more than if the tension wires had been left out, Van Egeraat raises doubts as to whether this slender construction was not originally too fragile and the wires were added later. This avoids too self-conscious a construction. These constructions, and especially the application of the materials, evoke doubt as well as tension, and it these moments of doubt that interest Van Egeraat. Something is not right, but it is often not immediately clear what that something is. The detail is of crucial

importance to provoke moments of this kind. On the one hand, he manages to make the strangest forms and remarkable material combinations look natural and obvious. On the other hand, the 'normal' things in a building are made to look strange precisely through the bizarre combinations.

The suggested naturalness is confined to external appearance. Van Egeraat is much less interested in the technical requirements needed to create this 'natural state'. 'Architecture is about taste, and in the detailing too it is like the art of cooking. What matters in a very good restaurant is what a dish looks like and – much more important – what it finally tastes like. No one wants to know how it is made. The same is true of architecture.'[10]

How this detail strategy works can also be seen from the design for the town hall in Alphen aan den Rijn (2002), where the enormously overhanging entrance hall seems to be supported by a system of sloping wooden columns.
→ 24 Of course, this is impossible; the wood is only used as a casing around the steel columns. But the tension, the moment of uncertainty, has already been evoked. Besides, that tension does not disappear just like that. This detail, and the same is true of the other essential details in his buildings, has been done so well that it does not give away anything about its actual state. So the uncertainty remains. The perfect detail – the fact that the columns do look as if they are made of wood – ensures that the effect continues to buzz for a long time afterwards.

1. B. Lootsma, 'De eeuwige jeugd van Mecanoo. Projecten in Boedapest, Stuttgart en Rotterdam', de Architect, 1994, no. 11.
2. R. van Toorn, 'Architectuur om de architectuur. Modernisme als ornament in het recente werk van Mecanoo', Archis, 1992 , no. 11.
3. D. Sudjic, 'Not neither nor but both and', Erick van Egeraat six ideas about architecture, Basle 1997.
4. E. Melet, 'De goed van het bestaande, detaillering en materiaalgebruik bij Mecanoo', de Architect, 1994, no. 11.
5. E. van Egeraat, D. Sudjic, 'Architecture, temptation and solace', Erick van Egeraat six ideas about architecture, Basle 1997.
6. See note 5.
7. D. Sudjic, Cool Hot Medium, Berlin 1997.
8. E. Melet, 'Intrinsieke spanning. Techniek bij Erick van Egeraat', de Architect, 1997, no. 4.
9. See note 8.
10. Erick van Egeraat in conversation with the author.

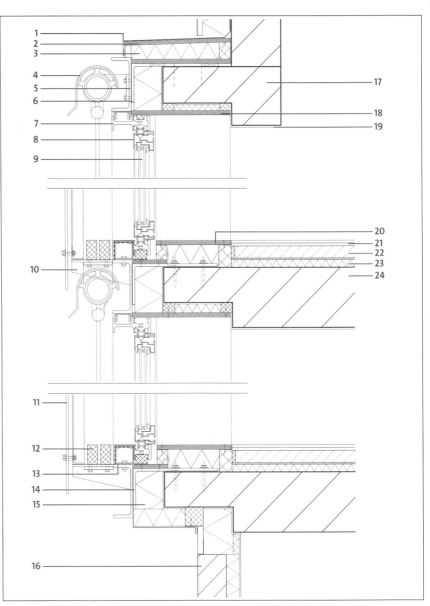

Section through wooden balcony
1 wooden railing
2 40 x 10 mm steel plate
3 16 mm dia steel tube (solid)
4 western red cedar boards
5 toughened glass
6 10 mm thick steel plate
7 wooden floor boards bolted to IPE
8 IPE 300
9 UNP 200

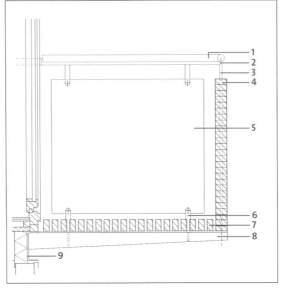

Glass façade
1 zinc cladding
2 water-resistant plywood
3 insulation
4 solar shading
5 UNP 180
6 steel angle
7 aluminium façade system, erected 'inside out'
8 aluminium frame
9 insulating glass
10 IPE 100
11 toughened glass safety barrier
12 35 x 65 mm wooden planks
13 66 x 55 x 3 mm box section
14 angle
15 insulation
16 concrete plinth
17 precast concrete panel
18 colour-painted plywood
19 render
20 removable plywood
21 floor finish
22 compression layer
23 insulation
24 wide-slab floor

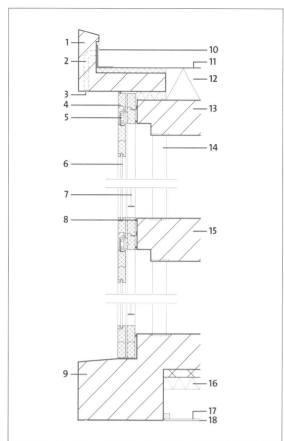

Façade detail of gallery at overhang
1 precast concrete roof edge
2 embedded water spout
3 15 mm dia throating
4 western red cedar siding
5 steel rail/guide
6 laminated glass
7 railing bars
8 sealant on backup strip
9 precast concrete
10 clamp profile
11 two-ply bitumen roofing
12 insulation
13 wide-slab covering floor
14 column
15 wide-slab floor, mechanically polished
16 insulation
17 20 mm fibre cement board
18 grey render

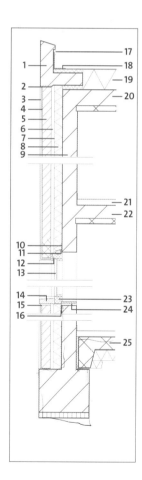

Section through stone façade
1 precast concrete roof edge
2 rebate at 1000 mm centres
3 10 mm slate
4 10 mm rendering coat
5 100 mm brickwork for rendering
6 30 mm cavity
7 vapour barrier
8 80 mm insulation
9 150 mm concrete
10 vapour resistant film
11 PVC foam tape
12 pine frame
13 insulating glass
14 slate
15 mortar bed
16 steel angle
17 clamp profile
18 double layer bitumen roofing
19 insulation laid to falls
20 wide-slab roof deck
21 50 mm finishing layer
22 wide-slab floor
23 67 x 80 mm pinewood frame
24 140 x 20 mm MDF window ledge
25 ribbed waffle slab floor

Erick van Egeraat ING Bank & Nationale Nederlanden head office Budapest 1994

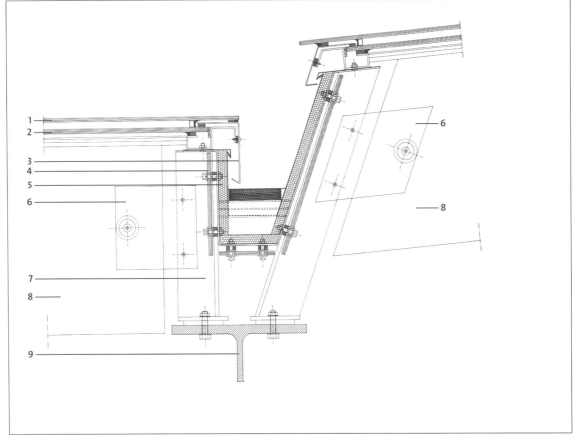

Detail of glass roof gutter
1 toughened glass
2 toughened, laminated glass
3 anodized aluminium section
4 glass
5 insulated steel gutter
6 stainless steel fixing plate
7 stainless steel supports
8 laminated glass beam
9 structural framework

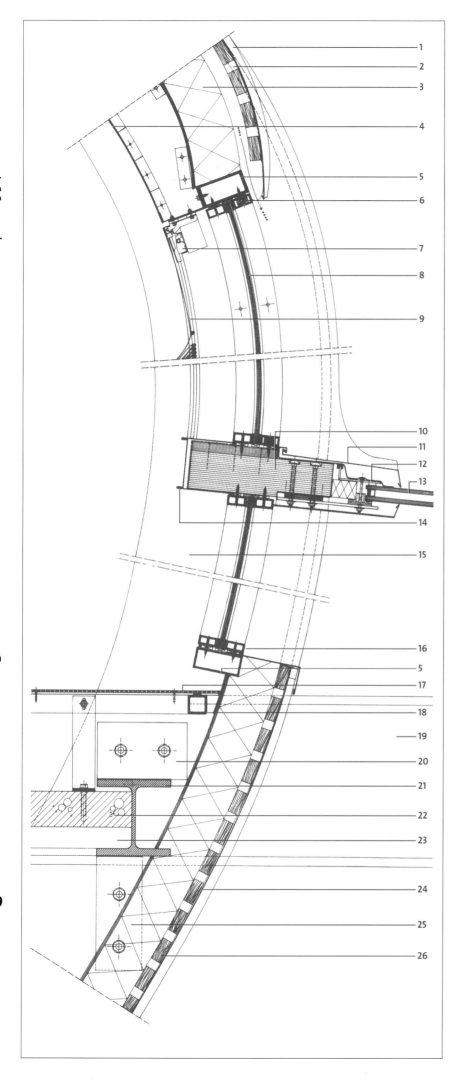

Restaurant with view of 'whale'

Junction zinc 'whale' and glass roof
1 zinc cladding
2 timber framing for mounting zinc
3 insulation
4 canvas
5 50 x 100 x 5 mm aluminium box section
6 20 x 40 x 3 mm curved aluminium box section
7 motor for solar shading
8 curved toughened glass
9 solar shading
10 glulam beam for glass roof fixing
11 zinc coping
12 EPDM membrane
13 glass roof
14 zinc cladding
15 glulam timber truss
16 20 x 40 x 3 mm aluminium sections
17 perforated stainless steel plate
18 box section
19 HE 360A
20 fixing plate
21 HE 160 B
22 reinforced concrete floor
23 perforated steel plate
24 zinc cladding
25 fixing plate
26 battening

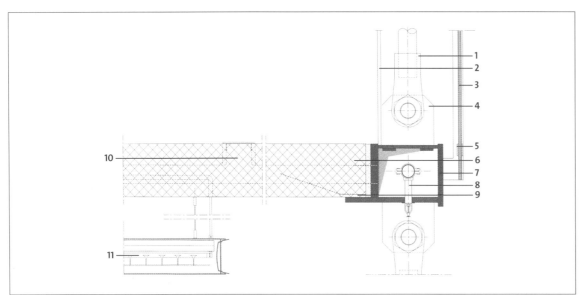

Detail of walkway suspension
1 M72 'willems' anchor
2 balustrade
3 12 mm laminated glass
4 mounting plate
5 glass clamp
6 precast concrete slab
7 integrated floor beam
8 sprinkler system
9 in situ slab with welded reinforcement
10 air inlet grid
11 fluorescent light fitting

Erick van Egeraat Ichthus College Rotterdam 2000

70

1 aluminium roof edge
2 UNP 160
3 HE 140 A
4 mechanism for adjusting façade
5 angle for fixing mullion
6 fixing plate for mullion
7 mechanically ventilated façade
8 plywood
9 roofing
10 insulation
11 profiled steel roof sheet
12 HE 180A
13 profiled aluminium cladding
14 air extraction from mechanically ventilated façade
15 HE 240A
16 air filter
17 integrated floor beam for intermediate floor

18 solar shading
19 air duct
20 openable section of façade
21 heating
22 perforated steel ceiling with acoustic insulation
23 Jatoba floor finish
24 hot-galvanized grille
25 steel plate
26 T-section for seating grille
27 T-section
28 concrete floor
29 insulation
30 synthetic balloon for regulating ventilation
31 insulated metal ceiling on T-section

71

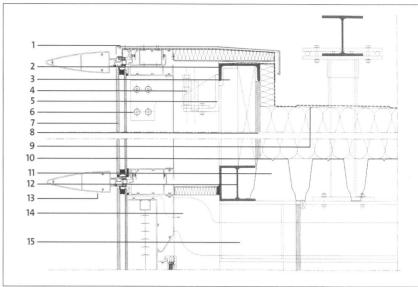

Roof edge on mechanically ventilated façade

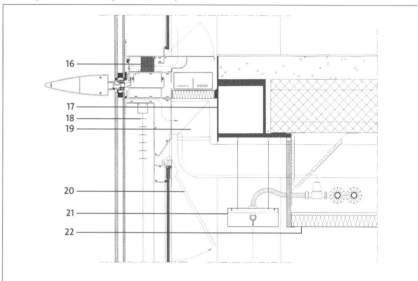

Mechanically ventilated façade at intermediate floor

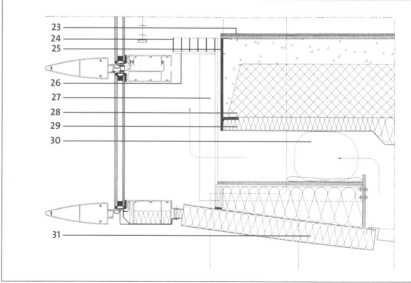

Junction mechanically ventilated façade and cantilever

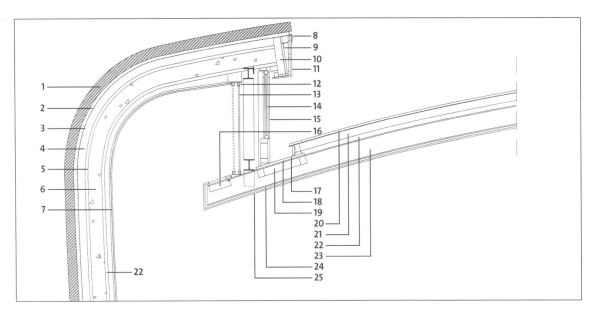

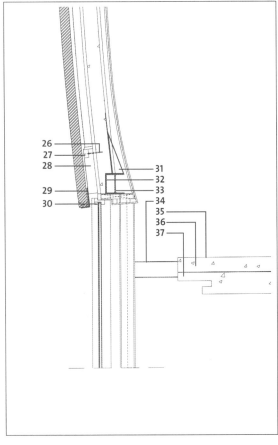

Erick van Egeraat Crawford Municipal Art Gallery Cork 2000

Junction glued masonry façade with glass front

1 glued masonry
2 cavity
3 bituminous asphalt
4 Halfen brickwork support system
5 profiled steel roof sheet
6 in situ concrete
7 plasterboard
8 zinc gasket
9 angle
10 insulation
11 plasterwork
12 40 x 30 x 40 mm U-section
13 35 x 25 x 35 mm U-section
14 insulating glass
15 aluminium frame
16 light fitting
17 copper gutter
18 18 mm water-resistant plywood
19 insulation
20 standing welted seam in copper roofing
21 curved glulam beams
22 profiled steel roof sheet
23 203 x 133 x 25 mm steel purlin
24 plywood battens
25 plasterboard
26 chemical anchor
27 Halfen brickwork support system
28 Halfen brickwork support system
29 100 x 200 mm steel angle
30 wooden glazing bead
31 steel wedge
32 welded-in plate
33 HEA 200
34 reinforcement steel (exposed)
35 mechanically polished finishing layer
36 compression layer
37 concrete floor

72

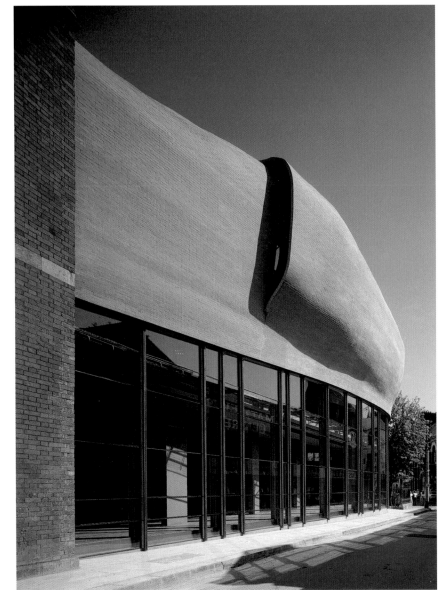

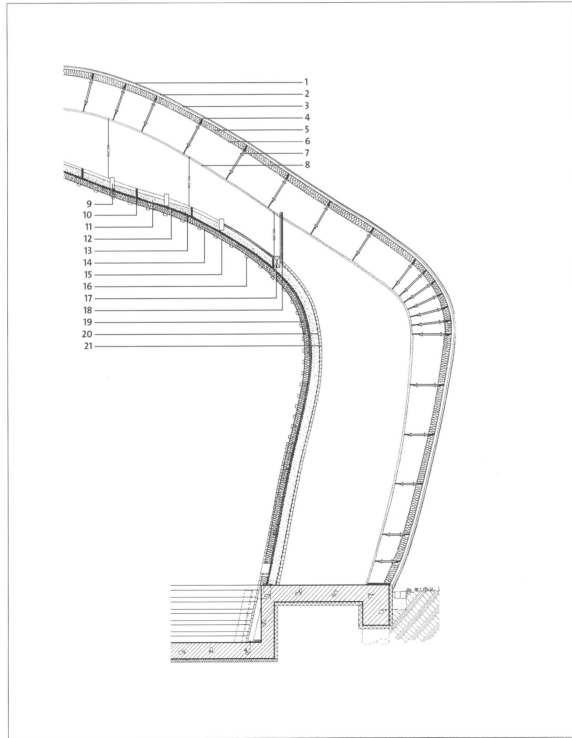

Section through façade
1 white copper cladding
2 PE film
3 20 x 50 mm pinewood battens
4 40 x 50 mm pinewood battens
5 100 mm mineral wool
6 PE film
7 25 mm plywood beams
8 25-50 mm shotcrete on lathing
9 75 x 200 mm wooden beams
10 20 mm local distributor
11 125 mm sand
12 PE film
13 25 mm plywood
14 Sonorex alu air mineral wool insulation
15 acoustic cloth
16 60 x 22 mm merbau slats
17 steel edge beam
18 40 mm plywood, 30 min. fire rating
19 70 x 50 x 6 mm L-section
20 damp proof membrane
21 merbau slats, no opening

1 aluminium coping
2 100 x 50 mm angle
3 aluminium water bar
4 U-section with welded strip
5 box section with welded strip
6 solar shading with steel cable guide
7 plywood, collapsible
8 mechanically ventilated façade
9 150 x 75 mm oval column
10 IPE 360 coated with fire retardant, wood veneer finish
11 plastic roofing
12 insulation
13 vapour resistant film
14 perforated steel profiled sheeting
15 IPE 240
16 air duct
17 expanded metal ceiling
18 cable duct
19 rubber mat, plywood sandwich panel with soundproofing
20 air conditioning
21 toughened glass sliding window
22 sprinkler
23 UNP 380 steel edge beam
24 holes for accessing sunken floor socket
25 finishing layer
26 compression layer
27 hollow-core slab
28 insulation with black coating
29 folded aluminium cover plate
30 50 x 50 mm U-section
31 aluminium sill
32 façade fixed to steel wedge
33 timber framing, insulated
34 smooth rendering
35 UNP 380
36 110 x 110 mm angle
37 110 x 110 mm angle
38 parquet floor
39 composite decking
40 HEB 450 (tapered)

Roof edge on mechanically ventilated façade

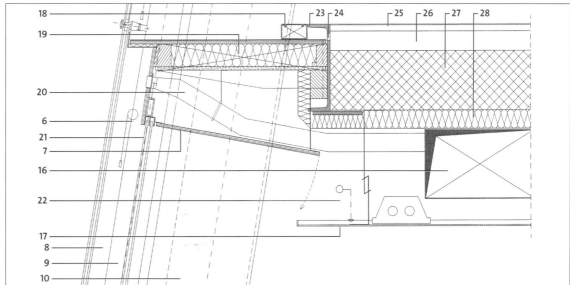

Mechanically ventilated façade at intermediate floor

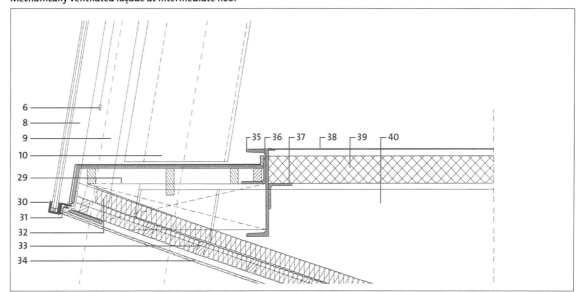

Junction mechanically ventilated façade and cantilever

Herman Hertzberger
Building order versus the grand gesture

Critics noted an about-turn in the work of Herman Hertzberger around 1990. The Benelux Merkenbureau → **1** and the Spui theatre centre → **2** (both in The Hague, 1993) showed that Hertzberger had abandoned the rigid structuralism of, for example, the Centraal Beheer insurance company building (Apeldoorn, 1972) → **3**, Vredenburg music centre (Utrecht, 1978) → **4**, or, to a lesser extent, the Apollo schools (Amsterdam, 1983) → **5** and the Ministry of Social Affairs (The Hague, 1990). Since the break in his oeuvre, Hertzberger is less forced in his approach to forms, constructions, the use of materials and attention to details. Hertzberger attributes this shift partly to a remark that his daughter made during a guided tour of the Ministry of Social Affairs. She found it a beautiful building, but said that it lacked a second theme. The second theme is a musical term to denote the counterpart to the forceful and heavy first theme. It makes the composition lighter and richer. Although the introduction and in some cases the dominance of a second theme have sometimes led to looser forms in his architecture, the structural elements have not disappeared entirely. However, as structural elements Hertzberger no longer confines himself to the at times corset-like construction, but he also uses other elements with freer forms. As a result, the structure and thus the hand of the architect have become less dominant.

In his older buildings Hertzberger aimed at building order. He argued that an building order was at stake if not only the combination of the parts of a building determine the whole, but also, vice versa, the separate parts emerge as a logical consequence of that whole. Every detail was related to the larger unity, and thus the architect had to be omnipresent to achieve that goal. At the same time, uniformity had to be (partly) avoided because not every part of a building has the same significance. This made it important that the structure of the building should be determined in such a way that it could accommodate every possible content.[1] The constructions formed the natural, structural elements of the building. They can be regarded as the warp, while the content, the materials, formed the woof.

The design of a single structure was mathematically complicated. It is not for nothing that critic Herman van Bergeijk claims that Hertzberger's process of thought starts with the structure and not with the choice of materials for the façade.[2] To structure the design process, Hertzberger placed a grid on top of the design,

no matter how complex the form was. Afterwards he conceived a 'construction kit' whereby the form of the building and the structure could be made as practically as possible. This construction kit was not only to support the building, but also to make the structure of the building legible both in the interior and in the façades. The constructional elements were therefore kept visible. The principle of the construction kit and the fact of keeping it visible, made it logical for the constructional elements to be prefabricated. Prefabrication provided concrete of such a quality that the elements could be applied cleanly. What you saw was a pure, honest, unfinished construction. In addition, it was easier to make didactic constructional details with prefab elements than with concrete poured in situ. Hertzberger wants details of this kind to make his construction, and with it his buildings, legible and comprehensible. He is convinced that this enhances the experience of the building.

De Drie Hoven home for the elderly (Amsterdam, 1974) and the Centraal Beheer building lent themselves particularly well to the construction kit method of building. These forms of buildings are relatively simple and are built up from rectangular elements that at most are linked or stacked in different ways. Nevertheless, it soon proved to be very difficult to design a structure that generated consistent architectural details both in the interior and in the façade. The problem was not so much with the principle of the construction kit, but rather with the idea that the structure had to be continued in the façade as well. This made the building easier to understand when seen from the street and prevented it from ending abruptly, by which the difference between exterior and interior was reduced. In the case of the Centraal Beheer façade, this resulted in an accumulation of constructional elements that, cased in grey bricks, made the façade forbidding, closed and rough. → **6** In addition, the buildings always had to be prepared for future extensions, and were thus not allowed to finish somewhere (which the critic Wim J. van Heuvel considers to be one of the characteristics of structuralism).[3] That is why the columns at the corners of De Drie Hoven have supports which have never been used. The two principles confer on the buildings a somewhat unattractive sense of being unfinished. → **7**

In the case of buildings with more complex forms, the construction kit, certainly as Hertzberger used it, proved to be too rigid. The unity and above all the legibility of the Vredenburg music centre in particular suffered from an overly coherent implementation of a single structure. The building has a capricious shape because Hertzberger wanted to create a transition from the ponderous Hoog Catherijne to the finely-meshed inner city. The kinks in the shape of the façade led to the use of round columns, which Hertzberger strongly favours anyway. The

76

Herman Hertzberger Building order versus the grand gesture

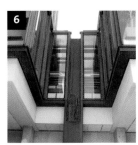

advantage of these columns was that, despite the constant changes of direction of the window fronts, the attachments of the window fronts to these columns could be kept more or less the same. To make these attachments simpler and technically better, Hertzberger proposes in his architectural lessons that the dimensions of round columns be increased.[4] Although this is certainly true, the accumulation of the wide columns, the resulting thick column heads, which have to remain in proportion after all, and the sturdy concrete beams has led to an exaggeratedly heavy constructional package.

Hertzberger also claims that the columns can be given more importance by making them 'free'. Although freeing columns can result in interesting spaces – which it certainly does in Vredenburg – the excessively consistent implementation of this order led to a number of recalcitrant details in the façade – at the corners of the uppermost floor, for instance, where a narrow strip of column still sticks out and a small strip of glass has been inserted between the grey B2 blocks and the column. → **8** The application of this constructional system did not lead to a genuinely successful choice in the interior of the Vredenburg either. The consistent filling in of the grid with sturdy columns, column heads and heavy beams ought to have created intimate spaces, but the system made the space too cramped.

A large number of the problems of the music centre are also present in the Ministry of Social Affairs, but there they are much less intrusive. → **9** The division of the mass into more or less independent, octagonal towers works better here in terms of urban planning, and the building order also guarantees the unity of the building despite the typical shape. The constructional intersections are relatively heavy in this building too, but they are in better proportion to the building mass as a whole than in the case of Vredenburg. While in Vredenburg the spaces seemed low and cramped because of the forceful construction, the ministry's hall roofed with skylights and the catwalks with glass sheets, which are supported by a slender steel construction and run over the entire length of the building, give it a friendlier look. → **10** The façade, moreover, is more attractive than that of Vredenburg or of the Centraal Beheer building. The glass of the parapet offers sufficient counterweight to the grey concrete and concrete bricks, and the corners are rounded by means of semicircular aluminium profiles,

which has softened the building. → **11** Although the consistent filling of the structure with light curtain walls at the sides of the islands of space that jut out has led to strange and unnecessarily complicated divisions of the window front, the Ministry of Social Affairs is a climax of Hertzberger's structuralism rather than a reason to go in search of a totally different architectural idiom.

Cultural U-turn

The remark by Hertzberger's daughter has been one of the reasons for him to deal less rigidly with the building order, but matters of a more practical kind played a part too. The increasingly strict demands regarding insulation made carrying the construction into and beyond the façade, for example, practically impossible, because this inevitably creates thermal bridges. Incidentally, this already proved to be a problem in the elaboration of the design for the Ministry. Where they join the window fronts, the concrete heads and columns have been 'incised', and those incisions have subsequently been filled with insulation material to reduce the thermal leaks.

Hertzberger's solution was a logical one, though it affected his architecture profoundly. He brought the construction (to a large extent) indoors. At the same time, as in the elaboration of the library and De Nieuwe Veste in Breda in 1996, he changed from a concrete to a steel supporting construction. As can be expected from someone who is tremendously influenced by the Maison de Verre by Pierre Chareau and Bernard Bijvoet (Paris, 1932), he already used steel constructions in almost all of his buildings, but they were always secondary constructions such as balustrades, walkways, stairs and accessories like lamps and benches. → **12** Following Le Corbusier and Aldo van Eyck, his main constructions were made of concrete. A steel construction was perhaps too eloquent for the original structuralism, in which there was no use of really large spans. Large spans did not fit in with structuralism because they are more difficult to read. However, now that the comprehensible fabric of beams and columns could no longer be extended consistently into the façade and Hertzberger himself was looking for a greater freedom of design, a second theme, the use of steel, a much lighter material, proved to be more suitable for the construction.

The use of detail in the new steel constructions was inspired by Henri Labrouste's Bibliothèque Sainte-Geneviève (Paris, 1850).[5] → **13** Labrouste gave his construction natural lines to bring about a smooth transition from the semicircular cast-iron trussed girders that supported the roof via slender iron columns and heavier concrete feet to the mass of the floor. This is how Labrouste linked the graceful roof construction with the solid ground. In addition, Labrouste ensured that the construction did not interfere with the spatiality. In fact,

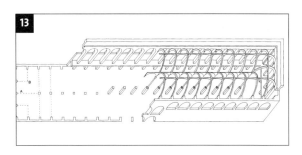

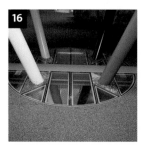

the spaces run into one another because the trussed girders point in two directions.

Hertzberger applied this tactic most clearly in the library in Breda. He placed clusters of sloping columns on circular concrete bases. Setting the columns at an angle – which Violet-le-Duc had once thought up for a market hall – is not a frivolity, but results in a practical construction. The columns are not just supporting elements, but they also provide the stability. What is more, such a system creates a large, free area at floor level, while the roof spans are relatively small. → **14, 15** The construction is lucid, and the connections of the storeys with the columns in particular are didactic. Large brackets in the floor beams are attached to projections from the column. This makes it clear how and where the column supports the floor, but it also leaves the column, its length, direction and thereby structure unimpaired. The importance of this can be gauged from the points where the columns intersect but do not support the intermediate floors of the entrance and the reading room/café. Here the columns poke through circular glass elements that have been incorporated in the floor. → **16** The façades do not stop the system of sloping columns either. The steel protrudes through the glass on the street side, and at the point where it sticks out a steel plate has been incorporated to keep the thermal partition shear. This looks like a throwback to the 'old' structuralism, but – unlike his older buildings – in this case this construction that has been taken outside does not tell you anything about the internal structure of the building. At most it says something about how the building – more precisely, the roof – is supported. → **17** In his extension of the Vanderveen department store (1998) in Assen, Hertzberger benefitted more from the plastic qualities of a steel construction. He placed large, steel elements on the roof from which traction cables support the extension on top of the existing premises. → **18** This steel construction is supported on concrete discs that also support the floors of the extension by means of cast concrete consoles. A completely glass container has been placed around this whose striking detail is the horizontal jambs that stick out on each side. This looks like an ironic reference to buildings like De Drie Hoven or the Centraal Beheer building, which also contained details intended to facilitate later extensions. At the same time, this detail also characterises the change in Hertzberger's conception. In the past he used

the construction to enable connections, now he uses the surface of the façade for the same purpose. Attention has shifted from the construction and the element to the surface.

While the two constructions discussed above are still legible, detaching the construction from the structure has given Hertzberger room to make the constructions more anonymous. In the Chassé Theatre (Breda, 1995) the columns are simply standards. → **19** They disappear into the floor without any visible detail. The connection can still be seen just below the wavy ceiling, but it is not clear to what the standards are attached. The construction of the theatre roof can only be seen from the outside. At the corners the overhanging roof is supported by exposed curved trussed beams and one supposes that they support the rest of the roof too. → **20a, 20b** Although the coloured columns give direction to the strangely shaped foyer, it is evident that this area, this building and Hertzberger's other buildings are no longer concerned with the structure of construction, but much more with the surfaces and the space between these surfaces.

Plastic structures

The disappearance of the constructions to a large extent behind the façades naturally has a great influence on the look of the buildings. The columns and beams determined the rhythms in the façades and inside walls down to the Ministry of Social Affairs. The lines were here so strong that the choice of materials among the different constructional elements could be determined mainly on the basis of use. The demands of the user of the building rather than its image set the tone. The fact that one grid was implemented in materials that were slightly different from those in the one next to it did not really matter. The structure prevented the visual disintegration of the building. With the disappearance of the construction as a structural element, Hertzberger was in danger of losing the freedom of choice of the materials for the fabric. To regain this terrain without delay, he drew his inspiration mainly from Le Corbusier's Obus plan (Algiers, 1932) → **21**, and in particular from his design for Fort l'Empereur. This block, that extends for kilometres and is more than one hundred metres high, was to include apartments as well as shops, footpaths and so on. The chaos was deliberately sought out, only to be exorcised again by the strong framework. After the Ministry of Social Affairs, Hertzberger follows Le Corbusier in using large and plastic structure to hold the chaos in check, limited though it is. The roof is the most important element in this process. It may be accentuated by means of obtrusive frames, as in the library in Breda and the Chassé Theatre, and have a similar function to the construction in Hertzbergers older designs. However, these new structures are livelier elements than the rigid,

Roof structure Chassé Theatre

structural constructions. The attractive wooden frame-work of the Montessori College Oost (Amsterdam, 2000) → **22**, but above all the corrugated, cut-open roof of the Chassé theatre are very friendly. → **23**

These new elements increase freedom of façade composition. The lack of the vertical and horizontal lines of the original structuralism can be used to achieve much more freedom in the choice of materials for the façade and sometimes even in figurative surfaces. The roof of the Chassé Theatre encapsulates all of the functions in a single gesture; thanks to the strong movement, the plastic structure, what goes on beneath it and how the materials of the façade are to be treated are really matters of little consequence. How tenuous the balance may be between chaos and structure can be seen from the Spui theatre centre (1993), one of the first projects in Hertzberger's 'poststructuralist' period to be completed. The structure proved by no means strong enough to curb the chaos caused by the many functions included in the programme (two auditoria, film club, video centre, shops, flats, café) and further accentuated by the large variety of materials used. Besides, the actual implementation of the design was substandard.

Palette of materials

The change in the look of the façade and the shifting of the grid to the surface have had remarkably little effect on the palette of materials. At any rate, the image and effect of the materials have remained more or less the same. Like those of the Maison de Verre, the façades still create the impression in the first instance of being enormously transparent. In fact, they are rather introvert, but the impression of an open building – one that does not end at the façades – is thereby created. The openness makes the building easier to understand. The trick lies in the application of materials with four gradations of density: transparent (glass), semi-transparent (coloured glass, glass bricks and Reglit), semi-opaque

(reflective glass, concrete blocks, plaster, button concrete) and closed (concrete, coloured masonry). Hertzberger uses these materials to compose façades with a certain layeredness and openness, in which the openness depends on the wishes of the users. A view, daylight and privacy are preferred to real transparency.

To distinguish the permanent (the structure) from the temporary in the Ministry of Social Affairs, Hertzberger used curtain façades with glass spandrels. → **24** The insulating material behind this glass has been removed from sight by painting the rear side of the glass white. This makes the glass semi-opaque, and produces a different effect to the Okalux glass that does let daylight through. This glass is semi-transparent and thus comparable to the glass bricks that are used somewhere in every one of Hertzberger's buildings, or with the Reglit with which a part of the façade of the Chassé Theatre is covered.

There is a very subtle play between apparently transparent but actually semi-transparent in the library in Breda → **25** and in the Markant Theatre in Uden (1996). The glass window fronts have been set at an angle. Although this increases the total surface area of the glass compared with what would have happened if the wall had been placed in the normal vertical position, it does not make the building any more open because the reflections on the sloping glass prevent direct looking in. Looking out, on the other hand, is no problem because the ground floor is below ground level. As a result, the visual axes of the people in the lending room of the library and the foyer are almost perpendicular to the line of the glass. Vertical glass would have frustrated that view outside.

A similar play to that with transparent and semi-transparent glass is also played with fully closed and semi-closed materials. This might explain, for instance, Hertzberger's predilection for the B2 concrete blocks. Unlike brick, this material is not completely closed, which makes it less solid. Furthermore, it is also a more neutral material than brick because of the larger dimensions. The walls have a less finely-meshed pattern than brickwork walls. However, when the blocks proved to be less durable than had been supposed, to be heavy pollutants and not very practical in use because of their rough surface, Hertzberger replaced them by materials with a similar look. Plastered walls have been used in many interiors for this purpose, as in the Chassé Theatre, the Markant Theatre and the Montessori College, or buttoned concrete walls, as in the extension of Centraal Beheer (1995) → **26** and the Vanderveen department store. → **27** These façades are more neutral and richer than the walls made of B2 blocks, and they have a friendlier look than the dingy B2 walls, which always looked a bit impoverished.

The effects of the materials are accentuated by the

treatment of detail. Distinguishing the structures and the elements with a short temporal cycle was relatively simple in the earlier works. The construction was of grey, heavy concrete, and the window fronts were light and slim in their dimensions, simply wedged, as it were, between the concrete elements. The colour scheme of the window fronts reinforced the distinction from the rest of the building – grey. In the Centraal Beheer building, moreover, the window front has been detached on the lower side of the façade by creating a recess in the façade. → **28** Such details are also used in his poststructuralist period to distinguish temporary from permanent, with the Benelux Merkenbureau as the most extreme example. Here the window fronts with reflecting glass are 'glued' onto the permanent grey structure like bay windows. Usually, however, Hertzberger uses much subtler details nowadays, such as in the library in Breda, where the lower and side parts of the aluminium window front slightly overlap the concrete, while the upper side of the glass disappears beneath a wide triangular swelling in the button concrete. → **25**

Obsessive details

Although the intended effect of the materials in the buildings has not changed radically in itself, the look of the façades has undergone a metamorphosis. Through the shift of attention from the grid to the surface and from the object to the space, the number of necessary details could be reduced. Under the motto of 'stimulating', Hertzberger created an exhausting number of details both in the interior and in the façade down to and including the Ministry of Social Affairs. He integrated areas and details in all of his buildings that were supposed to urge the user to take the initiative. He developed several strategies for this purpose. Some parts were not finished; this was left up to the users. Especially in the case of the housing in Kassel (1982), this led to excitement when the occupants took over their homes. In Vredenburg, however, this tactic backfired. Nobody appropriated the different areas in this public building to finish off the details. The poor details remained poor. In addition, Hertzberger conferred details on his building which provoked a certain type of behaviour. The asymmetrical placing of the steel columns on the concrete bases in the Centraal Beheer building, among others, so that the base could be used as a bench and thus become an area within the building, is a typically

Hertzbergian detail. The balance between the reticent and the guiding architect is at its best in the Apollo schools, and especially in the Montessori part of them. There are showcases beside the classroom doors in which the pupils' work can be displayed and which immediately make it clear to somebody entering which group works there. A semicircular transom in the glass front makes it possible to display objects, while the architect encourages the area near the window-sill to be kept empty – tiles are laid there which have been designed by the pupils in their first year. → **29** As in most of his buildings, many doors have large glass surfaces to lower the psychological threshold when entering. → **30** The openness of the door – exactly like that of the façade – was an indication of accessibility. Everything about this building shows that Hertzberger has devoted an incredible amount of attention to the treatment of materials and detail. Nowadays the decreasing budgets and the reduced authority of the architect have made it virtually impossible to work out the details of a building so intensively. Hertzberger has therefore effected a strategic withdrawal. In connection with the Chassé Theatre he stated: 'The sense of detail has degenerated incredibly on the part of the client. A reaction to that is to outplay, to introduce theatrical spatial elements in such a way that attention for the detail disappears.'[6]

These eye-catchers include the splendid staircases, fences and walkways. All of his buildings since Centraal Beheer include steel staircases, which in the course of time have become more exciting and more daring in terms of their construction. Hertzberger has no doubt been inspired by the delicate staircases that the smith Louis Dalbet made for the Maison de Verre. Just as the constructional structure has disappeared, so have the constructional details of this kind of element become (to some extent) more anonymous. The way the walkways are suspended is regularly kept in view. The staircases, however, have become almost incomprehensible rococo sculptures, and it is unclear how they attain their stability. The staircases owe their sculptural quality above all to the 'misshaped' balustrades that are often made from perforated and closed components. This play with closed and semi-open parts gives the staircase a highly surprising character. → **31** No matter how obvious the choice of materials for elements of this kind may seem, that of the balustrades in particular tends to change during the process under the influence of economic factors. In the first sketch for the Montessori College Oost there were steel fences, but glass turned out to be cheaper, and still in the end steel ones were chosen. This does not involve any reduction in the effect of the element. Hertzberger elaborates the details for these elements in the first instance independently of the materials. The structure and the rhythm of the staircases, fences and the attachments of

the balustrades to the floor have to be strong enough for the choice of the material that is finally chosen for the fences not to matter. → **32**

Hertzberger follows the same strategy when it comes to the choice of materials for the spaces. He creates frameworks, as he did before 1990 as well, in which there are many possibilities. The frameworks, however, are no longer made using the rigid structuralist grid, but primarily by the spaces themselves.

The hall of the Vogels primary school in Oegstgeest (2001) brings out the difference in Hertzberger's approach. While the Apollo school had an incredible number of details that elicited a certain behaviour, in the school in Oegstgeest Hertzberger framed the wooden staircase and the sunken steps with smoothly plastered walls and allowed daylight to enter attractively from all sides. That is really all that he did. This space too is fully used by the children as an area for play and contact, but now this is done much more on their own initiative and above all because it is such an enticing and airy space.

The strength of spaces of this kind means that the finishing materials and colours can be decided on at a late stage. → **33** Hertzberger sometimes accepts second choices if they do not affect the essence of the design – which lies in the spatiality and the effect that can be created with the different spaces.

By building in this way, Hertzberger has manoeuvred himself into a position in which he can still make the architecture that he wants to make in the present situation where the architect has less power. In fact, the buildings are not even very different from his older designs. He still wants to design spaces that stimulate the users to take initiatives, but nowadays he no longer tries to lay everything down in advance, but leaves space open for the unexpected. The surfaces are therefore neutral and have less details than before, without this negatively affecting the quality of the buildings. It is simply that less details are required. The wonderful walkways and staircases in the large areas not only accentuate the horizontal and vertical spatiality, but are also the ideal spots for meeting people. The elegant, second theme with the friendlier materials, less rigid constructions and increasingly refined steel staircases and walkways has overshadowed the heavy first theme. The result is that the buildings have become more exciting, and above all more lively.

1. H. Hertzberger, *Lessons for students in architecture*, Rotterdam 1991.
2. H. van Bergeijk and D. Hauptmann, 'Structuur en gebaar. Recent werk van Herman Hertzberger', *de Architect*, 1994, no. 2.
3. W.J. van Heuvel, *Structuralism in Dutch Architecture*, Rotterdam 1992.
4. See note 1.
5. H. Hertzberger, 'Henri Labrouste, la réalisation de l'art', *Technique et Architecture*, 1987-1988, no. 375.
6. P. van Assche, 'Het verhaal van het onverwachte. Het Chassé-theater in Breda van Herman Hertzberger', *Archis*, 1996, no. 1.

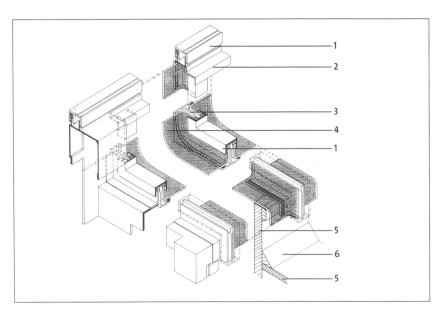

Junction roof light and gutter
1 aluminium cover strip
2 aluminium sill
3 aluminium profile
4 plastic roof light
5 woodwork
6 gutter

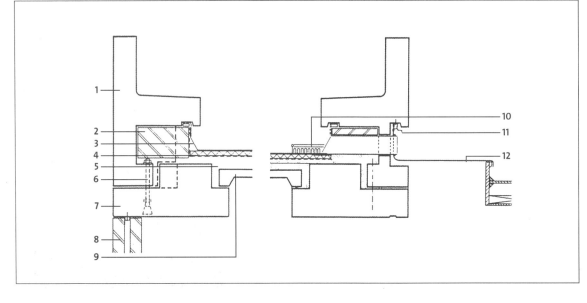

Roof edge with connection to roof light
1 precast concrete roof edge
2 masonry
3 roofing
4 insulation
5 in situ concrete
6 anchoring roof edge to beam
7 precast concrete beam
8 concrete block masonry
9 concrete beam
10 rainwater outlet with gravel guard
11 aluminium clamping strip
12 plastic roof light

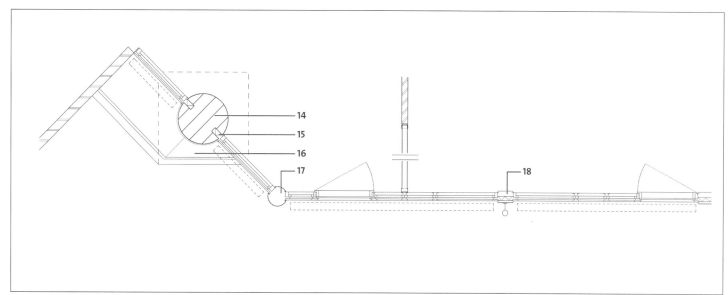

Curtain wall – horizontal

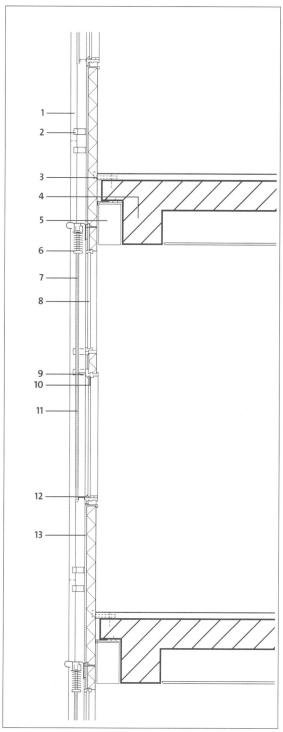

1 60 mm dia pipe with built-in security lighting
2 spacer for pipe
3 steel bracket for fixing spandrel panel
4 precast façade beam
5 cove for wiring
6 solar shading (automatic + manually operated)
7 guide rail for solar shading
8 Okalux light-diffusing insulated glass

9 powder coated aluminium frame profile
10 rubber sealing profile for double glazing only at window
11 insulating glass
12 integrated relay for turning off ventilation system when window is open
13 sandwich panel; inside: powder coated steel plate; outside: Crepie coloured glass

painted on the inner face
14 550 mm dia precast concrete column
15 thermal break by means of plastic profile
16 precast column head
17 220 mm dia angle cover profile
18 powder coated aluminium flat cover profile

Curtain wall – vertical

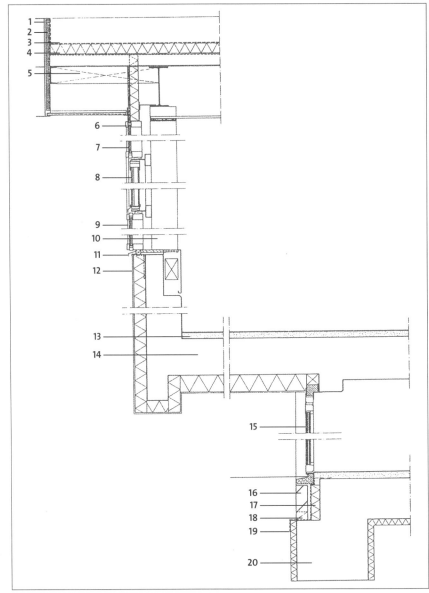

Façade with exaggerated eaves and glass planks

1 cornice of aluminium profiles
2 water-resistant plywood
3 roofing
4 insulation
5 steel structure
6 aluminium façade system
7 insulating glass
8 glass planks
9 insulating glass
10 column
11 sill
12 insulated plastered façade
13 compression layer
14 concrete intermediate floor
15 glass front
16 masonry
17 insulation
18 weephole
19 vapour resistant film
20 concrete foundation beam

Detail of roof edge: rooftop unit overhang
1 roofing
2 insulation
3 vapour resistant film
4 profiled steel roof sheet
5 aluminium glazing bead
6 cleat
7 sound deadening layer
8 UNP 220
9 steel plate
10 UNP 80
11 cleat
12 pre-formed aluminium sheet
13 cleat

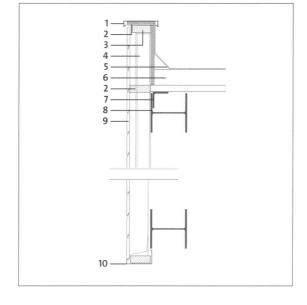

Details of wooden frame
1 aluminium cap
2 okoume plywood
3 wooden cleat
4 steel structure
5 roofing
6 steel roof
7 angle for fixing steel roof
8 HE 240 A
9 wooden tongue-and-groove boards
10 2.5 mm aluminium sheet

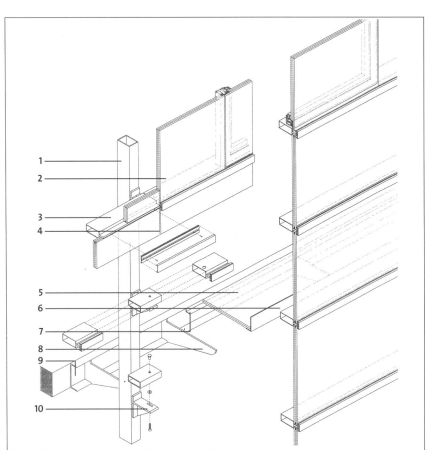

Detail of glass façade
1 80 x 120 x 10 mm box section
2 glass (6-12-5)
3 aluminium profile
4 structural sealed joint
5 laminated glass
6 50 x 100 mm angle
7 50 x 50 mm angle
8 10 mm thick steel bracket
9 UNP 200
10 60 x 180 x 10 mm angle

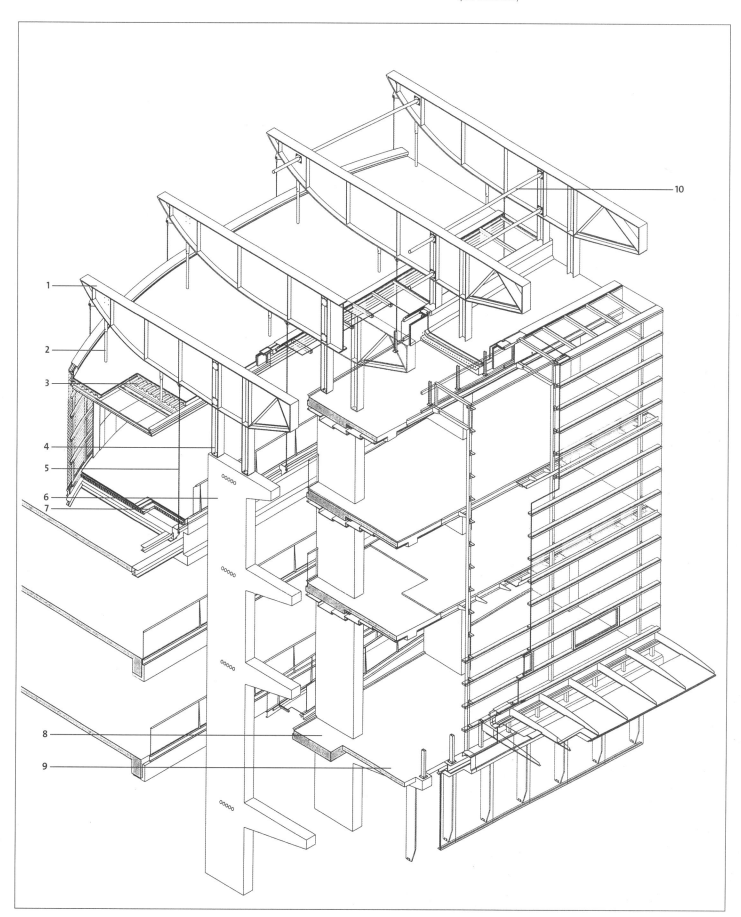

Construction details
1 steel element composed of sheet steel and double T-sections
2 76 mm dia tie rod
3 concrete floor on profiled steel sheeting on HEA 140
4 HEB 300-section
5 M30 steel cable
6 concrete slabs (in situ, 400 mm thick)
7 hollow-core slab floor on HEA 280
8 concrete floor (350 mm thick)
9 concrete floor (60 mm thick)
10 steel tie rod

Herman Hertzberger Extension of the Vanderveen department store Assen 1998

87

Mecanoo
Desirable detail

When Rem Koolhaas left his chair as professor at the Technical University Delft in 1990, he organised the symposium 'How modern is Dutch architecture?', and thereby launched the debate on the modernity of Dutch firms of architects.[1] Partly inspired by the question raised by Koolhaas and to legitimise the way in which Dutch architects were forced to deal with the legacy of Modernism in building practice, critic Hans van Dijk introduced the term 'Schoolteacher's Modernism'.[2] Picking up the thread from the architect Herman de Kovel, who had already claimed in 1980 that modern architecture should free itself of idealistic intentions, fascination with technology and social commitment,[3] Van Dijk arrived at the thesis that Dutch architects did make use of the heritage of the great Modernists, but that the ideologies of the heroic Modernists had been relegated far into the background. This was partly due to the complicated infrastructure (laws, regulations, organs) within which the Dutch architects had to work. Van Dijk mentioned Mecanoo as one of the firms that managed through an open acceptance and appropriation of that infrastructure to transcend its constricting effect.[4]

This positive criticism referred to the council housing projects of Mecanoo, the collective that was set up in 1984 by Roelf Steenhuis, Chris de Weijer, Erick van Egeraat, Francine Houben and Henk Döll, with as its highlights the Kruisplein young people's flats (Rotterdam, 1985) and the Hillekop housing project (Rotterdam, 1989). Mecanoo showed that it was still possible to construct very well made buildings with the inadequate budgets that were normally available for projects of this kind. The special element lay partly in the extremely clever way in which the flexible ground plans were fitted together, in the embedding in the city, and in the way in which the architects appropriated the public space around the buildings and included it in the design as part of the complex.

They also earned appreciation for the striking use of materials and perfection that were without parallel in council housing projects. The façades of the Kruisplein complex, for example, are partly plastered. → 1 This was a remarkable choice in terms of urban planning – the complex is situated in a rather neglected and chaotic part of Rotterdam with mainly prewar brick houses – and the material was virtually unknown at the time. While the façades of homes were often given a layer of plaster abroad, postwar homes in the Netherlands were made with bricks. Achieving a higher level of abstraction – in which not the individual housing unit but the block as a whole would attract attention -, as well as – at a more banal level – the technical advantages of a plastered façade were what led Mecanoo to choose this material. → 2 This finishing layer could be used to cover the often badly and irregularly bricked walls of council flats, with their big pointing and conspicuous rough details.

Despite the well-earned praise, because everything exuded a freshness and dedication to want to control everything to perfection, Kruisplein also has many characteristics of a first-born. The autonomy of the surface or the volume, which Mecanoo still tries to achieve in its present-day buildings, are frustrated in this building by the large number of different elements. For example, the window front of the apartments consists of many small windows and a door, and is otherwise filled with Trespa panels in different sizes. → 3 They make it too busy to really work as a graphic element, and besides the programme of details for the shop window fronts took insufficient, or no account of the advertisements that every shop wants to display. → 4 As a result, this part now looks pretty cluttered and incoherent.

The Hillekop complex is a logical successor to Kruisplein. → 5 The complex consists of a small blue block of flats, a yellow plastered ribbon with housing units, and a tower block, and it is the latter that particularly displays an evidently greater degree of control in the choice of materials. The tower block is facetted on the front, so that all the residents have a specific view of the docks. The facetting of the façade was not a concession by the architects – as can be seen from the rear, where a pure, round concrete form has been constructed – but it was a deliberate and strongly architectural choice. → 6 The façade thereby acquired an exciting set of vertical lines as well as a robust look that goes with the docks. There are two natural and logically positioned recesses in the concrete façade, making the plastered façade come to the fore. This makes the volume look as if it is made of two slender discs and that the concrete disc has been pushed in front of the plastered façade like a mask. → 7 The thinness of the layers is also emphasised at a lower level of scale. The layer of plaster has a different structure in the reveals than on the façades, and the concrete bricks have been bevelled at the corners.

Japan

While it was still working on the Hillekop plan, Mecanoo elaborated a design by Alvaro Siza for homes in the Schilderswijk in The Hague (1986-1987), and Francine Houben and Erick van Egeraat went on a study trip to Japan. Both events appear to have had a major influence on the subsequent oeuvre of Mecanoo. From Siza they

In the house cum studio, the strategy of visually continuous rooms, the use of untreated materials, the combination of very cheap materials (untreated concrete) with expensive ones (teak) – which confers on both an unusual effect–, the similar striving to combine light and heavy in order to accentuate them both through the contrast, and the detail as an autonomous composition, all work excellently. Large glass walls connect the inside with the outside, while the handling of details gives each glass façade a character of its own. The one between the studio and the Japanese garden is virtually lacking in detail. The teak window frames are set in the concrete. → **10** The combination of smoothly finished concrete (indoors), the wooden frames and the rougher concrete with form spacer holes (outdoors) is a typical example of a carefully composed and photogenic detail. The absence of detail and thus of materiality of the glass façade brings the garden into focus as a part of the house. Visible details are avoided as far as possible in the rest of the house too. The materials snuggle up to one another or are loosely laid on top of one another. Moreover, the doors – and there are plenty of them, because each room has two different entrances – are not treated as real doors, but can be seen rather as movable, ceiling-high panels in the wall.

Like the wall facing the garden, the glass façade of the first floor consists of a single large sheet of glass, but the balustrade in front of it prevents the 'no façade' effect from being produced here. → **11** The narrow mouldings of the balustrade frame the view of the Kralingse Plas, and from a distance the balustrade and the glass form a visual whole. It looks like a single three-dimensional façade.

The details in the interior are very reticent and calm, but the exterior has more eloquent details, betraying the influence of the early work of Koen van Velsen. The metal roof, for example, extends a good way beyond the volume as a sort of frame within which the house is composed, and the supporting construction is visible. The hole in the roof and the continuation of the construction at that point – a detail that recurs in many Mecanoo buildings – accentuates the presence of the supporting profiles. → **12** The termination of the dark and thus heavy-looking padouk panel just above ground level may be a reference to Van Velsen's library in Zee-wolde, where the heavy concrete façades are accentu-ated by allowing them to 'float' above the ground. → **13**

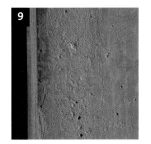

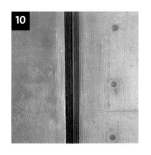

learned a sensitive use of materials and more freedom in dealing with the ground plans. While before this collaboration the Mecanoo architects racked their brains until the ground plans had the shape of a rectangle, Siza taught them that there was nothing wrong with allowing the volumes to have bulges, and that a fixed style only works constrictively and makes it impossible to respond adequately to each situation. In Japan Van Egeraat and Houben came into contact with a different way of composing surfaces and spaces. Instead of a clear break between building and surroundings and between the different spaces in the buildings, the transitions in Japanese buildings are softer, and in particular the transition from the home to the designed garden has to be kept as seamless as possible. Transparent and translucent screens provide visual connections, so that in spite of its often small dimensions, the building still acquires a striking spatiality. It was also in Japan that they discovered the potential of natural and untreated materials. The detail turned out to be used in a different way too. In Japan it is not a purely functional element, but offers the possibility of introducing a new composition at a smaller level of scale. Buildings can become more layered as a result. While closer inspection of Hillekop shows it to be unambiguous, the home cum studio (Rotterdam, 1991) – the first and probably the strongest example of Mecanoo's freer style of design – offers the viewer who examines it more closely an extra layer, that of the composition of the details. → **8** The importance of the composition at the smallest level of scale can also be seen in the way in which the home is presented. Besides the usual architectural photographs, the house is always documented by means of a series of slides on which the details are photographed close up. → **9, 10** In this way details become elements that are less connected with their context and have thus been prised loose of their traditional meaning as parts of the whole. They are not by definition purely functional, but beautiful.

Aesthetic Pragmatism

The freedom that Mecanoo created for itself was justly praised, but in the following projects the criticism shows a Mecanoo-tiredness. The ground plans are still clear, attractive materials are chosen for the buildings, and the handling of detail is, on the whole, good. However, critic Roemer van Toorn claims that 'more than ever, the

texture of the material, the effective detail and the innocent honesty have degenerated to become a festive ornament',[5] where ornament is a term of abuse. And Hans van Dijk, who had called Mecanoo a textbook example of 'Schoolteacher's Modernism', now found the excessive orientation of Mecanoo architecture towards visual enjoyment one of the major examples of an anodyne category that he called Aesthetic Pragmatism: 'Every question about the deeper meaning of architecture and about how architecture should operate in society has disappeared in this style.'[6] According to Van Dijk, this style has the following characteristics: 'The materiality, the tangibility, the sensory quality, is also underlined [besides "by treating the materials as naturally as possible"] by the attention paid to textures and colours. The separate screens and planes emphasise the separateness of the composing parts and make it unmistakably clear that the building is "put together". The composition to which that leads, emphasises that it is a question of a constructed object and not of cerebral or abstract concepts which must be illustrated by it. It is a matter of staging sensual perceptions, not proving theoretical positions which have perhaps collected too little credibility on the verbal circuit. And it is not at all a matter of fundamentally questioning the role of architecture within the changing play of social forces.'[7] In Van Dijk's view, Mecanoo produces 'the most sophisticated, indeed most beautiful, buildings within this mainstream'. The reason for this, he argues, lies in the fact that Mecanoo carried out a thorough typological investigation for council housing in the 1980s and has acquired a lot of experience. 'These are experiences which Mecanoo can nowadays make "careless" use of. In doing so this group frees capacity to focus attention mainly on the visual presentation of their buildings and the expansion of their stylistic repertoire.'[8]
The public library in Almelo (1994), which is specifically mentioned by Van Dijk, certainly does have an incredibly

rich variety of materials. → **14** Critic Herman Kerkdijk finds this tiring: 'The quantity of visible details derives from the strategy of being able to experience the building as an adventure not only from afar but also at close quarters. [...] This intensity of information at every level of scale provokes a certain irritation: there is so much to see, but so little to experience. [...] Everything has been thought about, in a very controlled and very professional way, but so patently that the building

acquires an exhausting quality. Sometimes you are dying for an untidy detail.'[9] Of course, a building can go down under the weight of its details. This is what Norman Foster manages to do in his iciest buildings, but then he uses mainly steel and glass as materials – not exactly lively materials. The library in Almelo, on the other hand, contains a mass of different materials, some of which improve with age (zinc, copper), others are weathered but, provided they are well detailed, also improve with age (concrete), while others remain intact (Colorbel enamelled glass panels and black brick). So the materials will prevent the building from becoming rigidly perfect and dead. Moreover, the number of screens and elements of different materials calls for an equally large number of details. Of course, it is debatable whether the building should have been covered with so many different materials – probably not, but Döll simply wants each element of the building to be legible in the façade. Besides bookshelves and depots, the building houses a radio station, café, information centre and theatre, so the materialisation does have a message to convey. Mecanoo has managed to use details to create the impression of separate blocks, as in the house with studio in Rotterdam. The different elements seem to meet one another by chance; nowhere is the encounter between different materials smoothed away in the details. On the one hand, this prevents dingy details made of too many different materials, while on the other hand it guarantees the autonomy of the surfaces. The blocks themselves have a strict programme of details. An attractive effect is produced by the concrete fans whose extremely thin, concrete discs extend beyond the surface of the roof, as well as being slightly detached from the square. → **15, 16** Finally, the glass wall has been set in a deep recess. The combination of all those elements produces a dynamism, even if it would have been more attractive to hide the construction or details of the steel columns on which the fans are supported better. The intersections in the black masonry are hard, and the detachment of the curved copper screen works well. The enormous window with the deep reveals and the peepholes placed irregularly are also effective. They both accentuate the thickness of this screen that is suggested at the sides, producing a splendid contrast with its raised status. → **17** Less effective, on the other hand, are the third type of window and the protruding window in the masonry façade. Precisely because the building already has so many different things, the architect should have been more sparing with trivial elements of this kind. Many other Mecanoo buildings also match Van Dijk's description. They are built up from what look like independent façades in which the choice of materials or the treatment of detail often refers to something in the surroundings. Restaurant Boompjes (Rotterdam, 1990), that is situated beside the water, has a corrugated roof

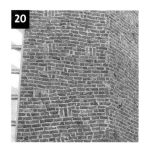

covered with wood, and awnings that have to be raised like sails. → **18, 19** The Isala College (Silvolde, 1995) has an outside wall made of reject bricks from the nearby brickworks, the use of a lot of wood is logical in a setting where there are so many trees, and – with a bit of imagination – the zinc can be taken as a reference to the River IJssel. → **20** The laboratory in Wageningen (1992) has grey brick masonry and wooden façades, materials that are also used in the neighbouring houses.
Mecanoo also sets out to turn the different surfaces into independent objects. By means of a specific, often sloping position of the horizontal and vertical jambs, the large glass walls acquire such an arrangement that attention is diverted from the individual pane of glass to the surface. Francine Houben calls these jambs the musical notes. Restaurant Boompjes has a glass wall of this kind, and the glass façade of the library of Delft Technical University is accentuated as a whole through the surprising positioning of the black jambs. → **21**
Mecanoo applies the same strategy to brickwork façades. Extremely thin cross joints have been applied in the Wageningen laboratory, making the individual bricks merge to form a single whole → **22**; in Silvolde the bricks are laid as if by a drunk, a bonding that ensures that the masonry façades form an unmistakable surface. → **20**
'The masonry bonding and the colour, contour and composition of the joints have more influence on the plastic quality of the masonry than the type of brick does.'[10]
Finally, as Van Dijk indicated, the different surfaces remain as independent as possible. The almost non-chalantly sawn off wooden planks in one of the buildings in Wageningen, for example, continue just beyond the glass façade. → **23** The sculpturally shaped gym of the Isala College, lined with wooden planks, is attached to the zinc aula in such a way that it looks as if the gym can be fitted into the aula. In other, less dramatic cases, the façades extend just beyond the side walls, or strips of glass are used to keep the façades apart.

Volumes instead of surfaces

In the course of time Steenhuis, Van Egeraat and De Weijer have left the collective to begin their own firms. Döll and Houben, the remaining Mecanoo members, pay no heed to the criticisms by Van Dijk and Kerkdijk. They see perfection as a sort of trade mark of Mecanoo, and have little in common with architects who give more importance to the concept than to a perfect building. After all, the client is not waiting for conceptually interesting buildings with technically weak details. They also adhere to the specific use of material, that is primarily intended to please the senses and to create atmospheres. However, the Isala College and the Faculty for Economics and Management (FEM, Utrecht, 1995), as well as the buildings that Mecanoo designed afterwards, reveal evident changes in the Mecanoo signature. The volumes are no longer constructed from more or less independent surfaces, but the often plastic volumes are more often covered with a single continuous material. The corner details are particularly important in this connection. Down to the Isala College confrontations of materials were avoided to demonstrate the independence of the surfaces and materials, while in the FEM the front and side façades are connected by means of unusual but simple corner details. The aluminium slats, for instance, are continued smoothly around the corner by means of mouldings at right angles, and equally attractive, almost furniture-like corner details have been devised for the wooden façades of the Zen garden. → **24, 25**
At the same time, this building consists of a series of very simple details. Details have become practical things again, and they are not just there to achieve beautiful connections or compositions. This makes the façades calmer. Thin façades in different materials were used for the FEM, behind which the actual wind-proof and water-resistant wall is set. The advantage of this strategy is that one series of details was sufficient, as the steel profiles set against the 'genuine' wall are used to attach the façade material that determines how it looks. The façades enable the constructional wall to disappear behind the wooden, metal or aluminium screens. Not the window opening or the end of the wall attracts attention, but the façade composition, and that is how Mecanoo wants it. All the same, each façade – both the outside and the patio façades – has been given an atmosphere of its own.
The library of Delft Technical University (1997) and the entrance to the National Heritage Museum in Arnhem (2000) are logical continuations of the FEM. In concept, the library of the Technical University was not to be a building. It lies behind the monumental Van den Broek and Bakema auditorium, and Mecanoo did not want to enter into competition with this building. The idea was to rip open the ground to create functional spaces below

ground level. How are you to handle the materials and details of an idea like that without its becoming precious? In connection with this building, Kerkdijk expressed the hope that the idea of a non-building would mean no details either.[11] That is not what happened. Mecanoo does not design buildings without details or materials, even if the choice of materials is a very sober one by Mecanoo standards. Only glass was used for the façades, but they have not become 'non-façades'. → **26** The black horizontal profiles placed at random ensure, just as in the other Mecanoo glass façades, that the three glass façades are experienced as surfaces. → **27** In addition, these ventilation façades are set at different angles for optimal reflection of the surroundings. The glass becomes a field, sky or street of glass, but is barely, if at all, transparent. The interior only radiates outwards when the lights are turned on. The roof is not detailed like a small field. It has a rigid metal frame and towers way above the glass façade in the Schoemakerstraat. The entrance to the building consists of a wide incision that grows progressively narrower and is made out of heavy concrete. → **28** It is not exactly an entrance to a 'non-building', but it is very effective because it dramatises entering the metal-coated hall on a gradient. Of course, this is a perfect example of architectural striving for effect, but it is beautiful. A similar effect is achieved by the 143-metre long wall that separates the National Heritage Museum from its surroundings. → **29** In a loose adaptation of Alvar Aalto, Mecanoo decided to use forty different types of brick and even more joints and types of bonding to form a gigantic mosaic. The wall contains brickwork quotations from Berlage, Staal, Neutelings and Mecanoo itself. While Mecanoo tries to turn other façades as far as possible into a single entity, this wall works much more as a sort of dazzle painting. Each brick and each joint reflects the light in a particular way, so that the gigantic dimensions of the wall are hardly experienced as such. An enormous red sliding door has been set against the wall. The bright

red door of the National Heritage Museum has become an independent element, because the rails are visibly attached to the brickwork and through the steel strips painted white from which the door is suspended, that attracts more attention than the enormous wall. → **30** Behind the wall is the glass pavilion – glass to avoid obstructing the view of the park as much as possible. The glass is held in place by wooden jambs that are enormously accentuated on the park side. If the building is viewed from an angle, the fully transparent façade looks closed. The thick, heavy jambs have been slightly detached from the concrete. This is a clever detail in terms of maintenance – the light and thus relatively weak larchwood was chosen for the jambs – but the seam also accentuates the thickness of the jambs. The calm that Mecanoo wanted this building to have can also be seen from the roof, which naturally overhangs considerably again but has not been detached from the rest of the volume. The wooden planks that line the ceiling on the inside and which keep most of the necessary infrastructure out of sight are also applied on the outside, and since the glass runs between the wood, as it were, a strong relation is created between inside and outside, and the glass façade virtually disappears. The corner detail, or rather the lack of one, is another strong point. The jambs are considerably detached from the corners, so that only the glass turns the corner, resulting in an optimal transparency.

While the National Heritage Museum, the library of the Technical University, and for example the flats beside the Brouwersgracht (Amsterdam, 1998) → **31** create the impression of a more reticent use of material by Mecanoo, the St Mary of the Angels chapel (2001) in the St Lawrence cemetery in Rotterdam shows that Mecanoo still uses festive materials when necessary, which is perhaps typical in this case in light of the function. → **32** The form and choice of materials for the chapel match the gym in the Isala College, the copper boulder of the National Heritage Museum that accommodates HollandRama, and in fact the conference room of the main office of the ING bank in Budapest (1994), which although designed by Erick van Egeraat dates from when he was still a member of Mecanoo. The distorted wall of the chapel is coated with brightly gleaming copper. Since the doors are coated with the same material, the impression is created of a single curved and continuous wall that floats above ground level. This idea is strengthened because the slender steel columns that can be seen above and below the wall, for even the overhanging roof has been prised loose from the volume, also function as elements on which the doors hinge. → **33** The walls have hardly any other details. Unlike the other, more organic Mecanoo buildings that are – or appear to be – visibly covered with a uniform coating, the chapel roof is an autonomous element. Not only has

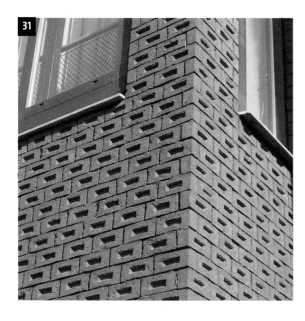

31

a piece of glass been introduced between the roof and the wall, but the ceiling has been painted gold. → **34, 35** That the building is not reduced to kitsch is mainly due to the fact that the details are not coddled to death. The light switches and the door handle, for example, seem to have been chosen from a standard DIY range. → **36** Nothing has been done to hide this, and it is precisely banal elements like these that bring the chapel back to the ground. The handling of technical details also seems to have become somewhat more nonchalant. It is no longer necessary for everything to be perfect and smooth. Details are absorbed in the volume, so that one material flows seamlessly into another. The independent, eye-catching details seem to have disappeared from the oeuvre. Everything indicates that Mecanoo has grown up. It makes buildings that are pleasing and radiate a certain atmosphere, and the more subordinate role of the details – in an architectural, but not in a technical sense – contributes to the less exhausting quality of the buildings. They are genuine volumes instead of compositions of elements. Whether the buildings should be classified as 'Schoolteacher's Modernism' or Aesthetic Pragmatism hardly matters, and certainly does not bother Mecanoo. Mecanoo wants above all to make beautiful and desirable buildings, and that is all.

1. R. Koolhaas, in: B. Leupen, W. Deen, Chr. Grave (eds.), *Hoe modern is de Nederlandse architectuur?*, Rotterdam 1990.
2. H. van Dijk, 'Het onderwijzersmodernisme', *Archis* 1990, no. 6.
3. H. de Kovel, 'De moderne architectuur leeft', in: H. de Haan, I. Haagsma (eds.), *Wie is bang voor nieuwbouw...*, Amsterdam 1981.
4. H. van Dijk, 'Dutch Modernism and its Legitimacy', in: R. Brouwers (eds.), *Architecture in the Netherlands. Yearbook 1991-1992*, Rotterdam 1992.
5. R. van Toorn, 'Architectuur om de architectuur', *Archis* 1992, no. 11.
6. H. van Dijk, 'On stagnation and innovation. Commentary on a selection', in: R. Brouwers (eds.), *Architecture in the Netherlands. Yearbook 1994-1995*, Rotterdam 1995.
7. Ibid.
8. Ibid.
9. H. Kerkdijk, 'Afscheid van een uitputtende architectuur', *Archis* 1995, no. 7.
10. E. Koster, 'De aaibaarheidsfactor van architectuur', *Architectuur/Bouwen* 1992, no. 9.
11. See note 9.

32

33

34

35

36

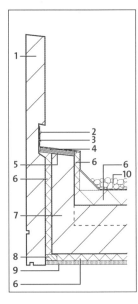

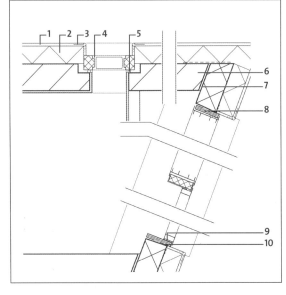

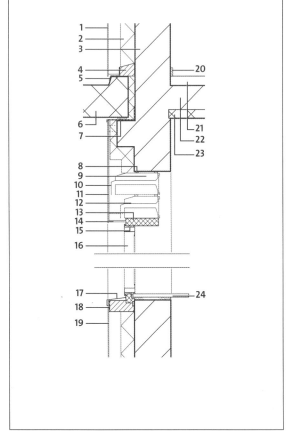

Roof edge
1 precast concrete roof edge
2 clamp profile
3 lead
4 roofing
5 water-resistant plywood
6 insulation
7 concrete roof slab
8 cleat
9 wood wool cement slab
10 gravel

94

Horizontal corner detail
1 plaster coat
2 insulation
3 plaster stop
4 glass brick
5 sealant on backup strip
6 calcium silicate brick
7 non-shrink mortar
8 sub-frame
9 DPC membrane
10 PVC foam tape

Façade detail at junction with balcony
1 10 mm Ornimat façade panel
2 insulation
3 in situ concrete wall
4 cleat
5 lead
6 concrete balcony
7 felt
8 sealant
9 acoustic baffle
10 fabric strip
11 Ornimat façade panel
12 acoustic baffle
13 45 x 190 mm wood beam
14 steel grille
15 Mavotex sealing tape
16 aluminium frame
17 drip
18 Bastik profile
19 Ornimat façade panel
20 plinth
21 cement screed
22 precast concrete floor
23 insulation and soffit finish
24 window ledge

Façade with terrace with bamboo screens

1 60 x 30 x 5.5 mm glass plate on T-sections
2 steel bar
3 two halved UNP 140
4 UNP 180 with welded stub ends
5 insulating glass
6 two halved UNP 140
7 rail for electrical control
8 20 x 50 mm duct fixed to strips
9 25 x 50 mm duct
10 bamboo stakes fixed with self-tapping screws
11 perforated aluminium
12 timber beams
13 25 x 40 mm angle
14 60 mm T-section
15 IPE 120
16 flat tingle
17 roofing
18 gravel
19 insulation
20 sloping screed
21 zinc on water-resistant plywood
22 insulation
23 concrete roof slab
24 IPE 220
25 render on plasterboard
26 insulation
27 parquet
28 compression layer
29 concrete floor
30 IPE 240
31 column

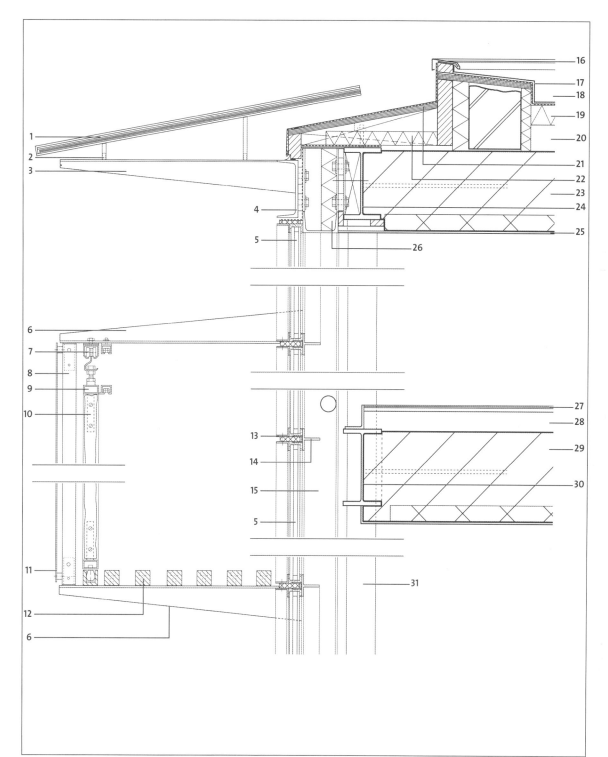

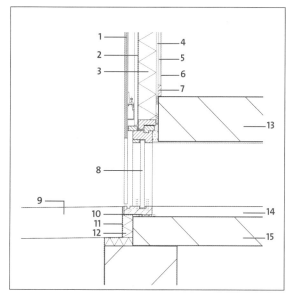

Detail of sliding patio door on rear elevation with steps of concrete stair

1 Bruynzeel panels attached invisibly using Justimax system
2 water repellent film
3 insulation
4 moisture barrier
5 two plasterboard panels
6 render
7 natural stone plinth
8 sliding door
9 in situ floor
10 blue Belgian limestone
11 bitumen
12 insulation
13 precast concrete stair
14 fair-face cement screed floor
15 insulated precast floor

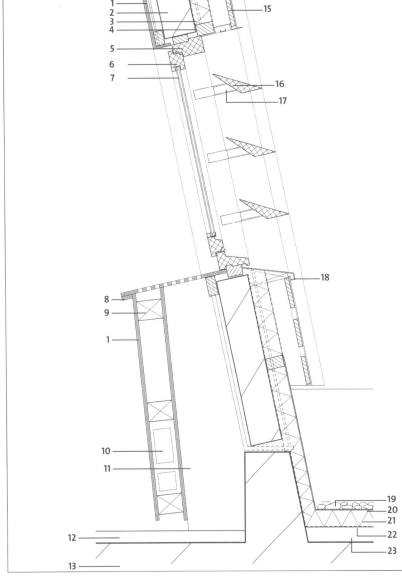

Zinc roof structure with solar shading of Oregon pine louvres
1 birch plywood
2 gas concrete
3 insulation
4 moisture barrier
5 67 x 139 mm Oregon pine
6 56 x 90 mm Oregon pine
7 insulating glass
8 2 x 19 mm MDF for grooved window ledge
9 cleat
10 convector
11 airconditioning duct
12 cement screed
13 concrete
14 zinc cladding
15 battening
16 Oregon pine slats
17 stainless steel fixing brackets
18 zinc drip
19 gravel
20 roofing
21 insulation
22 moisture barrier
23 sloping screed

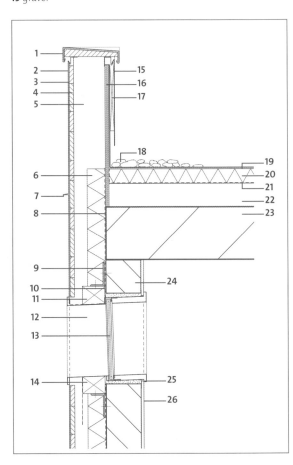

Copper façade at 'peephole'
1 profiled copper coping
2 copper façade cladding
3 bituminous glass fibre
4 25 x 114 mm planks
5 67 x 129 mm beams
6 insulation
7 copper realized with single lock seam joint
8 vapour resistant film
9 angle iron
10 DPC membrane
11 cleat
12 copper
13 insulating glass
14 cleat
15 copper sheet
16 water-resistant plywood
17 ventilation
18 gravel
19 roofing
20 insulation
21 vapour resistant film
22 sloping screed
23 concrete
24 calcium silicate brick
25 plaster stop
26 render

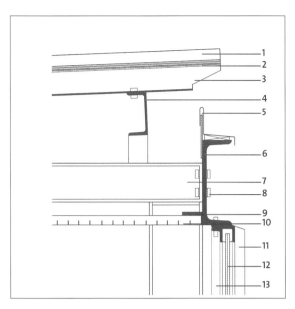

Roof edge of glazed connecting corridor

1 cover strip
2 laminated glass
3 100 mm glazing section
4 UNP 120
5 drip
6 UNP 240
7 HE 120 A
8 stainless steel bolts
9 welded strip
10 grille
11 120 x 8 mm steel strip
12 laminated glass
13 angle iron fixed to strip and UNP-section

Junction of north façade with glass and grass roofs

1 aluminium guard
2 water-resistant plywood
3 cleat
4 mineral plaster (15 mm) on 100 mm insulation
5 overflow
6 cement fibreboard
7 plinth profile
8 plaster stop
9 aluminium sub-frame with drip
10 cover strip
11 insulating glazing
12 glass roof box section
13 plaster stop
14 vertical wooden rails
15 horizontal wooden rails
16 moisture barrier
17 underlay
18 titanium zinc gutter base
19 upstand to prevent soil etc from falling into gutter
20 concrete tile
21 vegetation layer
22 roofing
23 insulation
24 vapour resistant film
25 roof structure

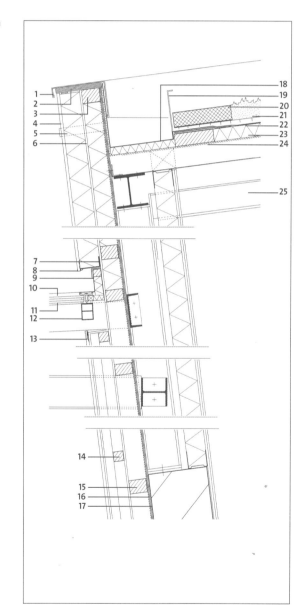

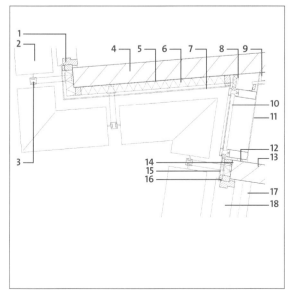

Horizontal detail of east façade with aluminium louvres

1 aluminium louvres
2 framing timber
3 support structure with post for louvres
4 calcium silicate brick
5 waterproof film
6 insulation
7 cement fibreboard
8 DPC
9 metal stud construction
10 infill panel
11 50 x 6 mm steel strip
12 Airex sealing tape
13 calcium silicate brick
14 waterproof film
15 cement fibreboard
16 rail
17 window ledge
18 sill profile

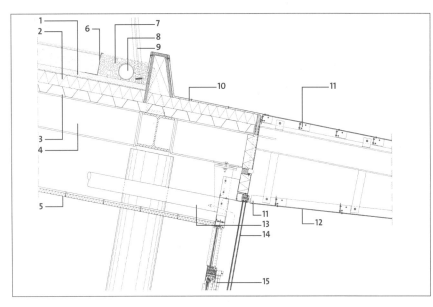

Junction grass roof and energy efficient façade
1 grass roof
2 90 mm insulation
3 profiled steel sheet
4 steel structure
5 acoustic ceiling
6 90 x 180 x 20 mm Cor-ten steel angle
7 black gravel
8 drainage
9 steel balustrade
10 pre-formed aluminium sheet
11 aluminium T-section
12 perforated aluminium sheet
13 outer leaf of façade
14 used air exhaust from façade
15 solar shading

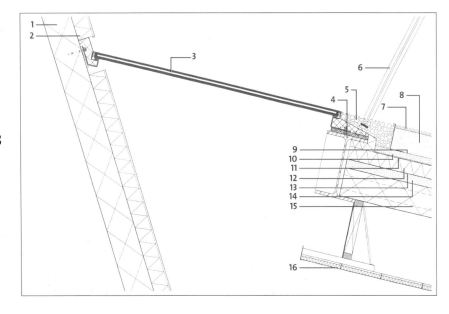

Junction grass roof and concrete cone
1 precast concrete cone
2 insulated rendered façade
3 toughened and laminated glass
4 HE 450 A
5 black gravel
6 steel balustrade
7 grass
8 substrate
9 filter membrane
10 clay chippings
11 EDPM membrane
12 90 mm insulation
13 vapour resistant PE film
14 levelling layer
15 hollow-core slab floor
16 acoustic ceiling

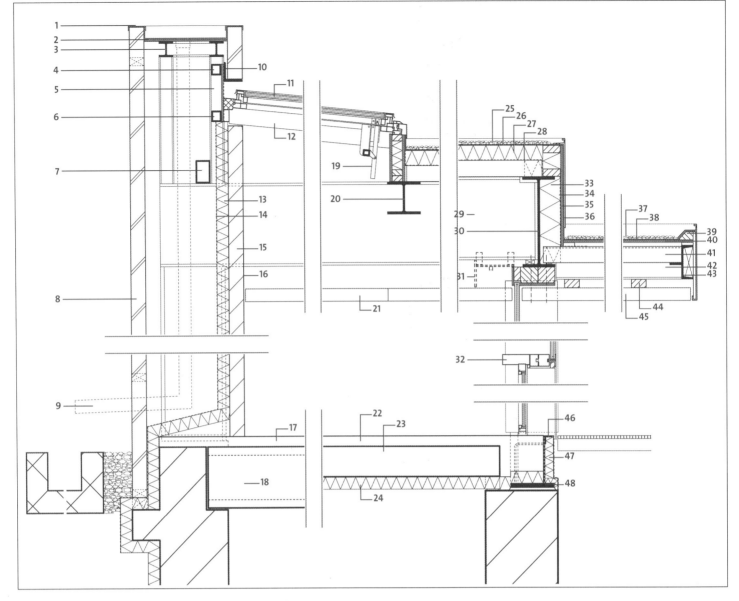

Section through entrance pavilion

1 zinc guard
2 water-resistant plywood
3 HEA 100
4 70 x 70 x 5 mm box section
5 composite HE 100A
6 70 x 70 x 5 mm box section
7 150 x 100 x 6 mm box section
8 brickwork (several different bonds)

9 water spout
10 120 x 120 x 10 mm angle
11 laminated glass
12 sky light structure
13 insulation
14 vapour barrier
15 calcium silicate brick
16 clay plaster
17 precast mechanically polished compression layer
18 uninsulated hollow-core slab

19 motor for opening roof light
20 HEA 220A
21 support system for suspended ceiling
22 precast mechanically polished compression layer
23 hollow-core slab
24 insulation
25 gravel
26 roofing

27 insulation
28 damp proof membrane
29 IPE 550
30 IPE 600
31 curtain rails
32 façade panel
33 insulation
34 breather membrane
35 water-resistant plywood
36 zinc cladding
37 gravel

38 roofing
39 tilting fillet
40 water-resistant plywood
41 steel roof decking
42 HE 220A
43 UNP 220 with welded strip
44 rails
45 small, unplaned Oregon pine beams
46 trimmed IPE 100
47 insulation
48 mounting plate

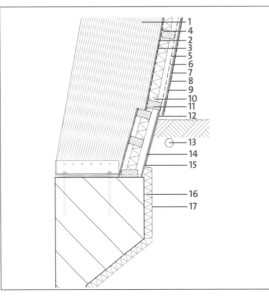

Detail of connection between copper 'egg' and ground plane

1 laminated pine trusses
2 12 mm plasterboard
3 damp proof membrane
4 laminated curved pine purlins
5 waterproof breather membrane
6 20 mm battens
7 2 x 10 mm plywood
8 bituminous mat
9 0.7 mm copper
10 insulation
11 pine purlins
12 0.7 mm copper
13 drain
14 18 mm water-resistant plywood
15 roofing
16 rigid insulation
17 roofing

Horizontal junction of façade and door

1 render, painted blue
2 10 mm masterboard
3 moisture barrier
4 120 mm mineral wool
5 battens
6 damp proof course
7 horizontal battening
8 vertical battening
9 copper (TECU®-Zinn)
10 copper folded over to cover reveal
11 copper plating
12 draught proofing
13 copper plating
14 plywood trim
15 steel column
16 ball-bearing hinge

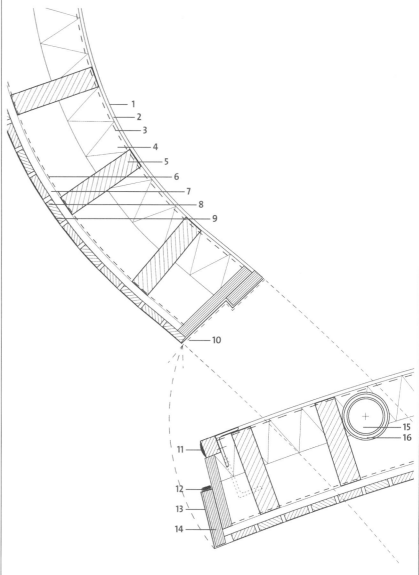

Junction copper façade and projecting roof

1 EPDM roofing
2 insulation
3 19 mm underlay
4 timber and steel girders
5 IPE 400
6 mineral wool
7 moisture barrier
8 battening
9 10 mm masterboard
10 6 mm render, painted gold
11 mounting plate welded to column
12 curved insulating glass
13 drip
14 UNP 220 wall beam
15 render, painted blue
16 10 mm masterboard
17 moisture barrier
18 battens
19 120 mm mineral wool
20 insulation at glass only
21 aluminium plaster stop
22 curved glazing bead
23 steel column
24 drip
25 damp proof course
26 horizontal battening
27 vertical battening
28 copper (TECU®-Zinn)
29 cavity opening closed with perforated copper

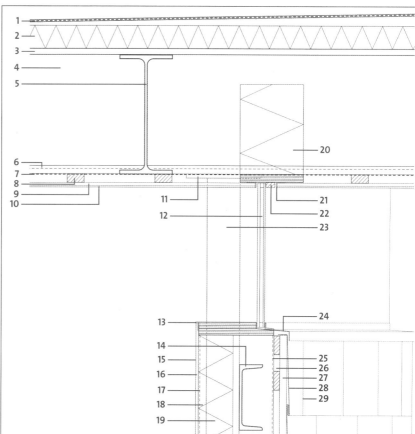

MVRDV
Accentuating the effects

MVRDV designs surrealist buildings. They may look normal at first sight as you drive past. The porters' lodges in the Hoge Veluwe National Park (1996) look like traditional little houses with a sloping roof → **1**; Villa VPRO (Hilversum, 1997) → **2** looks like a contemporary, blown up variant of Villa Savoie (Poissy, 1929) by Le Corbusier; the view from the rear of the WoZoCo (sheltered housing complex, 1997) in Amsterdam looks like a block of flats → **3**; the Dutch Pavilion Expo 2000 in Hanover looks like a stack of rough floors, or perhaps a flat. → **4** However, it soon becomes obvious that there is more to these buildings. By stretching the different edges of the stone, metal and wooden volume very gently, and by covering the roof and façade with the same material, plastic shapes have been created at the entrance to Hoge Veluwe Park. Villa VPRO turns out to be a continuous, sculptural concrete slab supported by a forest of columns and hollowed out at different points to allow the daylight to enter. Bizarrely huge, overhanging wooden boxes containing complete flats are attached to the access balconies of the WoZoCo. The Expo pavilion comprises a stack of different landscapes, with a forest on the fourth floor.

Besides being surrealist the MVRDV buildings are also extreme with their grandiose, almost dramatic gestures, although MVRDV is not out, or only out, for the effect. Winy Maas, Jacob van Rijs and Nathalie de Vries use their buildings to explore the possibilities of continuous surfaces and try to investigate the limits of what is still, or could be, a building. Buildings as cities, cities as buildings; buildings contain landscapes, landscapes are built. The detail plays an important role in heightening the intentional effect and determining the boundary of the volume.

The major influence of landscape in the buildings seems to come from Winy Maas – a landscape architect as well as architect – while the attention for the materials and for the details and their effects appears to derive from Nathalie de Vries. Maas and Van Rijs used to be members of OMA, where above all concepts were examined and the detailing of the buildings, at any rate for the outside world, played a subordinate role. De Vries worked for a few years with Mecanoo before MVRDV was set up. This Delft firm of architects spends much less time on developing new concepts, while the choice of materials and details for the buildings is done with great sensitivity. However, this division of labour proves not to

be the case. From the – often unjust – criticisms of the treatment of the detail in the work of OMA, Maas and Van Rijs learned that an architecturally weaker detailing diverts attention too much. De Vries, Maas and Van Rijs all recognise – like Koolhaas since the completion of the Nederlands Danstheater – the strength of the detail. Details can accentuate the effects of the concept, of the building, but badly implemented details can also undermine the idea.

The generally high level of the technical side of their buildings is partly connected with the collaboration with engineering consultants like Bureau Bouwkunde and ABT. After MVRDV had won the competition for Villa VPRO, it was more or less obliged to let Bureau Bouwkunde work out the technical side of the design. The client demanded this in the light of the lack of experience of the architects, and probably also because Maas and Van Rijs were former OMA architects. Since this project, Bureau Bouwkunde has often collaborated with MVRDV. Thanks to this cooperation, MVRDV does not have to worry about the technical aspects of the details, nor does it have to go (too far) into the constantly changing and stricter regulations. Although the growing number of completed projects no doubt leaves technical traces behind, the design process can still be carried out with genuine or feigned naivety. The idea behind this deliberate disregard for the technical aspects is that this kind of knowledge can work like ballast during the design stage and limit spontaneity and artistic freedom. Putting technical knowledge in parenthesis makes it possible to continue to develop architectural concepts that seem almost impossible to implement. The lack of knowledge is used as a kind of excuse, but what at first sight appears to be an impossible design is no less serious for all that. The next stage is to challenge the consultants to make the impossible happen. Each solution the consultants come up with that compromises the original concept is discussed, and afterwards alternatives are devised by MVRDV itself that are closer to the concept. Those solutions may not always be technically feasible either, but in this way the architects challenge the consultants to go further than they did before and to leave the trodden path. Moreover, they give the consultants technical ideas which are generally felt to be new and refreshing. There is always more possible than appeared at first sight.

So MVRDV elaborates the designs in a different way from, say, Neutelings Riedijk. Neutelings Riedijk also operates as a pure design studio and leaves the technical elaboration of the designs to Bureau Bouwkunde. Neutelings Riedijk, however, considers that architects should operate far more as engineers than as designers, and enters into discussion with consultants on the basis of technical insight. MVRDV tries to stimulate its consultants as much as possible, while at the same time

giving them a large measure of responsibility. This way of working can also be seen in the details of the buildings. Neutelings Riedijk designs most of the details itself – at any rate the contours of the details – before putting them technically in order. MVRDV consults more intensively to make clear what it wants and what kind of an atmosphere it is aiming at; it only designs the really important architectural details. Even in the case of what look like complex buildings, such as Villa VPRO, it turns out that there are only a few details designed by MVRDV, from which the other details can be derived. Of course, every detail is checked to make sure that it fits in with the concept.

Sculptural buildings

The precise architectural details prove that this strategy is successful, but the first project to be completed, the three porters' lodges in the Hoge Veluwe Park, also shows that the technical knowledge of MVRDV is quite considerable. The details of these lodges were designed by MVRDV itself. Although they are small, the lodges are complicated architecturally. The demands with regard to thermal comfort, security and daylight were high, and in addition MVRDV wanted them to reflect the wonderful combination of functions of the park. That park contains the Kröller-Müller Museum, which is why the lodges are a mixture of a traditional house, like others that can be found in the park, and a sculpture. The architectural complexity is a consequence not only of the distortion of the volume, but above all of the architectural desire to create the entire building volume in a single material. This emphasises the sculptural character of the buildings. In the first instance MVRDV designed one brick building, a wooden one – two materials that are an obvious choice in the light of the premises – and one made of glass (which is less logical). The latter material led to the creation of an image that is absorbed by its surroundings. The glass volume was also financially possible because at that moment the KPN (Dutch Post

Office) decided to make the counters of its post offices friendlier and to remove the bullet-proof glass that separated the employee from the customer. This bullet-proof glass – one of the demands of the client – could be used for the lodge. Rob Nijsse, a constructional designer for Adviesbureau ABT, devised the completely glass construction and a clever system of open joints between the sheets of glass laid like roof tiles to provide enough ventilation and to prevent the glass volume from overheating. The lack of privacy of the counter staff and the fear that the glass volume would still be too warm and would encourage vandalism, led the client to turn down the design. The third lodge is covered with corten steel instead of glass.

The glass volume would probably have been the most fascinating, it would also have been the richest in terms of visible details. Glass, after all, simply requires many joints. It is precisely the apparent lack of detail that makes the buildings which were constructed so architecturally and technically exciting. The material encases the volumes almost seamlessly. This suppression of the effects of the detail – combining the different materials as tightly as possible in a single surface and hiding as many technical aspects as possible from sight – recurs in most of MVRDV's designs. This is also logical given the firm's striving for continuous surfaces, since every shadow disrupts the continuous lines.

MVRDV was not particularly aiming for a continuum in the Hoge Veluwe Park. However, a sculpture calls for the same approach to detail. The material has been smoothly curved at the transition from façade to roof, and the bricks, for example, had to be sawn into exactly the right shape. → **5** The archetypal houses have also been stripped of typical technical elements like drainpipes, the gutters are concealed, and the openings in the façade (windows, doors and counters) are finished with the same material. → **6, 7** The seamless detailing of the porters' lodges suggests a massive volume of stone, steel and wood when the shutters are closed. Only when the shutters are open is it clear that the lodges are functional 'things' instead of sculptures. When they are open, the shutters are extra sculptural elements. They are parts that have been folded almost like origami.

Inconsistent details

The lack of detail in the skin of the porters' lodges creates the idea of a sculpture. In the case of the WoZoCo in Amsterdam, the flat wooden façade of the suspended flats is designed to accentuate the dramatic effect of the enormous wooden boxes that seem to be hanging from the glass access corridor. → **8** That is why the boxes are also covered with wood on the underneath, the drainage has been incorporated in the cavity wall of the boxes. As a result they seem to be made of solid wood. In reality, of course, the boxes are as light as possible. → **9, 10**

103

The light steel skeleton is covered with wood, fire-proof plaster boards and insulation material. This makes the boxes fire-proof and sound-proof. MVRDV would have liked to keep the steel skeleton in view in the interior, which would have enriched the interior as well as making the suspension of the flats in the flats themselves 'tangible'. However, giving the steel braced beams a fire-proof and sound-insulating covering would have been too expensive for this council housing project. The covered steel is now only visible in the flats hanging at right angles to the main volume.

The boxes themselves have practically no detail, but the attachment of the boxes to the concrete disc is visible. This seems inconsistent, because it seems to reveal the real nature of the boxes that has been so carefully camouflaged in the exterior. Strangely enough, this detail turns out to contribute to the desired effect. → 11 By making the contours of the enormous steel beams from which the box hangs visible, instead of incorporating this construction in the floors of the access balconies, the box gains in sturdiness, at least in the access corridors. This disturbance at the level of the detail, in contrast to the smooth and anonymous skin, draws attention to the force required to suspend the boxes and accentuates their weight.

The detail as datascape

The materials and details of the porters' lodges in the Hoge Veluwe Park and the wooden boxes of the WoZoCo is worked out from the exterior to the interior to enhance the effect. MVRDV followed the reverse direction in designing Villa VPRO. → 12 The idea behind it was to create a single continuous concrete floor in a compact volume which could be divided up as required and would facilitate different atmospheres. The green surroundings – although the building lies in the Mediapark in Hilversum and is surrounded by large office blocks, it also borders on a relatively large expanse of greenery – inspired MVRDV not only to make the

building a continuum, but also to keep the boundary between building and surroundings as vague as possible. The building was not really supposed to have a contour, so the architects decided that the distinction between inside and outside would have to be formed by the air, with air curtains providing a thermal barrier. This idea is a typical example of the level at which MVRDV initiates the technical discussions. No doubt no façade is the purest materialisation of the concept of a continuous surface, but it is also an idea which they knew in advance could not be implemented. Not only do the regulations prohibit a solution of this kind, but the maintenance of such an air curtain also requires an enormous quantity of energy. By setting very high stakes, MVRDV creates room for manoeuvre so that in the end they obtain more than what is normal, while at the same time the partners are given the idea that they have to an (important) extent won in the debates.

After the air curtains proved to be impossible, MVRDV thought up a detail to reflect above all the fact that the volume that has been cut off at fairly arbitrary points. In this detail, the glass façade would run in front of the rough 'nipped' off concrete. This would reveal the interior of the concrete slab with the plenum beneath the raised floor. This detail was not accepted either, this time from fear of an uncontrolled pollution between the glass and the concrete leading to a visual impoverishment of the building. The architects regretted this, as they consider that such maintenance-related details generate extra attention. In other words, by deliberately integrating dangerous details like this in a building, the building is kept clean better. In the field of urban planning MVRDV has implemented this in the plan for an industrial estate near Eindhoven, where the different buildings are pushed together so that they no longer have a rear side, which is often so neglected (1998-2003; Flight Forum, total plan). → 13 Loading and unloading are done on the representative front side of the building. These areas will receive more attention in the technical elaboration, and they will also be better kept. After all, they form an important part of the image of the company that has its quarters in the building.

The detail that has now been implemented in Villa VPRO disrupts the idea of the continuous surface. → 14 However, it is questionable whether this was the right approach to the detailing of the definitive façade. That the strategy was clearly changed in the course of the process can be seen in particular from the choice of glass. While the façade was as inconspicuous as possible in the first two variants, MVRDV finally gave in to technical demands and covered the villa with 35 colours of glass in 35 different gradations of transparency. The glass is opaque where the sun has most effect and where balconies with the striking rubber awnings were not possible for architectural reasons. → 15 The sides that

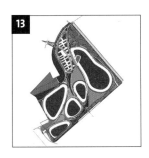

catch the least sun have transparent glass. Between these two extremes is woven a skin of gold, green, blue and red sheets of glass. The opaque types of glass in particular are remarkably solid-looking, making the volume not only much more closed, but also much heavier than in the original design. When seen in this light, the fact that the joint between the sliding glass walls of the façade and the concrete sheets is much less seamless – the relatively high ground sill of the sliding doors considerably disrupts the character of the continuous slab, whereas a rail set in the concrete would have achieved a smoother transition – is actually not so bad after all. → **16**

The composition with coloured glass has two interesting side-effects. To quote from the MVRDV book *Farmax*: 'the façade is now composed out of thirty-five types of glass, since the different heights and positions cause different heat loads and make cooling demands on the glass elements. [...] The façade has become a "result", a data-scape of demands.'[1]

Moreover, the coloured glass panels give the different areas an identity within the continuum, that is accentuated in the façade by means of a prefab concrete strip. Variation is brought to a uniform surface in a more or less similar way in the rear façade of the WoZoCo, though there was a greater need for it here. Villa VPRO already presents an exciting image through the continuous floor; the façade of the WoZoCo was in danger of becoming a normal, and thus fairly boring façade for a block of flats. Through the depth, the breadth of the balconies, and above all the virtually continuous variations in the colour of the polycarbonate plating used for the fences, the façade acquires an unprecedented dynamism and each of the flats also acquires an identity of its own – for those in the know, because for passers-by this façade camouflages the exact arrangement of the block. → **3** Since the wooden façade has almost exclusively balconies and storey-high doors with a window here and there and because the positions of

the balconies look fairly arbitrary, it is impossible to read off from the façade where the different units start and stop. Thanks to the large variations, this façade confers on the WoZoCo the identity of a gigantic block.

Hiding the details of materials

In the enormous Silodam (2002) housing project in Amsterdam, MVRDV achieves the effect of the individualisation of the block by using a wide range of contemporary materials, including wood, steel, concrete, corrugated sheeting and masonry. → **17** Each type of home and function has its own material, whereby the façade looks like an amazing coat of many colours. In architectural terms, the medium seems too heavy to be able to implement the original vision of a tight volume. While MVRDV used the detail in the other buildings to accentuate the effects, in the Silodam the detailing tempers the noise from all those materials. Since the firm was not trying to create a noise, all of the materials are placed as far as possible in the same surface and are only separated by one another by a minimal profile. → **18, 19** To achieve this, the differences in depth of the different materials are largely absorbed in the cavity wall. The astonishing result of this approach to detail is that the many materials are almost fused as one. Apparently, by not working out the details specific to each material, the materials are robbed of some of their specific characteristics. Only the texture of the different materials remains visible, but the skin is tight. And so MVRDV once again achieves its goal. The textures indicate the different types of home, and in combination with the location the individual flats become identifiable within the gigantic block and thereby receive identity. At the same time, the detailing prevents the complex from disintegrating into all sorts of small units.

So MVRDV knows how to weld the façades of its buildings carefully into a unity in spite of what are at time bizarre shapes and the diversity of materials. In the most important interior to date, however, that of Villa VPRO, the architects seem to have slipped up, and not just because of the complaints about the poor acoustics. The plethora of all kinds of disparate things does violence to the planned openness of the compact volume. → **20** The forest of columns, stability crosses and shafts which have no supporting function because of the construction system and are thus only for the vertical transport of the pipes and cables, and a large number of emergency exits that move like 'green snakes' through the body of the building have silted up the volume. As if this was not bad enough, many different materials have been used in the concrete volume for more or less identical functions. There are plastic safety devices next to or opposite steel cables; 'ordinary' wooden handles hanging from steel cables next to steel handles, or even tree trunks as handrails. In addition, according to plan, every VPRO

employee has taken over his or her area and arranged it in his or her own way. There is not a seconds peace for the eye, which is also the result of the fact that the building volume has been broken open in many places with 'precision bombardments' to create patios. Not only do they facilitate the entry of daylight, but they also create extra external areas with a friendly atmosphere of their own. Finally, the grass roof intrudes on the volume as well.

The building is too dynamic for an office in which people are simply supposed to get on with their work.

The detonating detail

The reason why MVRDV opted for excess in the case of Villa VPRO – certainly not all of the material applications can be attributed to their lack of experience, and besides they were no longer so inexperienced by this time – perhaps lies in the Expo pavilion in Hanover. This design can be regarded more or less as the MVRDV manifesto. The 'building' consists of six stacked landscapes: dunes on the ground floor, a gigantic lake on the roof, and a genuine wood in the middle. This intensive use of space meant that most of the 9000 m² site could be left as it was. The pavilion has no façades – this is what MVRDV wanted for Villa VPRO too. Of course, its purpose allowed this. Constructed nature in Hanover is only separated from the unnatural surroundings of the trade fair site by simple security devices. Demonstrating that nature can be manufactured and produced, and perhaps that is how it should be, is the third important statement after the intensification of the space and the creation of continuous surfaces. The pavilion therefore seems to have little or nothing in common with Villa VPRO. Besides, the pavilion has hardly any detail. It consists of stacked, extremely fascinating, almost dangerous constructions, but at the lowest scale level, that of the detail, they are barely refined. However, the crudity of the detailing suddenly makes a lot clear on the forest floor. Uncamouflaged in the middle of the forest stands a fire

hose, and the banal exit signs and even more banal sprinkler heads hang without any attempt having been made to incorporate them in the design. The joints of the supporting tree trunks make the intentions of MVRDV even clearer. In the first instance the trunks seem to be a part of the wood that have accidentally grown in such a way that they support the upper storeys. The illusion of an organic, natural construction is directly detonated in the details. → **21, 22** The soil has been removed from around the base to make the steel construction that fixes the tree trunks to the concrete plate clearly visible, and the joint at the top has been clearly brought into view as well. All these features, this noise, show that the wood is not a real wood; the wood becomes a building, and the effect of the wood fifteen metres above the ground in a built volume is enormously intensified. Perhaps that is how the noise in Villa VPRO should be seen as well. The Villa is not an ordinary office building, and was never intended to be one. People have been brought together in the new VPRO building who used to work in small villas scattered here and there in Hilversum and Amsterdam. The new Villa was to be a reflection of all those different villas with all of their specific atmospheres, and in this sense Villa VPRO can be seen as a very small city instead of a fairly large building. Building becomes city. The details, the confusion, the dynamism seem to be attuned to those of a city. That does not alter the fact, though, that by wanting too much and by wanting to be present, even if this building is to be seen as a city, there is still too much noise in too small an environment.

By now MVRDV seems to have learned from the confusion of the Villa. The limits of what can be made are extended further and further and the concepts remain exciting, but there seems to be more of an equilibrium. In the buildings with bizarre elements, therefore, the choice of materials has become somewhat more reticent, as in the 3-D Garden block of flats in Hengelo, for example (1999-). Every resident is allocated a 100 m² balcony that hangs from the volume in impossible ways. → **23** Some balconies even have a swimming pool. The effect of all those overhanging balconies is very strong, which makes it possible to tone down the materials used for the tower blocks. They will probably all be covered with wood.

As for the Ypenburg housing units (2001), the accent is precisely on the use of materials. → **24** Within the rigid frameworks of the Vinex housing estates, even MVRDV cannot do much more than a few centimetres of architecture. The houses have been given the shape of a roof that, as a roof should be, is covered with a single material. The occupants could choose from a variety of materials: cast polystyrene, traditional Dutch roofing tiles, or vegetation. Every superfluous ledge would destroy the impression of a continuous covering.

Gutters, even concealed gutters, were architecturally taboo. In terms of detail, this principle was even more complicated than in the case of the porters' lodges, because the permanence of the appearance of the homes, and thus their ease of maintenance, had to be guaranteed, and in particular the drainage of rainwater had to be taken proper care of. MVRDV won the discussion by arguing that the house should actually be detailed like a roof. Hence rainwater was drained off by means of simple gutters at the foot of the roof, i.e. at ground level. Incidentally, MVRDV received permission for this unusual solution because it turned out to be easier to implement and less expensive than concealed gutters. → **25**

The development within the oeuvre can also be seen from the various designs for the Nijmegen Polytechnic (1997-2001). → **26a, 26b** In the first instance MVRDV had the idea of using columns in the central hall to give places an identity of their own. Constructional engineer Rob Nijsse was asked to devise a large number of different columns. The result was series of columns of unusual materials (glass, car tyres) and series of apparently collapsed or almost collapsed columns. → **27** There was a danger that the interior would become anecdotal, like that in Villa VPRO. MVRDV did a U-turn. The school can now be seen as one enormous box that has been carefully hollowed out. The idea of a hollowed out mass is strengthened because all the surfaces will be covered with the same material. The concrete is first covered with a layer of polyurethane, which will be finished with a bright blue plastic. The blue is to give it a 'heavenly' look, and the façades must have a 'cloudy' look. That is why MVRDV departs from the flat detailing. The reveals are as deep as possible, whereby the polyurethane and the plastic are continued in the notches, and the frames are painted in the same colour. What this building would have looked like (it is very unlikely that it will actually be built) can be seen on a smaller scale in a studio/home, Thonik Studio, in Amsterdam (2001).

A bright orange layer has been applied on top of a small hollowed cube. → **28** Even the letter-box is detailed as just a slit in the surface.

In technical terms the detail is just as anonymous as the details of the suspended wooden boxes of the WoZoCo. Both the Polytechnic and the studio/home create the impression of a solid volume, and they also emphasise the squelchy nature of the façade.

As all these examples show, there are actually only two or three architectural details through which MVRDV accentuates the surrealist character of the building. Unlike what one might expect, they are relatively small details, unlike the much rougher details of Neutelings Riedijk. Neutelings Riedijk makes sculptural buildings that can be made using rougher details – 'details and profile' – MVRDV makes puzzling buildings. Technical amateurishness is fatal in buildings of this kind which challenge reality. It is precisely by deploying the architectural detail, in which interference sometimes plays an important part, with precision with regard to both place and form, that MVRDV manages to preserve the illusion of the bizarre in the buildings intact.

1. W. Maas, J. van Rijs with R. Koek (ed.), *MVRDV. Farmax, Excursions on Density*, Rotterdam 1998.

Otterloo
Sectional elevation of brick volume
1 150 mm precast concrete
2 insulation
3 masonry
4 transparent plastic
5 zinc gutter
6 hydraulic arm
7 brick-clad shutter
8 double glazing

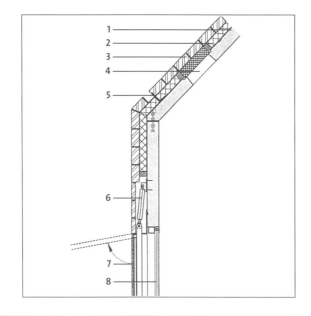

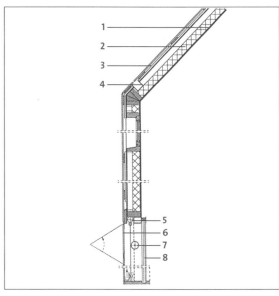

Arnhem/Rijzenburg
Sectional elevation of timber volume
1 timber frame
2 insulation
3 western red cedar
4 zinc gutter
5 fluorescent lighting
6 wooden shutter
7 motor
8 double glazing

Hoenderloo
Sectional elevation of steel volume
1 wooden frame
2 insulation
3 3 mm Cor-Ten steel
4 roofing
5 PVC gutter
6 ventilated cavity
7 hydraulic arm
8 shutter in Cor-Ten steel
9 double glazing

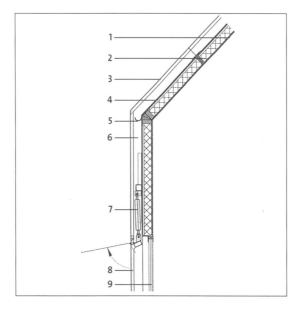

Section through cantilevered wooden boxes

1 aluminium edging strip
2 two-ply roofing
3 western red cedar drop siding
4 sloping insulation
5 profiled steel sheet
6 rainscreen
7 insulation
8 HE 160A
9 fire-resistant cladding
10 framing, separate from steel structure
11 DPC
12 2 x 12.5 mm plasterboard
13 2 x 10 mm Fermacel
14 100 mm mineral wool
15 levelling course
16 hollow-core slab floor
17 50 mm insulation
18 2.5 mm plasterboard on rails; rails against felt
19 aluminium tilt-turn window
20 sanitary and rainwater pipes
21 steel balustrade
22 water-resistant plywood
23 suspension frame for hanging wooden 'box' from gallery flat
24 IPE 200
25 HEB 260
26 fire-resistant cladding
27 insulation
28 plywood
29 concrete column
30 western red cedar drop siding on framing

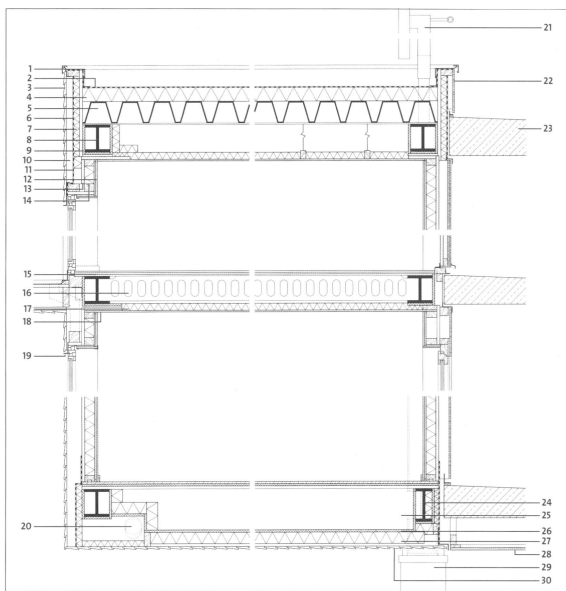

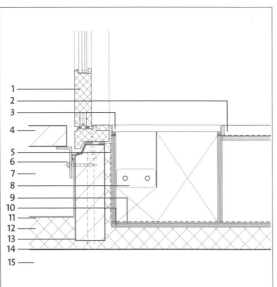

Junction timber façade panel and patio

1 sliding hardwood door
2 anhydrite floor on prefab system flooring (inc. soundproofing)
3 hardwood grille in edge profile
4 concrete tile
5 DPM
6 galvanized angle
7 water collection area
8 convector
9 DPM
10 plywood
11 two-ply roofing
12 120 mm insulation
13 precast concrete slab
14 insulation at dowels in concrete
15 in situ concrete

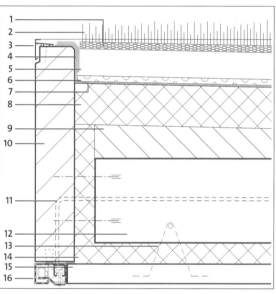

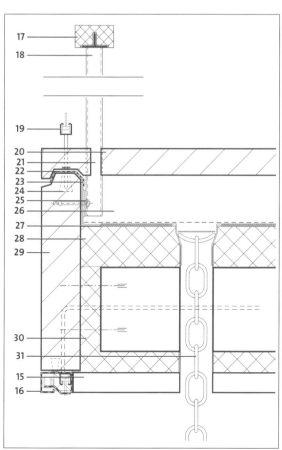

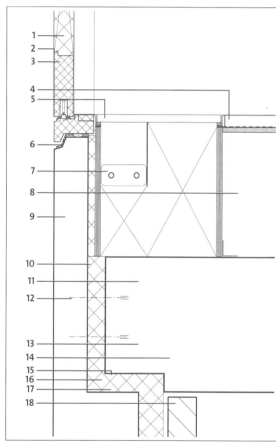

Junction vegetation roof and façade with rubber solar shading at one of the window-washing balconies
1 vegetation mat
2 vegetation
3 aluminium edging strip
4 lead
5 80 mm substrate
6 17 mm drainage mat
7 two-ply roofing
8 hard plastic foam sheeting
9 sloping layer
10 precast concrete edge
11 cast-in electricity cable for solar shading
12 in situ concrete
13 stainless steel anchorage for concrete façade panel
14 60 mm hard plastic foam sheeting
15 in situ concrete slab
16 top rail solar shading; electrically operated on east façade
17 hardwood handgrip
18 80 x 40 x 5 mm T-section
19 bottom rail solar shading
20 precast concrete tile
21 30 mm dia holes
22 rubber support strip
23 lead
24 cast-in cleat
25 rubber strip
26 water collection area
27 three-ply roofing
28 sloping insulation
29 precast concrete edge
30 60mm high performance insulation
31 water runoff via chain (instead of downpipe)

Junction of window wall and ground
1 46 x 67 mm mullions
2 aluminium cladding
3 timber sliding panels
4 anhydrite floor on prefab system flooring
5 hardwood grille in edge profile
6 lead
7 convector
8 plenum
9 in situ concrete edge
10 hard plastic foam sheeting
11 in situ concrete
12 stainless steel anchorage
13 85 mm glass wool, double-sided glass fibre
14 100 mm calcium silicate brick
15 PE film
16 insulation
17 local supports

18 calcium silicate brick, spring anchored

Detail of façade at rain curtain

1 scaffold leg
2 hot-galvanized steel roof
3 stainless steel strip
4 filter
5 stainless steel pre-formed gutter
6 downpipe
7 rain curtain
8 feeder pipe for rain curtain
9 cast-in-place pond rim
10 hot-galvanized steel plate
11 150 x 100 mm steel duct
12 steel girder with layer of shotcrete
13 water supply for rain curtain
14 steel cable for guiding water
15 filter
16 hinge
17 steel gutter bracket
18 50 x 150 mm hot-galvanized steel duct
19 suspension bracket for duct
20 pond
21 EPDM membrane
22 cement screed
23 hollow-core slab floor

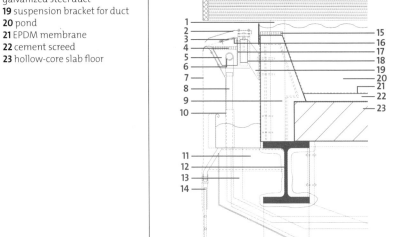

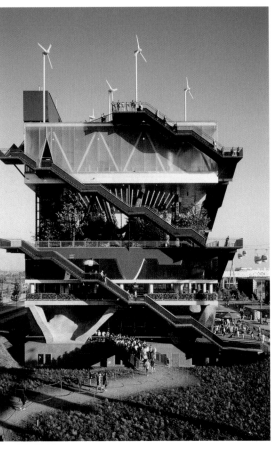

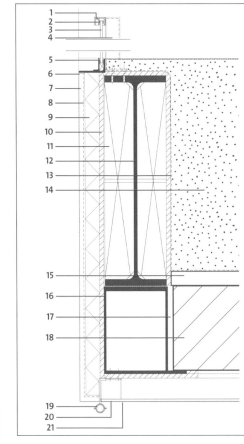

Detail of façade at forest level

1 50 x 37 x 5 mm hot-galvanized U-section
2 15 x 30 x 3 mm hot-galvanized L-section
3 12 mm safety glass
4 70 x 70 x 4 mm hot-galvanized duct
5 glass fixing
6 sealed joint
7 30 mm shotcrete
8 lathing
9 70 mm fire-retardant polystyrene
10 20 mm fire-resistant cladding
11 cleats
12 steel edge girder
13 waterproof layer
14 humus
15 compression layer
16 integrated steel floor beam
17 non-shrink mortar
18 hollow-core slab floor
19 tubular section
20 water-repellent plasterboard
21 stucco

Structural set-up of forest level with tree trunks as columns

1 pre-tensioned hollow-core slab floor
2 705 x 705 x 50 mm steel plate
3 10 mm thick stiffening plate
4 650 x 650 x 50 mm steel plate
5 25 mm thick steel plate
6 705 x 705 x 50 mm steel plate
7 tree trunk contour
8 705 x 705 x 50 mm steel plate
9 650 x 650 x 50 mm steel plate
10 elastomer

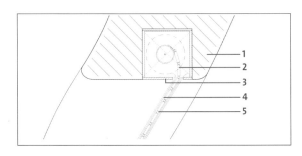

Detail of integration of fire-resistant hatch in concrete dune

1 sprayed concrete
2 fire-resistant roller shutter
3 fire-resistant cladding
4 guide rail
5 roller shutter profile

MVRDV Dutch Pavilion Expo 2000 Hanover

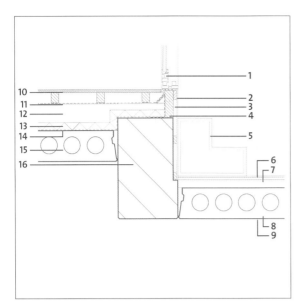

Vertical connection between aluminium sliding door and terrace
1 two-part aluminium sliding door
2 wooden parquet floor
3 framing
4 wooden beam
5 precast steps
6 American white oak
7 cement screed
8 hollow-core slab floor
9 soffit of hollow-core slab floor treated with oil
10 robinia planks
11 polyurethane roofing
12 sloping cement screed
13 insulation
14 DPC
15 hollow-core slab floor
16 concrete beam

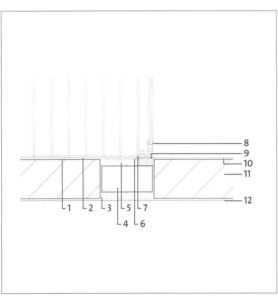

Junction aluminium sliding door (terrace) and orange wall
1 stucco with glass fibre
2 polyurethane façade finish
3 insulation
4 column, inverted concrete portal
5 insulation
6 angle bead
7 sealant on backup strip
8 two-part aluminium sliding door
9 5 mm rubber strip
10 10 mm stucco and glass fibre mat
11 300 mm Tasta blocks
12 polyurethane façade finish

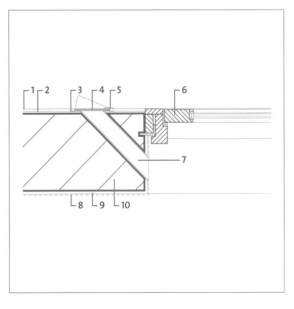

Horizontal façade detail at letterbox
1 second stucco layer
2 first stucco layer
3 stainless steel frame as stucco profile
4 lockable glass flap, self-closing
5 hinge flush with the wall
6 wooden frame in polyurethane colour
7 inside of letterbox finished with polyurethane
8 polyurethane façade finishing
9 stucco with glass fibre
10 300 mm Tasta blocks

Junction between brick façade and precast concrete façade
1 brickwork reveal
2 12 mm MDF
3 aluminium drip
4 plasterboard
5 PE film
6 framing
7 insulation
8 10 mm OSB
9 reinforced/perforated foil
10 PUR
11 lead
12 L-section
13 weephole
14 fixing of L-section to concrete structure
15 outer leaf concrete sandwich panel
16 insulation (part of sandwich panel)
17 PUR

18 inner leaf concrete sandwich panel
19 anhydrite floor
20 fixing of façade to concrete structure

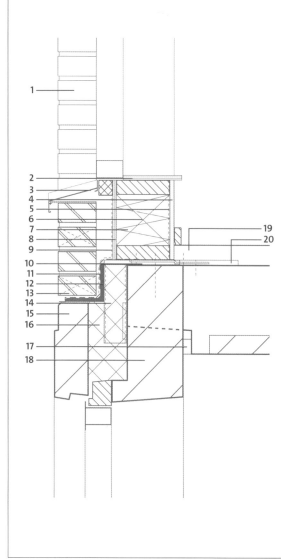

MVRDV Silodam apartment block Amsterdam 2002

114

Junction between façade with wooden spandrel and façade with aluminium cladding
1 insulated top-hung window
2 wooden frame
3 safety glass
4 12 mm MDF
5 aluminium profile
6 10 mm OSB

7 precast concrete slab
8 fixing to background structure
9 rock wool
10 in situ concrete
11 reinforced/perforated foil
12 L-section
13 wide-slab floor
14 plasterboard
15 PE film
16 140 mm insulation

17 framing
18 10 mm OSB
19 aluminium pre-formed panels
20 lead
21 MDF
22 aluminium spandrel panel
23 plinth
24 fixing to concrete floor
25 50 mm anhydrite floor

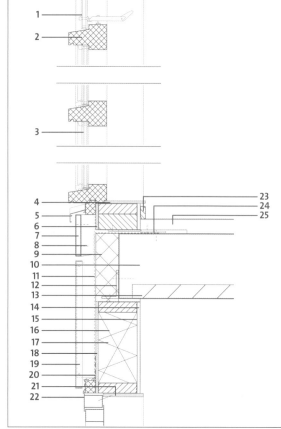

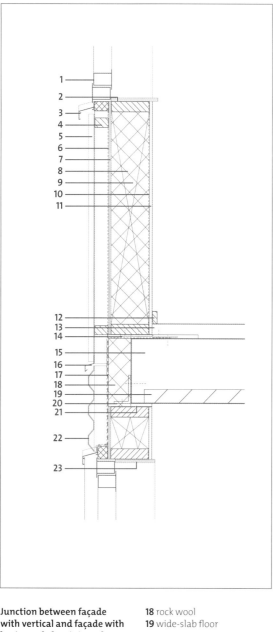

Junction between façade with vertical and façade with horizontal aluminium sheet piling

1 aluminium frame
2 12 mm MDF
3 aluminium drip
4 cleat for fixing profiled sheet piling
5 vertical aluminium profiled sheet piling (42W-960)
6 reinforced/perforated foil
7 10 mm OSB
8 140 mm insulation
9 framing
10 PE film
11 12,5 mm plasterboard
12 plinth
13 50 mm anhydrite floor
14 fixing of façade to concrete floor
15 in situ floor
16 aluminium profile
17 sealing tape (Matuband)
18 rock wool
19 wide-slab floor
20 L-section
21 PUR
22 horizontal aluminium profiled sheet piling
23 12 mm MDF

OMA
From no details to
NO-Details

'No money, no details, just concept.'[1]

'For years, we have concentrated on NO-Detail. Sometimes we succeed – it's gone, abstracted; sometimes we fail – it's still there. Details should disappear – they are old architecture.'[2]

These quotations from Rem Koolhaas admirably show how thinking about the detail has changed inside his Office for Metropolitan Architecture (OMA). NO-Details, according to Koolhaas, are abstracted details in which it seems as though a seamless transition is effected between one material and another, resulting in tightly demarcated volumes. These are the most difficult details to work out and to build. No details, on the other hand, are unmade, or more accurately, undesigned details. They are not architectural details. 'No money, no details' was Koolhaas' reply to the criticism of the building of the Nederlands Danstheater (The Hague, 1987). → **1**

Convinced of the fact that an architect must strive for 'material authenticity' and that the detail in an architecturally important building must bear the signature of the architect, thereby ruling out the use of standard details, the Dutch critics attacked Koolhaas en masse.

The Danstheater certainly does have few architectural details that can be called accents. The budget (a good 18 million guilders for a building of 54,000 m^3) was insufficient to give every detail an architectural significance. Besides, the building had to be designed and constructed very quickly. Finally, as Koolhaas later admitted, OMA had not mastered building at that time. In spite of the low budget and the lack of time and experience, the Nederlands Danstheater already contains traces of the later OMA detail strategy. Where there was apparently more supervision of the building, it is lacking in detail just as Koolhaas wanted. The treatment of detail that was applied makes the Nederlands Danstheater look as though it consists of three more or less independent elements that have been juxtaposed without any visible connections between them: the sculptural, black hall → **2**; the cheery façades adjacent to it on the Spui side → **3**; and the golden cone that forms a link between the Danstheater and the music theatre designed by Van Mourik Vermeulen Architecten. → **4** The detail strategy is most effective in the case of the screen with the work of art by Madelon Vriesendorp. Because of its dimensions and the invisible link with the side façades, this can be considered more

an autonomous work of art or a movable piece of décor than a façade.

At other points, however, the subcontractor appears to have had serious difficulties with the OMA objective of no details, and to have fallen back onto traditional solutions. For instance, the golden cone has acquired a rather precious aluminium eaves, and the windows in the side façade look as though they have come from council housing and are unnecessarily unrefined. The interior too reveals a number of features where the architecture cried out for distinctive details. It is especially regrettable that the sharp architectural details are lacking in the skybar. The bar seems to be balancing on a tube and to be prevented from falling over by a tensile rod and a steel cable. The design of the attachment of the tensile rod to the floor is reasonable, but the suggestion that the skybar is balancing is destroyed because the tube has been allowed to enter the ceiling and these elements are plastered together in a cumbersome and awkward way. → **5**

In spite of this rather clumsy detail, however, the skybar is still a constructionally interesting object, as clever as all of the constructions in the oeuvre of OMA. The constructions are partly used to determine the atmospheres of the different spaces. Besides Koolhaas' fascination with techniques of this kind, he has another important reason to use constructions and installations architecturally. Installations and (to a lesser extent) constructions take up space in the building where the architect has for a long time had little or no influence. 'It is astounding that a part of the building that takes up almost one-third of the cross-section of a building and sometimes absorbs as much as 50 per cent of the budget eludes the architect and architectural thinking.'[3] Koolhaas successful converts the installations and constructions in his buildings into architectural instruments.

Architectural engineering

Probably the attempt to integrate installations and constructions was one of the reasons why Rem Koolhaas sought an intensive form of cooperation with the constructional designer Cecil Balmond from the Ove Arup engineering firm. Koolhaas intended this cooperation to result in a new firm – not a firm of engineers or architects, but something in between. The ongoing cross-fertilisation between architects and engineers could lead to totally new types of buildings, constructions and installations. However, this far-reaching merger did not go ahead because the directors of Ove Arup were frightened of losing their own identity.[4]

The present cooperation between OMA and its advisers, in which intensive consultation is already held at the stage of developing the concept of the building, has also

resulted in a series of interesting constructions. A newly developed and unusual constructional principle is used for each building, and in the buildings that combine different functions, a different construction is even used for each space. This is logical in view of the fact that the construction is not just the supporting structure, but also determines the mood. Like the Educatorium (Utrecht, 1997), for example, whose most striking feature is the construction in the largest lecture hall where the reinforcement forces its way out of the concrete sheet. → **6** In the Dutch Embassy building (2001) in Berlin, the strategy of the atmospheric construction is carried out in a more subtle fashion. The construction consists of more or less independent concrete discs nonchalantly stacked like a pack of cards, thereby giving each space a different constructional constellation – and making use of enormous spans – but the presence of the construction itself is calmer. It looks more familiar precisely because a single principle has apprently been followed. How different this is from the Kunsthal (Rotterdam, 1992), where, for instance, from the exhibition space above the auditorium you can see the concrete columns of this hall, the tensile rod supporting the balcony, and the orange wind bracings that connect the open girders of the largest hall. It can be stated without any doubt that the construction in the Kunsthal contributes to the picture of an orchestrated chaos. That OMA was aiming at concentrated chaos in this building can also be seen from the presence of the enormous orange steel beam resting on the canopy → **7**

Orchestrated chaos

Architecture critics Bart Lootsma and Jan de Graaf are right in stating that the construction of the canopy itself can be seen as a homage to Mies van der Rohe's National Gallery (1968) in Berlin.[5] → **8** The enormous orange beam, however, is certainly not an allusion to Mies. In the case of Mies, his constructions determined the rhythm of the building with great precision; Koolhaas's beam, on the other hand, sticks out no less than five metres. It looks as though he is turning up his nose at his critics. The beam is not exactly to size, it looks like a rather clumsy detail, but of course this 'chaos' has been deliberately introduced. You do not accidentally place such a long beam just like that. The same is true of many of the details in the Kunsthal. Koolhaas wanted this building to destroy the myth that OMA cannot build.

At the same time, however, OMA was engaged in developing new detail strategies, searching for new meanings for the detail more deliberately than when it was elaborating the Danstheater. First of all, the detail did not need to be perfect by definition. 'I have the feeling that the world at the moment does not benefit from perfection. That is why we try to prevent that, even in our best detailing.'[6]

Besides as an illustration of the Zeitgeist, OMA is also convinced that perfection is deadly dull and prevents unexpected things from happening – unexpected things that are enormously charged. No doubt a traditional approach to detail would have prevented the rain from running along the roof of the slope to the entrance of the Kunsthal and above the heads of the visitors. A ledge at the top of the underpass would have diverted the water to a less dangerous spot. However, not only would such a ledge disrupt the abstraction of the box, but this solution turned out not to be necessary either because the water runs tidily down the concrete columns.

The building is full of details that are not quite perfect. Sometimes it is obvious that perfection has been deliberately avoided, but sometimes the application of a little more precision – such as at the joint between the concrete and the travertine at the corner, or where the gradient intersects the overhead bridge – would have prevented attention from being diverted from the unusual fitting of the detail into the concept. → **9**

'The detailing of the Kunsthal is a mode of detailing that frees the attention for other aspects such as the way the ground is read, the sensing of abstractions, of transparency and translucency, of concrete and of the conditions themselves. The sensing of a whole instead of all that fixation on the joints and the encounters.'[7] Although the different materials could probably have been fitted more smoothly into a single surface – traditional sills disrupt the smooth surface too much at the moment – these façades of the Kunsthal do arouse the suggestion that the building has been cut out in a fairly arbitrary fashion. → **10** In addition, a special game is going on with the perception of the façade materials concrete and travertin. In particular, by making various joints with the glass, these materials look very thin at some points – where the different materials lie in one plane so that they acquire the visual thickness of glass – while at other points the mass of the façade is enormously emphasised. In the case of the façade facing the Museumpark, the thickness of the travertine skin is accentuated, while here the apparently heavy natural stone seems to float above the enormous expanse of glass. → **11** What looked at one moment like a very thin surface without any mass has an enormous weight at another point, so that the detail constantly accentuates the desired effect. The application of similar details to the different materials detaches the desired effect from

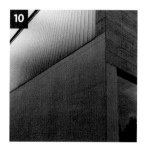

12

the traditional properties of those materials. Vice versa, when the same material is given a different treatment of the details, it acquires a completely different look. The accentuation of heaviness and the idea of a form that has been cut out and truncated at apparently arbitrary points are achieved not so much through the use of materials as through the handling of detail.[8]

Junkspace details

Koolhaas was forced to adopt a different strategy for the Grand Palais (1994) in Lille, a complex combining the functions of a conference centre, pop music venue and exhibition hall. The enormous dimensions of the building, the strategic position in the OMA urban development plan, the budget and the ideas formulated in 'Bigness' about the design of such enormous projects called for a different approach to materials and details.[9] Considered as a typical example of Bigness, the Grand Palais can be regarded as an enormous container in which the building does not react to the surroundings, but where the casing envelops a kind of city. Such a container is not given refined materials, and the infrastructure can remain rough because it is absorbed by the shell of the building: a lot of roughly finished visible concrete where the accentuated seams are only 'aestheticised' in the pop music centre → 12; and a façade consisting mainly of plastic and aluminium corrugated sheets whose profile has been specially chosen to be in proportion to the extreme height of the building and that can therefore be recognised from a distance as a corrugated sheet and not as a flat surface. These materials with an industrial or civil engineering look about them have been accompanied by an appropriate detail strategy.

Crude is not the word to describe the detailing. Rather, it looks undesigned – just as in industrial projects. Beauty does not here follow from solutions thought up in advance by the architect, but from the 'natural' solutions that have emerged during the building process and the unexpected things that have arisen in that way. However, the detail strategy of the Grand Palais has a double bottom. Partly through the industrial detailing, it looks as though the building can be dismantled again very easily. Everything that does not belong to the structure, to the permanent part, is visibly assembled on the concrete. It looks as though the Grand Palais has been detailed as a junkspace, the detailing of which

Koolhaas was to describe in a much later text as follows: 'Where once detailing suggested the coming together, possibly forever, of disparate materials, it is now a transient coupling, waiting to be undone, unscrewed; no longer the orchestrated encounter of difference but a stalemate, the abrupt end of a system.'[10]

The elliptical roof, for example, looks as though it is not really connected to the different façades, but rests loosely on top of them. → 13 This impression is created because the roof overhangs the façades, but above all by the way in which the corrugated sheet façades and roofing sheets are attached to one another. OMA used a steel profile which makes it look as though the roof can be raised and thus simply removed. The corrugated sheets with their robust bolts can be dismantled. The interior also contains many example of details based on the principle of being capable of being dismantled. For instance, the balustrades and landings on the staircases are made of simple T-profiles that are attached to the concrete in the most banal manner using a simple angular profile. Even the sprawling wooden staircase is detailed as a separate element that rests on top of the supporting sheet of concrete. → 14

Besides the industrial atmosphere of the infrastructure and the large spaces that give the building something inviolable, the Grand Palais also has a number of soft spots. The glass façade of the conference centre, for example, can be characterised as soft. The placing of narrow sheets of glass at different angles has created a sculptural façade because of the different reflections. The visitor to the building is also offered soft places. The small conference hall has been given a padded blue vinyl wall, and the largest a wall with a transparent coating of finished glass wool. The other striking feature of this hall is the dazzling ceiling constructed of transparent corrugated sheets placed so that the sound is reflected towards the audience. → 15 The detailing of these soft elements has not been made softer; it is just as no nonsense as that of the rest of the building.

Bordeaux

By now OMA has far exceeded the budgets for the Danstheater, the Kunsthal and the Grand Palais. OMA is building prestigious objects all over the world. The Casa da Música is currently being completed in Porto, OMA is constructing the new student centre on the campus of the Illinois Institute of Technology, an enormous library in Seattle, and an embassy in Berlin, as well as elaborating the winning entry for an auditorium in Cordoba. The question is what this means for OMA's treatment of detail and whether the short but powerful flow of chaos that Koolhaas allows in his buildings (according to Michael Speaks) and that is partly responsible for their fascination will also be given a chance in the prestigious projects.[11] Moreover, clients

13

14

15

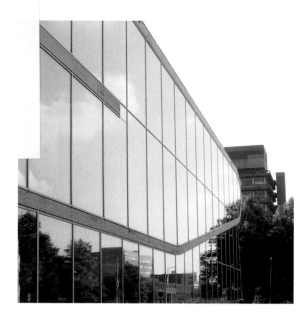

with large budgets want an architecturally interesting building that is also technically perfect and easy to maintain.

The Educatorium in Utrecht shows how difficult it is to find the right balance between the concept, on the one hand, that is so strong that an unforced but carefully controlled imperfection does not harm it, and the demand of the client, on the other hand, for a perfect and beautiful building. → **16** Almost everything in the Educatorium betrays an almost un-OMA-like attempt to control and give shape to every facet. It is undoubtedly the most finished OMA building to date.

The concept of the building (a covered volume created by inserting a hook into a rising curved form) is not affected by the particularisation of every corner and the designing of every detail, but the sublimity arising from the unexpected is less in evidence than in the Kunsthal or the Grand Palais. Besides, both the choice of materials and the handling of detail are architecturally questionable. For instance, the travertine covering of the concrete band that illustrates the concept of the building in the façade is meaningless. → **17** This is unlike what happens in the embassy in Berlin, where the aluminium bands are used in the façade to indicate the continuum, but the inside walls of this continuous structure are coated with aluminium as well. If the impression to be created in the Educatorium was that the building has been simply cut off at the façade, a concrete band would have done the job more effectively. In addition, cutting open the wooden covering on the inside of the arch does reveal its construction, but this honesty dissipates the force of this space because it is too distracting. → **18** Of course, this OMA building has its fascinating spaces too. The tremendously high 'corridor' between the two lecture rooms in particular has a mysterious beauty, perhaps also because the concrete wall was not perfectly cast here. Gravel pockets contribute to create a special atmosphere. → **19** The villa in Bordeaux (1998) shows a stronger balance

between concept, perfection and imperfection. → **20** This villa is barely finished or softened. It is a crude, but at the same time extremely cleverly constructed concept. The image is dominated by an enormously heavy brown concrete box that seems to lie on top of a glass volume. → **21** To emphasise the weight of the concrete box, the big hole in the top of the volume is covered with a concrete element the same thickness as the wall. An ingenious system with an axle and cogs ensures that the window can be opened easily in spite of its weight. → **22** The peep holes in the side walls have been left as holes without detail and seem to be placed in a completely arbitrary fashion. Nothing could be further from the truth, it is just that they are not used to create a façade composition. The holes have been introduced because the rooms needed daylight or a view at those points. The thickness of the concrete is tangible at these peep holes too. By the way, something went wrong when these elements were applied, as the resin that was supposed to make the holes waterproof has run down the concrete and left ineradicable marks. Nevertheless, the concept is so powerful that this unintentional imperfection does not spoil the look. It is an imperfection that Koolhaas finds fascinating.

Of course, the details of the glass façade were also important to evoke the idea of the floating volume. That is why large sheets of glass have been used that can almost all be slid open. Sliding sheets of glass entail less visible details than hinged elements. The most effective detail, however, is the fact that one glass façade has been set just slightly in front of the concrete volume. This makes the concrete's independence from the glass even clearer. Incidentally, this was a very troublesome detail for the engineers, because the large span and the weight of the storey would certainly have buckled the concrete. The glass has therefore been kept separate from the concrete, and the movement of the concrete is absorbed by a cast tenon and a steel plate glued to the glass. Equally ingenious, and much more important for the functioning of the villa, is the moving plateau that has been devised for the invalid owner and that has more or less become his world since his car accident. → **23** The ingenuity lies above all in the idea of the moving room by which the owner enters into a different configuration (office, living room) each time. He can also move on this platform to every floor. Such an object could have seriously impaired the abstraction of the floors, since safety regulations lay down balustrades. To avoid these facilities, the glass balustrades can be incorporated in the floors when they are not needed, and appear on command.

Layered details

The Dutch embassy building in Berlin and the Casa da Música make it clear that OMA has developed enorm-

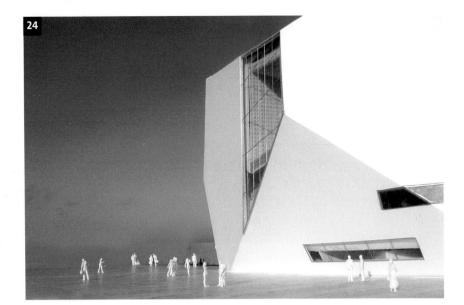

ously in the last few years. Particularly in Porto, the abstracted details are the high spot so far. The shape of the Casa da Música is rather like a diamond that has been hollowed out where functional spaces were required. → **24, 25** It looks like an unmistakable solitary body with the windows as razor-sharp incisions that are totally lacking in detail. The problem was how to join the roof to the façades without any detail, because the roof, unlike the façades, had to be insulated to keep the interior cool, and the expansion of the concrete had to be taken into account as well. There had to be a gutter too. In order to maintain the image of a sculptured body, a single large concrete plate has been laid on top of the insulating material and fastened at only a few points. This leaves the concrete free to move in any direction. The sunken gutter functions as a sort of wide expansion joint over which the concrete can slide.

The two enormous side façades of the Casa are of corrugated glass with an acoustic function. A detailing has been found for this difficult façade which allows an almost seamless transition from the concrete to the glass. The mouldings are incorporated in the concrete or hidden behind the façade casing. The problem here was that it must be possible (to some extent) to open the corrugated glass elements, and that curtains are necessary to make the hall dark enough. While curtains played an eye-catching role in the Danstheater, the Kunsthal and the Grand Palais, here the interior façade is so detailed that the curtains disappear in cavities in the wall. The camouflaging of the curtain resembles to some extent the way in which the balustrades are concealed in Bordeaux. The hatch to the niche that accommodates the curtains opens and shuts automatically.

OMA details increasingly include an extra, surprising layer which makes it possible to avoid utilitarian elements (balustrades, curtains with their infrastructure). This betrays the influence of Gerrit Rietveld, and enables the buildings to become even more abstract. This strategy is also applied in the embassy building in Berlin.

→ **26** The building has a continuous concrete floor that provides access to every room in the building. The continuous concrete slab and the structure created by it can be read in the façade, just as in the Educatorium. Besides applying an aluminium-covered band, OMA also decided to give this space a different type of façade from the rest of the building. The continuum has a structural glass façade, while elsewhere OMA applies ventilation façades with striking split jambs. Splitting the jambs is not a detail for detail's sake or just to give the façade a certain rhythm. OMA does not deal in ornaments. On the inside of this double jamb is a door that enables the users to make contact with the outside world. Unlike traditional ventilation façades, in which the openable parts always disrupt the rhythm of the façade and call for a series of extra, visible details, OMA has prevented this in a powerful and invisible fashion. → **27**

OMA also strives for perfect NO-Details in the embassy building. The aluminium plates with which part of the wall will be covered are detailed with precision. Every element that would normally disrupt the abstraction of the walls is incorporated in those walls. For instance, the handrails and door handles are negative shapes formed behind the aluminium plates.

Has this precise elaboration banned imperfection? 'We have to ask ourselves whether we can still operate with roughness. [...] We have to avoid the same sort of development as say, Gehry. I see Gehry as an example of an architect whose transition to bigger and more major briefs has turned him from maximum authentic into, let's say, a maximum fake.'[12] But this fear seems unjustified. Thanks to its increasing control, OMA can now direct the imperfection. The unusual, non-designed aspect of the buildings will remain; the imperfection is allowed at and it will be used at those points where attention is not deflected from the whole, the concept. By the way, this does not mean that the imperfect detailing is designed. That is impossible. As soon as a deliberate search is under way, or imperfection is even detailed,

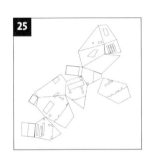

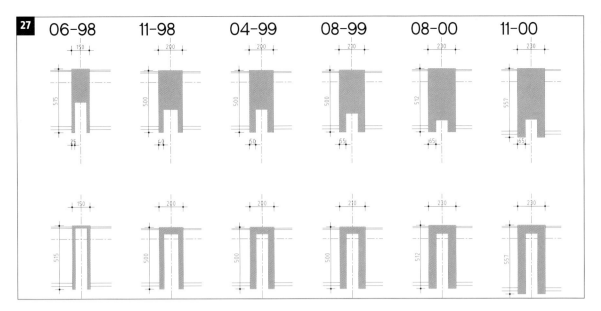

Study of the width and depth
of the mullions in the
mechanically ventilated
façade of the embassy in
Berlin

it naturally becomes a fake, a trick. Genuine and thus
dazzling imperfection can only arise when the reins are
dropped at the right moment, and the points at which
this can be allowed to happen have to be chosen with
great care. In the embassy in Berlin – as in all its
buildings – OMA alternates expensive and inexpensive
materials. The relatively expensive and smooth detailed
aluminium panels are juxtaposed with very cheap tiger
wood – a material usually used for shipping containers –
and the sloping concrete slab is cast in situ and left
unfinished in full view. The concrete in particular will
never be perfect and will always bear traces of the
manufacturing process; leaks will always leave patches
behind them.

Moreover, the concepts of the buildings are so complex
that perfection is virtually ruled out. The embassy is a
good example of this, as the subcontractor is continually
complaining that it is almost impossible to build. In
addition, OMA is constantly on the lookout for new
materials as no other firm is. The corrugated glass sheets
in Porto and the structural metal stocking that is to be
used in Seattle are cases in point. It is difficult to predict
what the detailing of these architecturally virginal
materials will be like. Finally, an abstract handling of
detail – no matter how well designed it may be – always
means that the surfaces will suffer to a greater or lesser
degree: the brown concrete box of the villa in Bordeaux,
for example, is growing patchier and patchier. In the
Educatorium too, the combination of the joints detailed
out of sight and the unusual shape of the building has
caused damage, though on an insignificant scale, to the
building: rain, which first flows across the semicircular
concrete shape, etches the sloping glass of the restaurant. The manufacturing process and time are given room
to affect the look of the building. By constantly going in
search of danger, Koolhaas manages to prevent the
roughness of the buildings from lagging behind or
becoming a trick.

1. A. Zaera, 'Finding Freedoms.
Conversations with Rem
Koolhaas', El Croquis, 1992,
no. 53.
2. OMA, R. Koolhaas, B. Mau,
SMLXL, Rotterdam 1995.
3. N. Kuhnert, P. Oswalt and
A. Zeara Polo, 'De ontplooiing
van de architectuur. Interview
met Rem Koolhaas',
de Architect, 1994, no. 1.
4. A. Graafland and J. Haan,
'A Conversation with Rem
Koolhaas', in: The Critical
Landscape, Rotterdam 1997.
5. B. Lootsma and J. de Graaf,
'In dienst van de ervaring.
Kunsthal van OMA in
Rotterdam', de Architect, 1993,
no. 1.
6. E. Melet, 'De perfecte
wanorde. Detaillering en
constructie Kunsthal',
de Architect, 1993, no. 1.
7. See note 4.
8. See also: U. Garritzmann,
'De ondraaglijke lichtheid van
bekleding', Oase, no. 47, 1997.
9. OMA, R. Koolhaas, B. Mau,
'Bigness', SMLXL, Rotterdam
1995.
10. R. Koolhaas, 'Junkspace',
A+U, May 2000.
11. M. Speaks, 'Artificieel
Modernisme', de Architect,
1995, no. 9.
12. See note 4.

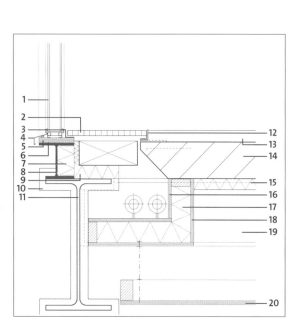

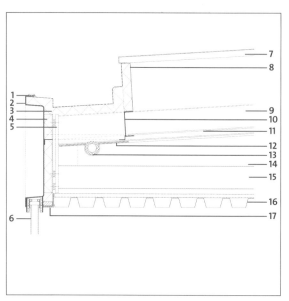

Vertical junction between glass planks of façade and roof with curved roof lights

1 aluminium profile
2 sand-coloured steel fascia
3 extruded foam insulation
4 insulation
5 truss end plate
6 glass plank
7 curved dome light
8 standing metal plate of dome light
9 HE 220 A truss
10 UNP 180
11 opaque glass plate
12 gutter housing
13 insulated rainwater pipe
14 twisted panelling, view
15 160 x 80 x 10 mm angles
16 perforated profiled sheet
17 white panelling

Junction between glass planks of façade with steel structure at portal

1 glass planks
2 hot-galvanized grille
3 35 x 35 x 5 mm angle
4 sill
5 plywood
6 bitumen fabric
7 baffles
8 HEA 160
9 insulation
10 fireproof cladding painted in sand colour
11 HEA 600
12 55 x 35 x 4 mm angle
13 compression layer
14 concrete floor
15 insulation
16 plywood
17 insulation
18 plywood
19 IPE 300
20 plywood with storm-proof fixing

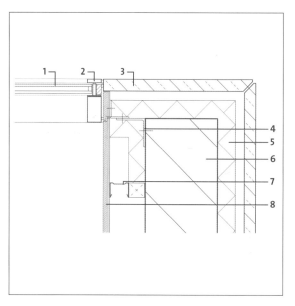

Horizontal junction travertine façade and glazed façade

1 insulated glass
2 aluminium façade panel
3 travertine
4 angle iron for fixing façade panel
5 insulation
6 concrete
7 plywood fixing
8 plywood inner wall

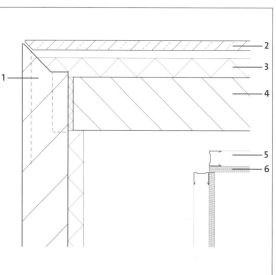
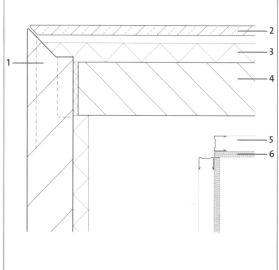

Horizontal junction concrete façade and travertine façade

1 black concrete
2 travertine
3 insulation
4 calcium silicate brick
5 plywood fixing
6 plywood inner wall

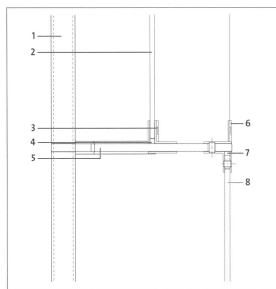

Detail glass façade
1 balustrade
2 canted toughened glass
3 stainless steel fixing
4 silicone joint
5 laminated glass (to absorb tensile stress)
6 stainless steel fixing
7 silicone joint
8 vertically placed toughened glass

Section through corrugated plastic sheeting
1 projecting roof
2 roof structure
3 junction façade structure/roof structure
4 corrugated plastic panel
5 corrugated panel fixed to background structure
6 steel column
7 stainless steel grilles

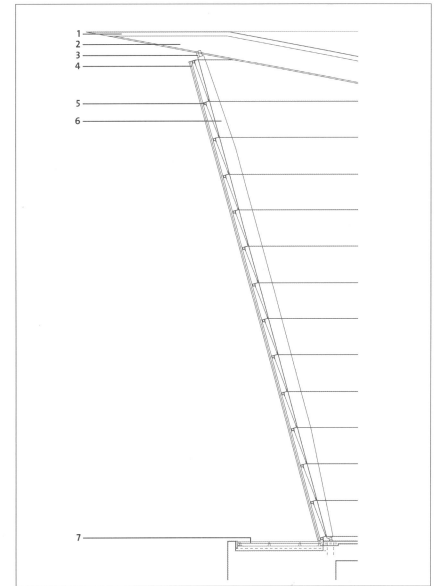

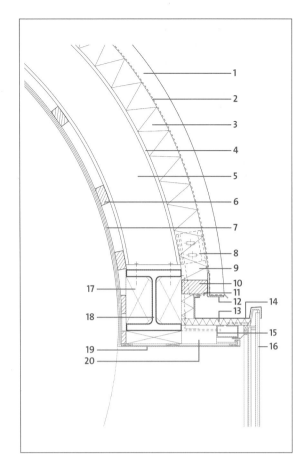

Junction curved concrete wall and window
1 sprayed concrete
2 elastomer layer
3 PU sprayed insulation
4 sendzimir galvanized steel sheet
5 IPE section
6 filler rails
7 3 x 4 mm (3-ply) plywood
8 70 x 70 x 7 mm angle with slotted holes
9 welded steel strip
10 46 x 85 mm wooden cleat
11 60 x 5 mm welded steel strip
12 80 x 60 x 8 mm angle
13 PU insulation
14 pre-formed stainless steel gutter
15 80 x 40 mm aluminium box section
16 laminated insulated glass
17 cleats
18 HEM-section
19 pre-formed aluminium sheet
20 steel strip

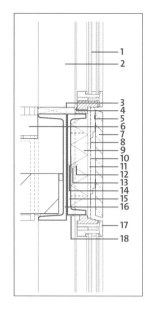

Junction glazed façade and travertine belt course
1 insulated, sound-damping glazing
2 steel column
3 pre-formed steel sheet, galvanized and painted
4 sealed joint
5 stainless steel strip
6 convector well
7 30 mm thick natural stone
8 breather and damp proof foil
9 70 mm thick rock wool
10 stainless steel suspension frame
11 perforated cement fibreboard
12 threaded end welded to UNP 400
13 washer with nut
14 nylon washer
15 UNP 380
16 UNP 400
17 aluminium curtain wall profile
18 pre-formed steel, painted

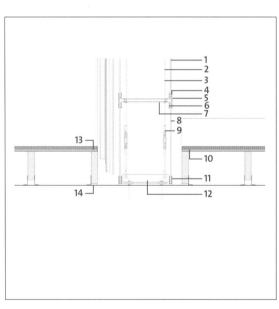

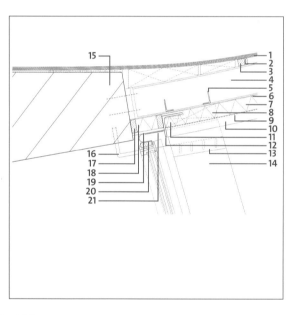

Junction curved concrete wall and sloping glass façade of canteen
1 3 x 6 mm form-fitting underlay
2 felt
3 framing
4 IPE-section
5 70 x 50 x 6 mm angle, fixed between curves
6 steel plate with coating
7 PU foam insulation
8 46 x 85 mm cleats for glass fin brackets
9 elastomer layer
10 sprayed concrete
11 nylon sheeting at junction of curves
12 120 x 120 x 12 mm angle, hot galvanized
13 welded stainless steel bracket with slotted holes
14 glass fin
15 concrete floor
16 20 mm thick rod in M16 anchor; one per fin
17 32 x 75 mm rails
18 mineral wool
19 cement fibreboard
20 rubber profile
21 1 mm thick stainless steel fixing clip

Lower detail of suspended double-glazed wall in largest lecture room
1 8 mm thick toughened glass coated with Asahi Lumisty film
2 8 mm thick monolithic steel tension cable
3 fixing of tension cables
4 5 mm thick neoprene gasket
5 120 mm dia stainless steel disc
6 stainless steel unit
7 35 mm dia stainless steel pipe
8 lower glass panel chamfered
9 turnbuckle
10 timber construction stair
11 50 x 20 mm U-section
12 70 x 70 x 8 mm steel T-section
13 timber construction C500 lecture theatre
14 silicone sealant

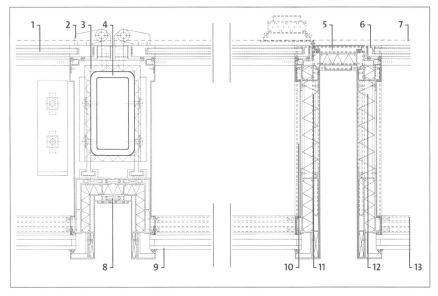

Horizontal section of mechanically ventilated office façade

1 glazed inner leaf of mechanically ventilated façade, single-strength safety glass
2 hinge
3 fire-resistant material
4 120 x 220 x 16 mm steel tube
5 insulated panel that can opened to let in outside air
6 aluminium façade panel
7 concrete floor
8 thermal separation
9 outer leaf mechanically ventilated façade (insulting glass)
10 'parking place' for vertical louvres
11 cross braces
12 insulated aluminium panel
13 aluminium strip

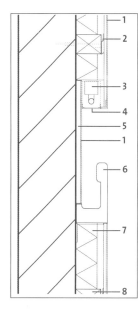

Handle integrated in aluminium wall of 'continuum', the area that provides access to all the rooms in the embassy

1 aluminium sheet
2 aluminium suspension system, tied to rear construction
3 lighting
4 2 mm plastic cover plate for lighting
5 non-combustible 'filler' material
6 milled aluminium handle
7 50 mm acoustic insulation
8 spacer

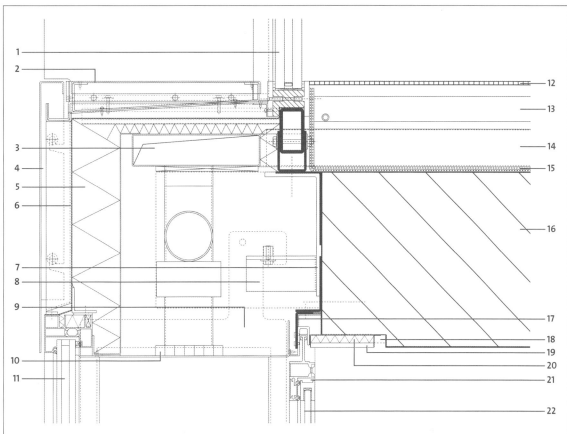

Junction between mechanically ventilated façade and glazed façade of continuum

1 insulating glass of continuum
2 aluminium cover plate
3 air duct
4 aluminium façade cladding
5 insulation
6 vapour resistant film
7 hot-galvanized L-section
8 hot-galvanized L-section
9 hot-galvanized façade auxiliary structure with adjustment mechanism
10 maintenance flap
11 insulating glass in mechanically ventilated façade
12 parquet
13 air duct in continuum
14 compression layer
15 impact noise insulation
16 in situ concrete
17 auxiliary structure for fixing glazed inner leaf
18 curtain rail
19 plasterboard
20 fire-resistant material
21 aluminium façade panel of mechanically ventilated façade
22 single strength safety glass

OMA Dutch embassy Berlin 2001

125

Detail of upper connection of cantilevered glazed façade

1 aluminium sheet
2 insulation
3 stainless steel section
4 aluminium plinth
5 brown concrete
6 silicone joint
7 laminated, toughened glass
8 laminated, toughened glass
9 20 x 38 x 4 mm Z-section
10 cast-in anchor
11 rails and aluminium sheet
12 grey concrete
13 finishing layer
14 cast-in ducting
15 insulation

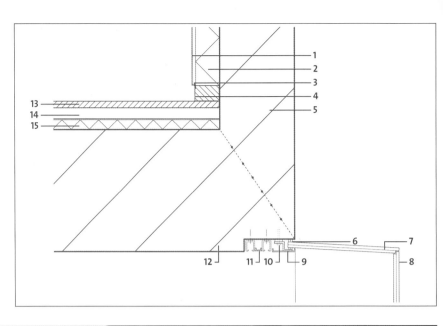

Detail of junction between floor and cantilevered glass façade

1 aluminium sheet
2 compression layer
3 cast-in ducting
4 insulation
5 concrete
6 aluminium sheet
7 laminated glass
8 40 x 40 mm angle
9 aluminium tube
10 60 x 8 mm aluminium plate
11 14 mm thick steel plate
12 HEA 300
13 rails
14 insulating glass

126

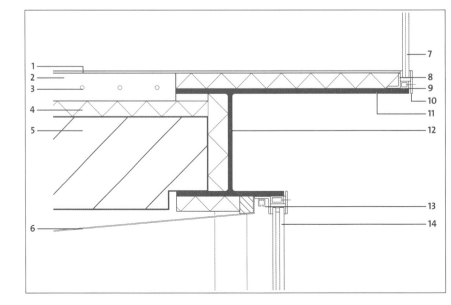

Detail of glazed peepholes
1 brown concrete
2 insulation
3 aluminium
4 cast-in anchor
5 silicone sealant
6 hinge
7 laminated glass
8 opening mechanism
9 20 x 50 mm angle
10 spacer

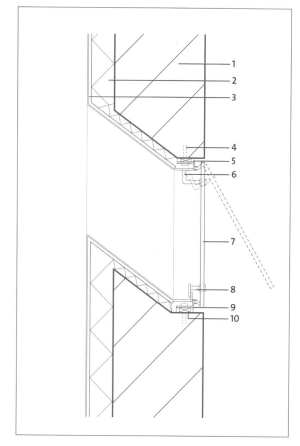

OMA Maison à Bordeaux 1998

**Detail of swing-aside
toughened glass balustrade
for lift shaft**
1 laminated glass plate
(balustrade)
2 mechanism for folding glass
plate up and down
3 fixing to concrete structure
4 concrete finishing
5 grey concrete
6 lift shaft
7 aluminium sheet
8 compression layer
9 insulation

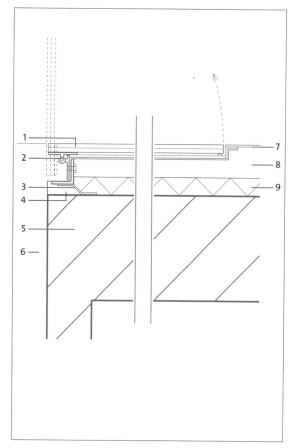

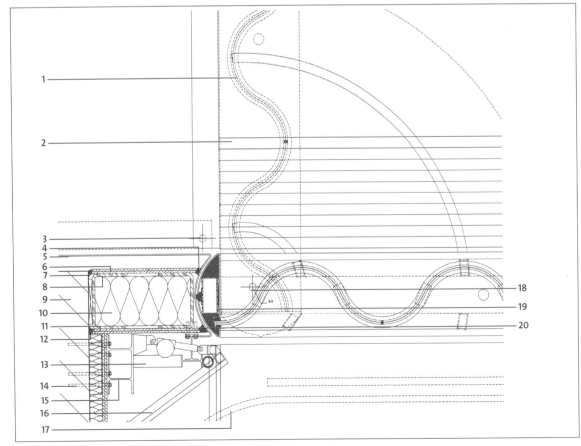

Detail of connection between swing-aside curved glass and recess for storing curtain

1 curved laminated glass
2 aluminium louvres
3 rotation point of pivoted door
4 silicone sealant
5 curved aluminium sheet
6 plasterboard
7 silicone sealant
8 box beam
9 reinforced concrete
10 acoustic insulation
11 plasterboard
12 silicone sealant
13 mechanism for opening recess
14 steel structure fixing
15 steel structure
16 recess door
17 curtain rails
18 rotation point
19 steel section
20 silicone sealant

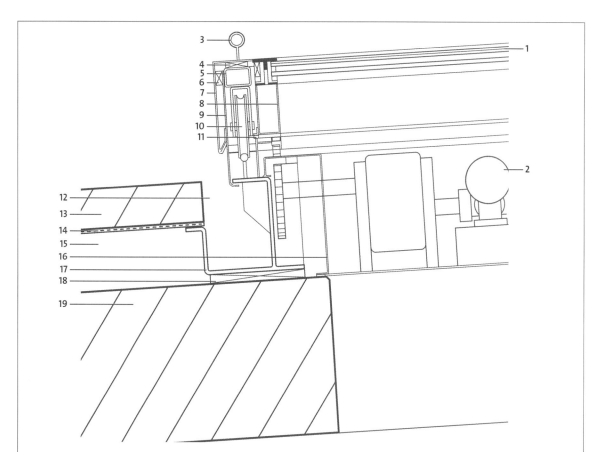

Junction swing-aside window and concrete roof
1 insulated glass, laminated glass on the outside
2 motor
3 safety ring for window cleaners
4 spacer
5 steel section
6 spacer
7 3 mm thick pre-formed aluminium sheet
8 extruded aluminium profile
9 steel fixing aluminium sheet
10 track for sliding window
11 brush
12 rainwater outlet
13 reinforced concrete
14 waterproof membrane
15 insulating material
16 aluminium sheet
17 steel section
18 spacer
19 reinforced concrete

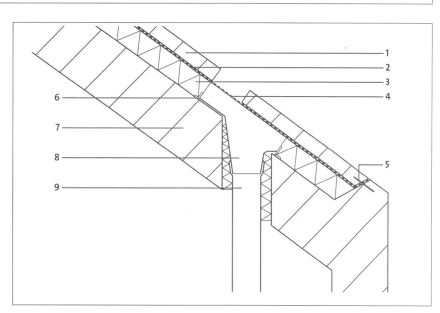

Detail of concealed gutter structure
1 reinforced concrete
2 waterproof membrane
3 insulating material
4 galvanized steel grille
5 rod
6 angle
7 reinforced concrete
8 zinc gutter
9 rainwater discharge

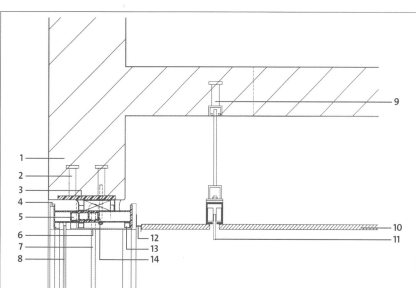

Details of vertical junction curved glass/concrete
1 reinforced concrete
2 steel anchor
3 steel plate
4 aluminium section
5 composite aluminium section
6 aluminium sheet
7 stainless steel cable
8 laminated curved glass
9 anchor for rails for cleaning system
10 wood ceiling finish
11 mechanism for cleaning system
12 aluminium sheet
13 aluminium section
14 fixing

Hans Ruijssenaars
Layered richness

Jokingly Hans Ruijssenaars calls himself an illegitimate son of Louis Kahn (1901-1974) and Johannes Duiker (1890-1935), two architects with highly individual but completely different styles. Duiker was an engineer as well as a Modernist architect who illustrated the play of forces in his constructions with great sensitivity. His plastic beams and columns are an integral part of the architecture (Open air school, Amsterdam, 1930). → **1** Louis Kahn was equally interested in the constructions, but above all for their architectural significance (First Unitarian Church and School, Rochester, New York, 1969). → **2** He was much less interested in the mechanics behind them and purity of materials, which is what engineers like Duiker were always striving to attain. He was particularly searching for constructions that would give his buildings a powerful look. The façades of the two architects are completely different too. Duiker used large glass surfaces and de-materialised the rest of the façades by plastering them. Kahn also made abstract façades, but their materiality was at least as important; his façades had to be genuine, solid and monumental, or at least appear to be so.

So the ideas of these two great architects on architecture – beaux-arts versus modern – differed enormously, and it seems almost impossible to develop a coherent signature of one's own from the two styles. Yet Ruijssenaars' remark is not out of the blue. That would be impossible anyway, because he knows the work of the two architects too well for that. He has carried out a thorough study of Duiker's work and has studied with Kahn. The fusion of both styles has been an evolutionary process in which Ruijssenaars has moved a step further each time. The climax so far is the library in Amstelveen, that combines the 'airiness' of Duiker and the materiality of Kahn with the subtle playing with daylight that is common to them both. → **3**

Negation of weight

Ruijssenaars' first really big building, the public library in Apeldoorn (1984), seems from the outside to be influenced above all by Kahn, but whereas Kahn tried to accentuate weight in the interior as well, Ruijssenaars tempered the weight in various ways, particularly that of the construction, while at the same time retaining its materiality. → **4** The library has a masonry construction. That looks like a direct reference to Kahn – although the cambered beams and tapered consoles are from the

vocabulary of Duiker –, but the reasons for adopting it were more banal. At the time a brick construction turned out to be simply less expensive than a concrete skeleton except in the cellar, where concrete columns were used because the pressure would have been too much for ordinary sand-lime brick. An advantage of brick is that it is a material with a past, but the disadvantage of brick columns is that they are more robust than concrete supports. To make the construction look less weighty, Ruijssenaars has split them up into three more or less independent sets of discs of which one set supports the façades, one the floor storeys, and one – an extremely delicate one – the roof construction. → **5** Ruijssenaars used the third, slender disc to accentuate the effect of the tall central area. Besides splitting them up, so that the forces were distributed and the discs could be made more slender, Ruijssenaars had the bricks whitewashed. This choice was also motivated for economic reasons, as less regular and thus cheaper bricks could be used. However, it does take away some of the weight – white objects simply look lighter than dark ones – while whitewashing, unlike plastering, leaves the texture of the material visible, as well as adding a layer to the building. While a layer of plaster is flat and smooth and thus neutral, whitewash is always less regular and the stripes from applying it are often still visible, giving this layer depth and materiality.

Finally, these white surfaces dramatise the effect of the enormous window on the top floor of the Apeldoorn library. The light is reflected downwards more effectively, and besides these white masses absorb most of the heat from the sun that enters the building and thus prevent the warmth from being oppressive in the public area.

Ruijssenaars uses windows in high positions in almost all of his utilities buildings. The best example is the sky light in a bank beside the Herengracht in Amsterdam (Bank Insinger de Beaufort, 2000). This sky light is situated on wooden 'sticks' arranged in a criss-cross pattern, forming a 'natural' extension of the tall, slender columns in the central hall. → **6** These kinds of tall windows not only provide the most dramatic lighting – especially in the tall areas that form the heart of Ruijssenaars' buildings and where the main access routes are incorporated – but they are also the most effective way to convey light inside since there is hardly any obstacle to the entry of daylight. This is unlike what happens with windows placed normally. Their position already reduces the amount of light, and besides there are always all kinds of things in front of these windows, both in the street and in the rooms themselves, which stop light from entering the building freely. So these windows always have a completely different function in his buildings from the windows positioned high up in the central areas, which primarily ensure that the light

can be used to its best advantage as an architectural device. The windows in the walls are there for the use of the building, that is directed to some extent by the architect. That is why Ruijssenaars designed wonderful brickwork window-sills for the library in Apeldoorn, inspired by Mackintosh or Dudok. → **7** Their detailing is severe, and they can be regarded as plastic continuations of the constructional discs that support the façades. The window-sills invite visitors to sit down and leaf through the books.

The construction – at least, the discs supporting the façades – has been rendered legible in the façade by means of window piers that are given an extra accent by the introduction of a sort of footing course between the piers and the rest of the façade programme. This turns out to be an effective detail that gives the building a certain timelessness. The steel drainpipes – which have been given a very plastic design at the rear of the building and form a sort of arch leading to the cycle rack – complete the strong vertical articulation of the building. → **8** At the same time, by making the construction legible in the façade, Ruijssenaars ensures that the building turns the corner in a 'natural' way. By definition a corner disturbs the rhythm of the façade, by using the constructional façade discs as a corner element, however, the rhythm is continued around the corner, as it were, in spite of the ultimate differences between the individual façades.

Layered structure

131 The next series of buildings look different to the library. First of all, they are airier than the sober, austere library because they consist of a number of elements that appear to be independent of one another thanks to the detailing. The library can still be set in the Modernist tradition, especially that of Kahn, but the later buildings with their white walls, arcades, roofed or open patios and independent towers, or the way they nestle in the urban pattern, look almost like Renaissance buildings from the

Mediterranean. Nevertheless, many of the elements with which Ruijssenaars composes his façades can already be found in rudimentary form during the development of the library. Apparently during and soon after designing the library, Ruijssenaars continued on paper to develop his own signature which departs from both the Dutch and the Modernist traditions.

The critic Herman Kerkdijk describes Ruijssenaars' way of working as follows in his article 'Een gewetensvolle architectuur' [A conscientious architecture]. He fills lots of sheets of A3 with small sketches in which he explores the urban planning context and the possibilities for the buildings, next to historical examples he sketches the buildings in cross-section, elevation and in the different ground plans, he tries to find the right construction principles and draws the most important details. Kerkdijk notes that Ruijssenaars draws much more than he can use in his buildings, and that during the design of one building the ideas and principles of the next one are already developed. 'The strange sensation arises that the next building is already hidden somewhere among all these possibilities, that it is already present as a possibility, but that it still "only" needs to be given shape.'[1] It is a natural consequence of such a design process that his buildings display large similarities, but that the resources grow richer and richer.

The main reason for changing his design process was that Ruijssenaars wanted to show how the different parts of his buildings are constructed to a greater extent than he had in the library. Kahn too showed how his buildings are constructed and how the forces are dealt with, but he then went on to abstract the different layers. Ruijssenaars wants much more to show the technical side – say the banal side. He detaches the different elements of a building or a part of a building from one another and makes them more or less independent. This enables him to tone down the transition from the building to the surroundings. This is at its most extreme with the roof. First of all, the roof itself is detached from the rest of the building volume. He applied a recess on the top floor of the library in Apeldoorn too, where this treatment of the mass of the building introduced a strong horizontal line as well as making room for the roof terrace and sky light and giving the building a less solid-looking façade on the side of the Vosselmanstraat. However, in that building he did not yet make the different layers from which the roof itself is constructed independent. In the housing project in IJmuiden (1992) → **9** and the CABO and ATO laboratories in Wageningen (1991 and 1993) → **10** Ruijssenaars used large glass surfaces to separate the roof from the rest of the building, but then went on to anatomise the roof in his detailing. The glass surfaces can be regarded as the transition from the heavy

but, as in the case of utilities buildings, a strong block. The details are deployed to camouflage the difference between the units. 'Detailing serves first the whole, and only in the second instance the home itself. [...] Especially now that the world can be known in isolation behind your own front door, it seems extra important to give form to something that hangs together or coheres outside it.'[2] The roof overhang is an important device for welding the block (almost 100 x 55 metres) together. → **14** It links all the housing units to one another. In addition, Ruijssenaars has constructed the façades with many small windows, and once again most of the masonry has been whitewashed. They are both devices to divert attention from the individual units.

An important detail to guarantee the unity of the block consists of the yellow brickwork frames. Since details that accentuate the individual units or components like windows are absent, these yellow frames ensure that attention is concentrated on the surface. At the same time, these bricks bring about a stronger connection between the different surfaces of the façade – they guide the surface around the corner, as it were. This is how Ruijssenaars preserves the unity of the building as a block and prevents it from collapsing into different surfaces. Moreover, the yellow brickwork creates a smoother transition from the white masonry on top of the dark bricks of the damp course. Sometimes he used a single brick-on-edge course, sometimes whole surfaces made of yellow brick. All the openings on the ground floor, for instance, are framed in coloured masonry. By setting all the frames in yellow or dark brown brickwork, Ruijssenaars once again does not emphasise the individual window as a hole in the façade – which is what would have happened if he had used yellow brick masonry lintels – but he uses the different colours of the masonry above all to create an exciting façade pattern and to focus attention on the block as a whole. He uses strips of this kind in the CABO and ATO laboratories with similar patterns to those in IJmuiden. In the ATO building, for instance, Ruijssenaars has created a delightful fabric of horizontal and vertical bricks that guide the building as a whole and its individual window piers around the corner. → **15** Once again, it is the compositional element that draws attention to the building as a whole.

The play with light and darker bricks in the Apeldoorn town hall (1992) has also a different meaning, which follows from the meaning of the masonry walls. → **16** In IJmuiden and the laboratories the masonry is the most prominent layer, while in the town hall it has become just one of the many layers. Here, more than in the other buildings, Ruijssenaars applied the strategy of dissecting the elements in the façade itself as well. The building is richly layered, which has given the strips of dark masonry two functions. First, the sloping lines are introduced so

building to the sky (not a building), although the overhanging roofs turn the windows into dark surfaces and give them more mass than Ruijssenaars may have intended. In terms of detail the glass is clever because Ruijssenaars wants the trusses – usually made of wood – that support the roof to stick out of his buildings in order to make those buildings legible. Glass makes it easier to achieve this detail than in a masonry façade because it is a way of avoiding thermal bridges without the use of very complicated devices. The trusses are tapered as they approach the roof edging to minimise the construction at the edges. To achieve his ideal – reducing the edges of the building mass to a few millimetres – he generally uses steel roof plates for the simple reason that they are much thinner than wooden panels. The thinner this line is, the softer is the transition from the roof – and thus from the building – to the sky. By the way, revealing the roof plating in all its nakedness – stripped of insulation, for instance – is only possible if the roof hangs over the building. → **11**

Besides tapering the trusses – which makes the construction lighter – Ruijssenaars introduces fine braced beams between the trusses and the roof plates in the IJmuiden housing project and in the laboratories. This makes the construction look airier, and these braced beams form a more attractive intermediary between the massive masonry building, the thin roof and the sky. Moreover, these braced beams introduce a new horizontal line in the surface of the roof. → **12**

132 Masonry patterns

It seems curious that Ruijssenaars used virtually the same roof details in the housing project in IJmuiden → **13** as in the two laboratories. After all, the functions of the two types of building could not be more different. However, Ruijssenaars probably designs in a less type-orientated way and uses detail much more in relation to the image of the building. In IJmuiden he did not want to make a series of linked, stacked individual housing units,

Hans Ruijssenaars Layered richness

that the brickwork façades are experienced as a single façade, just as in the other buildings. That is why the pattern has been continued at the transition from the front to the side walls, behind the balcony, around the windows, and at the sharp incision that marks the entrance. The way Ruijssenaars has set the window-frames in the façade without a reveal reinforces the experience of this part as a single surface. Moreover, he used glued windows so that no frames would be needed. This robs both the window and the masonry of some of their materiality, because the depth of the material has been smoothed away. The shadow lines that would have been created by the reveal would have broken the façade up too much, as well as causing extra noise in what is already a crowded façade. While the window-frame has been inserted as minimally as possible in the façade, indoors the window-frame has been made very eloquent. Ruijssenaars has rounded off the jambs of the window-frames on the inside, which makes them look like the younger brothers of the slender columns of the arcade. They soften the view, creating a sharper perspective.

However, Ruijssenaars uses the diamond pattern on the façade to make it less solid and less of a presence. → **17** The brick wall is almost 130 metres long, and although there is plenty of visual experience to be had from the layered façade, this section would have been too prominent if it had been painted completely in white. The pattern breaks the façade up into comprehensible parts. This eradicated the danger that such an enormous building might dominate its surroundings too much. → **18** The rear of the Apeldoorn town hall looks like the negative of the front. Ruijssenaars has used dark bricks as the main material, and horizontal white lines have been introduced at the rear instead of sloping ones. → **19** Combined with the many window-frames, this façade has so many different lines that the different storeys are camouflaged. It is transformed into a block. The choice of materials, and above all the colour scheme, fit in better

with the surroundings of the town hall, which consist mainly of masonry buildings. The significance of the front façade is completely different. Ruijssenaars did not want to harmonise with the environment here, but to create a flamboyant wall facing the square. He has achieved this ambition perfectly through the light colour, diversity of ornaments, and the remarkable tower.

Arcades

An important device to make the façades more layered is the use of arcades of slender steel columns that Ruijssenaars has been putting in front of his buildings ever since the CABO. These rows of columns have developed from the discs that support the entrance canopy and window piers of the Apeldoorn library. The piers, to put it very simplistically, have detached themselves from the mass in the later buildings. The support function is illustrated even more strongly by columns than by piers, even though the support function of this row of columns is actually limited in reality. Architecturally more important, however, is the fact that they bring about a more gradual transition from the public space to the building, just as the gradual 'stripping' of the roof effects a transition between the building and the sky. Ruijssenaars discovered this device towards the end of the 1980s. The first arcade can be found in his design for the town hall in Apeldoorn, but political conflicts prevented this building from being completed for five years. Ruijssenaars did place rows of columns in front of the CABO and ATO buildings → **12**, but the combination with these buildings, situated as they are in rural greenery, is less powerful than in the Apeldoorn town hall, the Stadserf Schiedam (1997) → **20**, the Hilversum apartment and retail complex (1998), or the public library and art library in Amstelveen (2001), where the columns form a wall around the square. Incidentally, the columns in the central area of the ATO are particularly effective, where their slenderness accentuates the enormous height of this space.

In his column in *Archis*, Willem Jan Neutelings calls Ruijssenaars' columns (as well as Jo Coenen's) exaggerated vanity, because he considers that the presence of columns reduces rather than reinforces the resistance to gravity.[3] Invisible support, he believes, is more exciting. However, Ruijssenaars barely seems to use his thin steel columns as genuine supports. They are not completely devoid of function, but they could also have been concealed as part of the construction, especially by an architect like Ruijssenaars, who integrates the construction in all of his buildings with great sensitivity to the play of forces but also for its architectural quality. In the two laboratories they only support the roof, in the Stadserf they alone provide the safety factor for the construction that bears the archive,

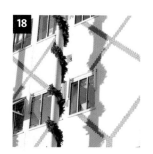

and in the Apeldoorn town hall only the balcony, that also functions as an escape route, rests on the columns. Technically speaking, the balcony could have been supported simply by consoles alone, making it possible to incorporate the support construction in the balcony itself and thus removing it from sight. In architectural terms, however, this option was not possible, because it would have become something bulging out from the façade instead of an extra, more or less independent layer in front of the façade. → **21** A continuous pattern of dark bricks behind the balconies accentuates the independence of the balcony from the façade even more strongly. The columns contribute to the suggestion of an autonomous element because they are not placed directly beneath the balcony – which would have merged the columns and the balcony to form a single element – but grip the balcony in a quasi-nonchalant manner by the upper ledge of its concrete body. The rest of the balcony seems to sag below this joint. The 'autonomy' of the ledge, and thus of the arcade vis-à-vis the balcony, is accentuated because the ledge extends a few grids beyond the edge of the balcony.

Despite what Neutelings claims, Ruijssenaars is thus not concerned to show off the supporting function. The columns are not constructionally necessary, and can thus be seen as one of the ornaments that Ruijssenaars deploys to obtain more layered façades, so that the transition from public to private passes through a number of stages. In this way he creates an intermediary between building and non-building. They are ornamental elements. This is particularly apparent in the case of the row of columns of the library in Amstelveen, that alone support the equally decorative canopy, and in the importance that he attaches to the detailing of the concrete column bases. Of course these are functional – they have to protect the construction from collisions – but they also provide Ruijssenaars with the opportunity to create sensitive, ornamental details. Metal wedges have been introduced into the concrete in Apeldoorn,

and the drainage of the steel column has been accentuated by a plate that protrudes above the concrete → **21**, while in Schiedam the upper side of the concrete has been inlaid with marbles → **22**, and the concrete columns in Amstelveen have been given a shiny metal band. → **24** Finally, the sturdy concrete base draws extra attention to the slenderness of the columns.

Appealing to the senses

Ruijssenaars' buildings need to be broken open in this way through the introduction of different layers because the buildings themselves are rather massive, an impression created not only by the size of the buildings, but also by the choice of materials for the 'main façades'. The large surfaces of painted masonry, as well as the frequent use of glass bricks, make his buildings heavy and apparently closed. Ruijssenaars uses the different layers, certainly by detaching the elements very clearly from the main mass, to make his designs less heavy and to create a subtle counterpart to the weight of the building. For this purpose he introduced not only the arcade and the balcony to the Apeldoorn town hall, but the two eaves pointing upwards – the one near the roof terrace is made of glass, and grilles are used near the edge of the roof – also create an extra layer. Their significance is made clear in the details. The steel supports for the glass, accentuated by their extra long legs, have been detached slightly from the masonry. In the library in Amstelveen, Ruijssenaars has hung plain reinforced glass to the consoles that jut out from the glass façade on the side of the square. Its function is to prevent the building from heating up too quickly in the morning sun, but at the same time it forms a fascinating extra layer that makes the edges of the building more diffuse. → **25** By using reinforced glass, Ruijssenaars ensures that the glass does not disappear completely from sight. After all, the glass has to be there and to have a structure in order to achieve the desired effect.

There is no sign of the apparently closed nature of the façades in Ruijssenaars' buildings. Subtly manipulated daylight enters from all sides. → **26** On the one hand, he deploys sculptural sky lights, as in the bank building in Amsterdam mentioned above, and on the other hand he hollows out his volumes or chops them up into pieces. In the town hall in Apeldoorn the light enters the central hall mainly through the roofed inner courts – the glass roofing elements are detached from the building in a similar way to the glass projections in the façade, and thus form independent units.

A lighting row has been constructed extending the entire length of the library in Amstelveen. As a result of the glass bricks used to construct the wall here, daylight enters the staircase evenly and attractively, and it also provides indirect lighting for the underground car park.

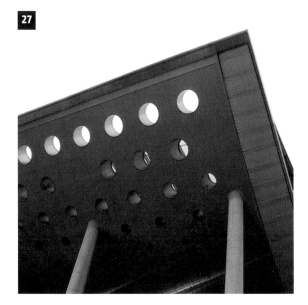

Hans Ruijssenaars Layered richness

Sky lights placed here and there, and above all the wooden glass façade, ensure that daylight enters in an exciting way. This façade is constructed of rough wooden beams placed crosswise. The construction was necessary to give the unusual form of the library a logical glass façade. The library is built on top of the flamboyant roof of a car park, and the roof of the library itself is not even either. → **27** This means that the height of the façade varies from 6 metres to a bare 3 metres, as well as being 70 metres long. A vertically and horizontally orientated façade was thus not ideal in architectural terms. That is why Ruijssenaars placed the wooden beams at an angle. → **28** Daylight enters the reading room in an unusual way because of the construction, and wood always exudes an unmistakable scent. Ruijsenaars discovered this side effect from the application of wood in the theatre in Padua, where the timber still has a pleasant aroma after centuries. The game that Ruijssenaars plays with the different scents that the wood in the theatre in Schiedam spreads is very subtle. Pine was used in the foyer and oak in the theatre – you can tell where you are from the scent. → **29, 30** The library in Amstelveen appeals to the sense of smell too, though to a lesser extent.

Its form, the way daylight enters, and the layered façade on the side of the square make the library in Amstelveen one of Ruijssenaars' most exciting buildings to date. It is also one of the buildings which show what he means when he refers to both Kahn and Duiker. Kahn's materiality is present without a doubt – and certainly not just in the masonry side wall – while the elegance, the use of the construction as an architectural device, and the large glass surfaces recall Duiker. At the same time, there are many other direct and indirect allusions, but it is above all a Ruijssenaars building. Using more or less the same elements each time in slightly different constellations and combined with new layers, he manages to give his buildings a timeless richness.

1. H. Kerkdijk, 'Gewetensvolle architectuur. Recente projecten van Hans Ruijssenaars', *Archis*, 1994, no. 3.
2. H. Ruijssenaars, 'Woningbouw te Velsen-Velsenbroek', *Bouw*, 1994, no. 1.
3. W.J. Neutelings, 'The sex appeal of gravity', *Archis*, 1999, no. 11.

Hans Ruijssenaars Public library Apeldoorn 1984

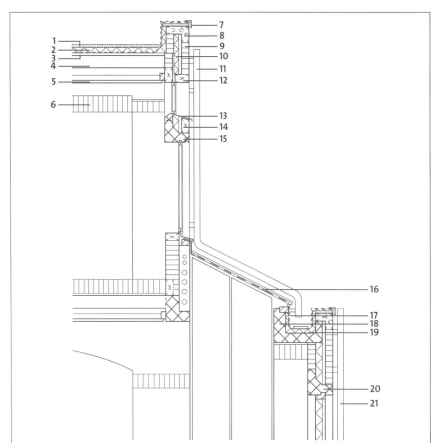

Sectional elevation at roof light
1 tiles
2 insulation
3 roofing
4 roof slab
5 ceiling finish
6 upright course
7 aluminium roof trim
8 upright course
9 façade masonry
10 insulation
11 rainwater discharge
12 upright course
13 drip
14 upright course
15 precast lintel
16 rolled wired glass
17 lead
18 precast concrete panel
19 insulation
20 concrete lintel
21 rainwater discharge

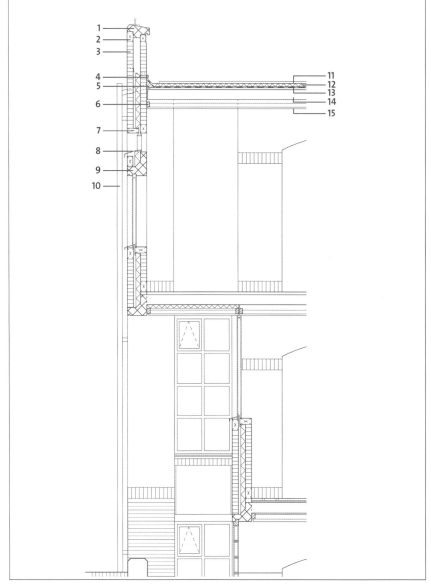

Sectional elevation of front
1 concrete panel
2 upright course
3 masonry
4 clamp profile
5 angle fillet
6 cleat
7 upright course
8 drip
9 precast concrete lintel
10 rainwater discharge
11 tiles
12 insulation
13 roofing
14 concrete roof slab
15 ceiling finish

Sectional elevation of front
1 two-ply roofing
2 insulation
3 profiled steel sheet
4 common grounds
5 ceiling panel
6 400 x 90 mm laminated wooden beam
7 22 mm steel pipe, orange/white
8 40 mm stainless steel pipe
9 upright course
10 steel post, charcoal grey
11 façade with clear glass
12 wooden inner frame
13 double glass with glass fibre
14 woodwool cement board on lowered ceiling section
15 concrete frame painted with white mineral paint
16 zinc bead with tingle
17 hot-dip galvanized trussed beam

18 ceiling panel
19 steel column
20 meranti façade panel
21 concrete tiles
22 insulation
23 180 mm concrete floor
24 40 mm dia stainless steel railing
25 15 x 60 mm sheet steel baluster
26 pre-formed aluminium coping with bead
27 plywood
28 cleat
29 upright course
30 precast façade panel
31 insulation
32 façade masonry painted with white mineral paint
33 solar shading
34 wooden frame
35 brick sill
36 galvanized spiral pipe for ventilation
37 façade grille
38 precast façade panel
39 precast concrete lintel
40 insulation
41 plywood
42 fixed light
43 plywood window ledge
44 plywood
45 insulation
46 masonry, coated with white mineral paint
47 side-hung window
48 freestanding column
49 ceramic water bar
50 dark purple masonry
51 black flat joints

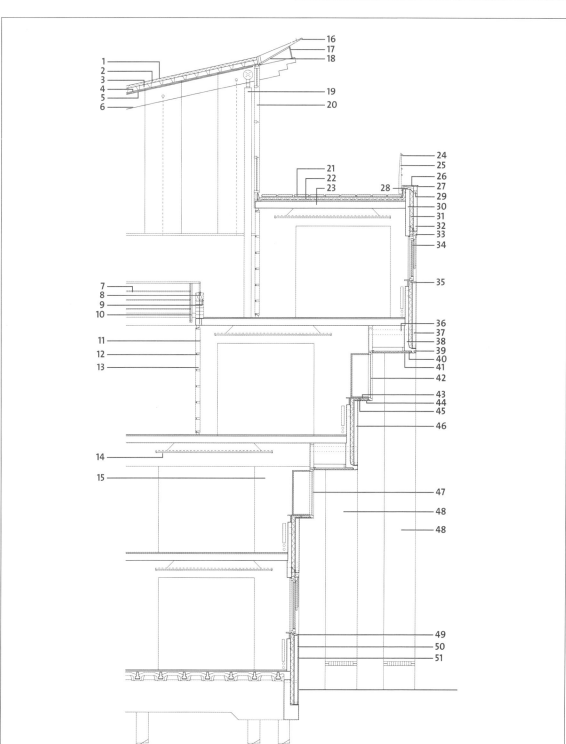

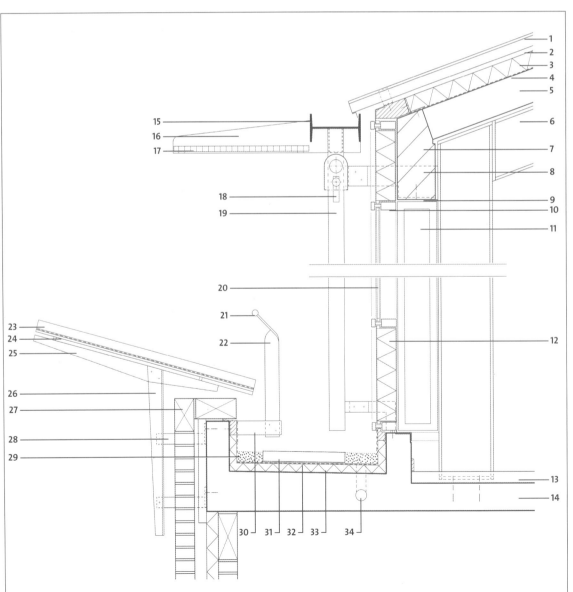

Roof edge with terrace
1 Kalzip roofing sheet
2 ventilation
3 insulation
4 PE film
5 roofing sheet
6 2 x UNP 280 trusses
7 concrete beam
8 10 mm thick steel strip
9 L-section
10 steel façade panel
11 laminated glass
12 insulated panel
13 compression layer
14 concrete floor
15 IPE 270 gutter
16 10 mm thick steel bracket
17 steel grilles
18 solar shading
19 rainwater discharge
20 insulating glass
21 pipe
22 70 x 10 mm steel strip
23 zinc cap
24 rolled wired glass
25 8 mm steel strip
26 80 x 40 x 6 mm bracket
27 upright course
28 steel strip for cornice
29 gravel
30 10 mm steel strip for balustrade
31 tiles
32 roofing
33 insulation
34 rainwater discharge

Typical horizontal detail of frame
1 horizontal soldier course as window ledge
2 insulating glass
3 timber mullion, rounded
4 side-hung frameless window
5 concrete column
6 insulation
7 vapour resistant film
8 façade tablet

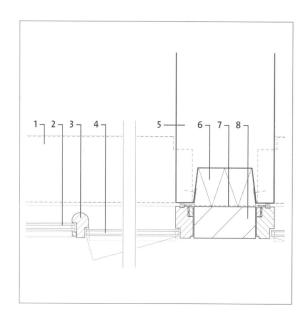

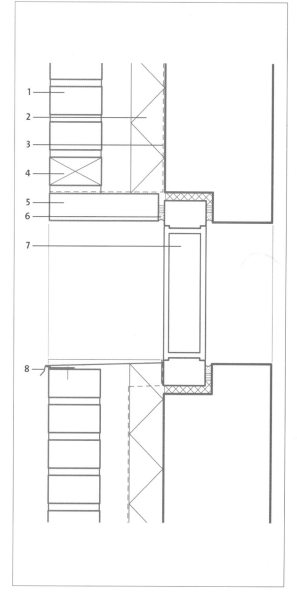

Façade at glass brick
1 façade tablet
2 insulation
3 vapour resistant film
4 weephole
5 façade tablet
6 sealant on backup strip
7 precast concrete unit with glass block
8 sill

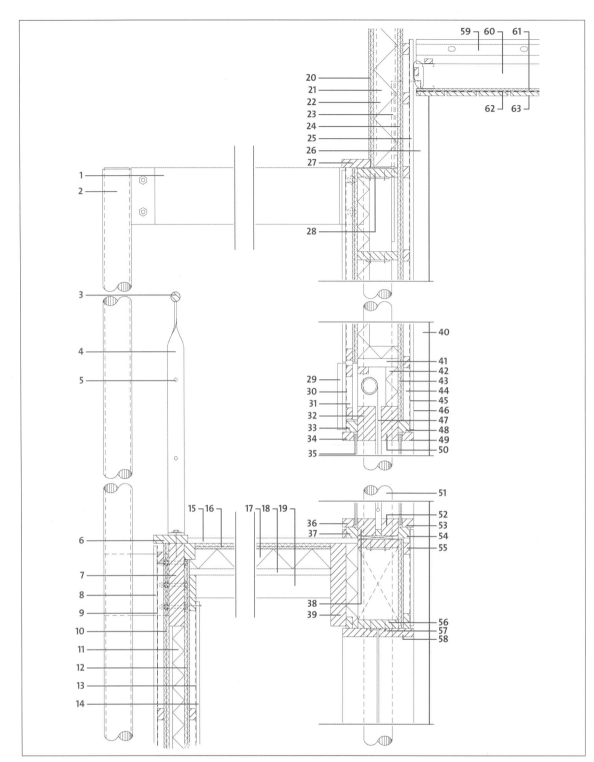

Details of wooden dividing wall of the gallery in theatre foyer

1 230 x 15 mm steel plate
2 121 x 6.3 mm steel column
3 handrail of planed pinewood
4 steel strip
5 steel wire
6 planed pinewood rail
7 65 x 336 mm wooden beam
8 sawn pinewood panelling
9 acoustic insulation
10 two sheets plasterboard
11 50 mm mineral wool
12 two sheets plasterboard
13 acoustic insulation
14 sawn pinewood panelling
15 22 mm underlay
16 two sheets plasterboard
17 80 mm mineral wool
18 woodwool cement slab on timber laths
19 floor joists
20 two sheets plasterboard
21 steel strip
22 100 mm mineral wool
23 steel strip
24 two sheets plasterboard
25 planed oak panelling
26 120 x 12 mm steel plate
27 cover fillet
28 mounting rail
29 sawn pinewood panelling
30 acoustic insulation
31 plywood
32 75 x 138 mm planed pinewood
33 50 x 45 mm planed pinewood
34 48 x 34 mm planed pinewood
35 fire-resistant glass (30 min.)
36 48 x 34 mm planed pinewood
37 50 x 45 mm planed pinewood
38 75 x 68 mm sawn pinewood
39 65 x 336 mm beam
40 120 x 12 mm steel plate
41 mounting rail
42 50 mm mineral wool
43 two sheets plasterboard
44 battens
45 acoustic insulation
46 sawn oak panelling
47 blackout screen
48 50 x 45 mm planed oak
49 48 x 34 mm planed oak
50 70 x 138 mm planed oak
51 121 x 6.3 mm steel column
52 70 x 69 mm planed oak
53 48 x 34 mm planed oak
54 70 x 138 mm planed oak
55 battens
56 mounting rail
57 lip welded to column
58 planed oak
59 metal stud ceiling suspended from steel hanger rods
60 metal stud ceiling hanger
61 plasterboard
62 acoustic insulation
63 oak ceiling

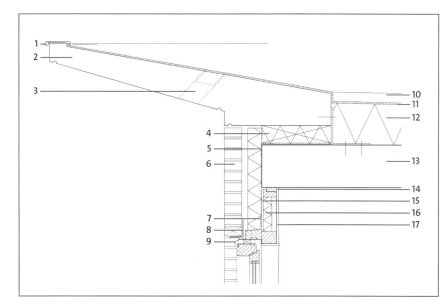

Roof edge
1 zinc roof trim
2 precast concrete roof edge
3 overflow incorporated in concrete canopy
4 bearing ridges
5 moisture-repellent strip
6 masonry painted with white mineral paint
7 adhesive strip
8 hot-galvanized angle
9 ventilation grille
10 gravel
11 two-ply roofing
12 insulation laid to fall
13 precast concrete slab
14 sealed joint
15 10 mm cement fibre board
16 insulation
17 12.5 mm plasterboard

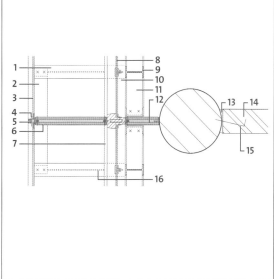

Horizontal detail of rolled wired glass screens (advertising strip)
1 80 x 40 mm T-section
2 50 x 80 mm steel tube
3 rolled wired glass
4 40 x 40 x 4 mm L-section
5 sealant on backup strip
6 2 x 20 mm Promatect boards
7 240 x 10 mm steel strip
8 rolled wired glass
9 IPE 120
10 top view of wooden rail
11 top view of UNP 120
12 10 mm Promatect strip
13 Promaseal
14 calcium silicate brick
15 anchor
16 tension wire

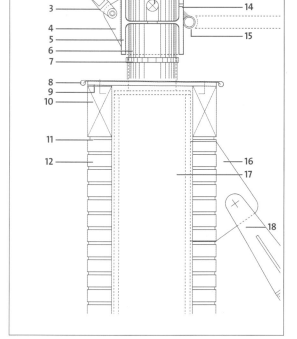

Column foot
1 16 mm dia rod
2 turnbuckle
3 10 mm steel plate
4 welded steel plate
5 HE 260 B
6 stiffening plate at junction
7 zinc secured with clamping strip
8 zinc cover with bead
9 plywood
10 soldier course
11 recessed joint
12 façade tablet masonry
13 drainage holes
14 holes for glass
15 sliding rail for window cleaning unit
16 anchor plate welded to column
17 steel column
18 140 dia stanchion for column

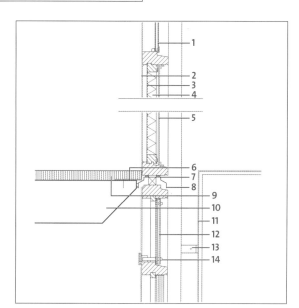

Façade detail at floor of apartments
1 insulating glass
2 plasterboard
3 vapour resistant film
4 insulation
5 enamelled glass
6 steel angle for cement screed
7 sealant on backup strip
8 ventilation grille
9 compression layer
10 intermediate floor
11 balcony screen; steel frame with rolled wired glass
12 top-hung window
13 screen fixing by means of strips
14 telescopic window stay

Hans Ruijssenaars Public library and art library Amstelveen 2001

Sectional elevation at glazed units
1 69 x 234 mm beam
2 40 mm pine plywood
3 wooden cleat
4 insulation
5 18 mm pine plywood
6 15 mm steel bracket
7 steel pipe
8 end plate
9 stainless steel forked joint
10 16 mm stainless steel bar steel
11 250 x 100 x 10 mm duct
12 two 35 x 35 x 3 mm L-sections
13 stainless steel brackets
14 stainless steel rails
15 pine plywood, with ventilation slits
16 2 mm thick gusset plate
17 two 35 x 35 x 3 mm L-sections
18 120 x 30 x 15 mm stainless steel, welded to bar steel
19 sandblasted glass
20 timber lower front
21 steel balustrade
22 steel strip
23 composite panel, coloured glass
24 lead
25 steel plate
26 steel bracket
27 150 x 100 x 10 mm L-section
28 60 x 60 x 6 mm L-section
29 grille
30 box section
31 hollow-core slab
32 corrugated aluminium sheeting

UN Studio
Details as structures

The Italian architect Carlo Scarpa (1906-1978) is praised above all for his craftsmanship, his feeling for using exactly the right materials in the right places, and his mastery of the different materials. He designed every join with much feeling in such a way that the values of all of the materials that come together in a detail are retained, and above all that the textures of the different materials receive special emphasis. The crossing point appeared to be the major element in Scarpa's work. Spatially, however, Scarpa's buildings are much weaker, and this deprives his architecture – by definition, a spatial art – of genuine interest. While still a student at the AA in London, Ben van Berkel with Caroline Bos tried to give Scarpa's approach to detail a more spatial, and thereby more architectural, dimension in the text 'The ideal detail: theme and motif'. 'It has been noted more than once that the spatial structure of Scarpa's buildings is not very compelling and that it is more the details that unite the components and thereby determine the structure. [...] [The detail assumes] the form of the Leitmotiv. The fact that Scarpa confers such independence on the detail has sometimes led to his work being interpreted as fragmented, lacking in harmony, and de-compositional. This is because people vainly persist in believing that the detail should occupy a subordinate position.'[1]

Not just the plea for a reappraisal of Scarpa's work, but above all the time at which this article was published, made it so remarkable. Important architects like Rem Koolhaas, Zaha Hadid and Daniel Libeskind were more concerned with the conceptual aspect of architecture at the time. The detail represented the banal side of architecture, that is, the building activity itself. Scarpa's predilection for the material and the detail – regarded by some as detail fetishism – was almost a taboo topic. In retrospect, it is as if this early article by Ben van Berkel was intended to clear the way for the striking role that the detail has come to play in his architecture. He seems to have been already trying to forge a link between the concept and the detail, because he had decided for himself that the detail can be an important means of giving buildings different structures.

Camouflaging the detail

In the first instance Van Berkel used the structures formed by series of details above all to add a layer to the casings draped over the functional volumes. Ben van

Berkel and Caroline Bos demonstrated the importance of this function of the detail in the text 'Storing the Detail' on the basis of a fictitious city full of buildings by the architects Oscar Niemeyer, Jon Utzon and Pier Luigi Nervi. 'It would be a place full of tension and dynamism. [...] It would be a city of brutal encounters with alienation resounding from its improbable angles and planes. But despite its thrilling quality there might be a certain aridity about this forbidden city, a sense of a couple of percentages of one dimension missing. [...] it was as much structural heaven as detailing hell.'[2]

To some extent Van Berkel actually invites the risk of the detail-free casing. Although his outer walls always bring about a connection between inside and outside, at the same time they form almost autonomous entities. Van Berkel largely detaches the casings from the function of the building, while guaranteeing their continuity by allowing the different façades and the roof to flow into one another. The necessary openings in the casing are almost independent elements that seem to poke their way through the casing, as if one layer is pushing its way through another.

The visual appearance of the casing with respect to the functional volume seems to be a direct consequence of the great influence of the computer on the design process. Van Berkel and Bos have been designing parametrically for years. Several parameters, especially the ones which cover the movements behind the existing structures, are fed into the computer, which then combines the input to arrive at the optimal form. It is almost natural that a process like this yields rounded shapes in which the different surfaces flow seamlessly into one another. However, Van Berkel's preference for continuous surfaces dates from the pre-computer era, as can be seen, for instance, from the Karbouw office building (Amersfoort, 1991), the REMU electricity substation (1993) → 1, and the Nijkerk business centre (1994) → 2 These (partly) sketched designs are also characterised by the lack of definitive or hard surface edges.

The authors of 'Storing the Detail' describe two ways of creating continuous outer walls. One way is by leaving out details, as in the case of the absence of roof details in the REMU power station, the Nijkerk business centre, or the Nuclear Magnetic Resonance laboratory (NMR laboratory, Utrecht, 2001).[3] The REMU building is nothing more than a distorted casing covering three

transformers. Van Berkel used lightly coloured aluminium plates and black basalt lava plates for the façade. → **3** The latter material looks heavy, but this was not the effect that Van Berkel wanted to achieve with this façade material. The natural stone is only used because it provides a strong contrast with the silvery metals; the two materials are polar opposites, and as such they represent the function of the building. A clever detail was devised to eliminate the roof edging: aluminium and rubber mouldings behind the plating make the walls leak-proof. Of course, the detail is very constructed and artificial, and in this sense it is certainly not unobtrusive, as Van Berkel and Bos suggest. Its architectural significance goes further than just the absence of the roof edging; it is easy to imagine that on the upper side of the building the façade material (the aluminium and basalt lava plates) has simply been reversed. The absence of a break suggests a continuation of the material into the roofing and thereby of an abstract volume that has been hollowed out. The merging of the different surfaces is visualised in a very striking way in the NMR building. The perfectly rounded corners convey the impression of folded, continuous slabs. → **4**

Detail of the new order

Draping a casing over the volume that is almost independent of the functional building, as in the case of the REMU building and the NMR building, is regarded by Van Berkel and Bos as a possible contemporary function of the detail. This detail of the new order replaces the classical ordering of façades. As a corollary of their first detail principle – the camouflage of the expected detail – this application of detail shows that details are not a small component of the whole. In this way details acquire a completely different dimension from their traditional role. Since the casing around the volume often camouflages the details, façades are often conceived as shells. Van Berkel himself cites the Acom

building (1993) in Amersfoort as an example. → **5** 'Here the detail is the imposition of a transparent screen over an existing small office building and simultaneously this detail, consisting of a revealing transparency, is all there is... There is no composition, for the original façade shimmers through the flimsy fabric of the screen.'[4] Seen in this light, the façades of the IJsselstein municipal office (2000; Reglit), Museum Het Valkhof (Nijmegen, 1998) and the NMR building (both glass), as well as the expanded metal façades of the Piet Hein Tunnel (Amsterdam, 1996) and the bridgemaster's house (Purmerend, 1998), are related to the Acom façade. Although they, unlike the Acom building, are new constructions, the nakedness of the buildings shimmers through the semi-transparent casings. The façade is a single detail consisting of different small details and through which the actual building, as it were – the building as a functional entity – is visible. This treatment of the façade confers on it a new meaning in terms of experience.

The glass façade of the IJsselstein municipal office is particularly unusual in this respect because of the different gradations of transparency, which increases uncertainty as to the function of the façade, the building and the different components of the façade. → **6** This effect is achieved by introducing a narrow strip of satin-smooth concrete between the Reglit and the window openings – which are distributed almost at random over the horizontal surfaces, thereby camouflaging the spatial organisation of each floor. The concrete is placed in the same surface and has the same smoothness as the Reglit. Van Berkel also makes use of the semi-transparency of the Reglit casing here to establish a link between the openings and the second casing behind the glass, for a rough structure that looks like concrete can be seen behind that glass. In fact it is the foam insulation material, but Van Berkel uses it to suggest in a subtle way that the building has two casings: a very prominent glass casing, and a second, concrete casing which protrudes near the window openings but is at the same time always present behind the glass. This façade thereby acquires a fascinating depth as a result of this combination of transparent material (glass), an impenetrable surface (the concrete), and a material with an unfathomable depth (the Reglit); it takes on volume and becomes three-dimensional. The three-dimensional effect is reinforced by the fact that the whole building, despite its having a number of different functions – the municipal theatre is incorporated in the same complex as the municipal office – is executed in the same material and with the same use of detail. The only difference between the front and the rear lies in the material of the window frames: the front wall has slender aluminium window frames, while the rear wall has sturdy wooden ones. → **7** The latter feature is Van

buildings that can be implemented properly, and he has also become much more reticent with regard to the materials of the buildings. The façades consist of two materials at most, in which the different materials are preferably placed one behind the other, making it possible to avoid difficult joints. The ensuing tension is no longer the product of the confrontations between the different materials – with all of the constructional risks this entails in the case of complex buildings like De Kolk – but arises from the choice of material and from the layered qualities of these materials. This layering – often achieved by the multiple application of glass with different gradations of transparency, as well as with perforated steel – already prevents the façade constructed from a single material from becoming too flat and monotonous.

Profiles

To enliven the façades even more and to give them an extra sparkle, Van Berkel structures his casings by means of different profiles. It is normal practice for the plates to be attached in or beneath the profiles, but in a Van Berkel façade the profiles go beyond the actual join. They seem to be a means of camouflaging the architectural details, accentuating the seamless quality of the casing even more, and the profiles confer relief and a specific direction on the casing. As Van Berkel himself put it in connection with the REMU building: 'The building's power is mainly in the effect of the detail, developed not as a solution to the material treatment but as its source. The avoidance of specific detail by link-ups between the material shifts emphasis to the sculptural impact of the projecting and receding façade planes.'[5]

The profiles of the REMU building are almost independent elements because they are constructed from two stainless steel U-profiles which hold an untreated strip of iroko in position. → **12** They give the façade an extra contour, but upon closer inspection they do more than that. This composite profile turns out to deepen the vertical and horizontal joins in the aluminium façade. This profile is only applied horizontally in the façade of natural stone, while more sober U-profiles provide the vertical lines here. This gesture is a sign of a fine sense of the façade materials used. By using the sensitive profiles vertically as well, the neutral and flat aluminium acquires more depth and almost as much value in experiencing it as the natural stone components of this casing. In addition, the continuous horizontal profiles ensure that, despite the differences in the use of material and in the angles at which the parts of the façade are set, the result is a folded but continuous casing. → **13** Finally, Ben van Berkel introduced the time factor into this building with this profile, and in this sense it is also a Scarpa-like detail. In the course of time the iroko will turn grey and thus come closer to the

Berkel's only concession to match his striking building to its surroundings.

More volume than building

The semi-transparent materials are used not only to create an impression of a deep façade or of a continuous skin, but also in a literal way to generate more building volume. Particularly with regard to the Piet Hein Tunnel → **8** and the bridgemaster's house in Purmerend → **9**, the expanded metals have no relation with the – limited – functional space. The material not only produces a moiré effect, but in the case of the bridgemaster's house it also enables the building to be experienced from a distance as a single sculptural body; it is only at closer quarters, and then only with difficulty, that the empty casing is distinguished from the genuinely functional spaces. The same effect is produced by the silk-screened glass of the NMR building. Kneading the casing like this is not entirely without its dangers, especially because the casing that covers everything often hides the architectural details from sight. Moreover, because Van Berkel tries to make his casings from a decreasing number of materials, there is a risk, as Van Berkel and Bos themselves showed in connection with the façades of Utzon and Niemeyer, that buildings will be created that are too much of a sculpture and too little of a building. This aiming for a more minimal use of material seems to be a consequence of the architectural and constructional disaster of De Kolk from 1996, a complex in the centre of Amsterdam comprising a hotel, shops and shopping streets. → **10** It was Van Berkel's first computer-generated design. In the attempts to cater for the predicted mobility in this part of the inner city of Amsterdam in a built structure, the result was a design with too many sloping surfaces intersecting at different angles, and above all too many different materials. The design was too complicated, and it was not carried out properly into the bargain. → **11** Since then, Van Berkel has been manipulating the computer images to arrive at

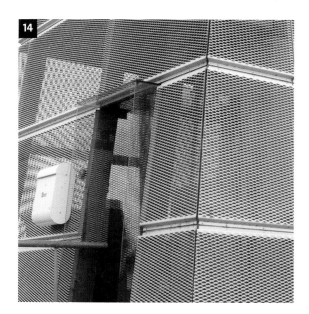

colour of the stainless steel, thereby toning down the differences between the materials. Of course, the profile remains clearly visible, but it is only at close quarters, when the different textures of the materials come in sight, that the building displays the actual beauty of its composition.

As in the case of the REMU building, where the profiles are used to unite the two totally different materials within a single sculptural gesture, the profiles of the Piet Hein Tunnel and of the bridgemaster's house accentuate the lines of the building. To this end deep horizontal grooves have been left between the expanded metal sheets on the bridgemaster's house → 14 and on the Piet Hein Tunnel. This causes the much narrower vertical seams between the different plates to disappear almost completely, giving the casing the horizontality which Van Berkel wanted. → 15 Although the details of these two constructions are very similar, they are essentially different. The expanded metal plates of the bridge-master's house have been bent inwards and attached to the construction behind them in the join, so that the attachment is overshadowed and loses its importance. The seams of the Piet Hein Tunnel are more ornamental, and in this sense they resemble the profiles of the REMU building. The seams (the profiles) are independent elements, which is confirmed by the protruding plates incorporated in the seam which presage the dramatic jutting out of the roof → 16 Like the REMU building, the Piet Hein Tunnel only betrays the layered nature of its sculptural body at close quarters. Only then do the composite profiles and the minute bolts fixing the expanded metal sheets to the profiles become visible. To offer the eye yet another layer as it zooms in, Van Berkel uses the smallest scale of the building: the bolt and the screw. The Acom bolts, the socket screws of the REMU building and those of the Möbius House (Het Gooi, 1998) provide an attractive scaling of the wrap-around casing which ends via more or less clearly marked profiles in these bolts. The bolts also make the buildings

intelligible, because it is as though they reveal at a glance how the casing is made, how the façade material, that normally clings invisibly to the volume, is supported. The bolts are the counterpart of the missing detail, in both constructional and architectural terms. The missing details create the impression of a continuum; the bolts and other attachments bring the building and casing 'back to earth', make them legible, breaking up the surfaces and conveying rhythm.

Big details

Based on the assignment, REMU, the renovation of the shopping centre in Emmen (1996), and the bridge-master's house in Purmerend are no more than volumes generated by casings. However, a new direction in Van Berkel's oeuvre can be seen in the Möbius House, the Het Valkhof Museum in Nijmegen, and the NRM building in Utrecht. On the surface, these buildings may look very much like his other buildings, but in these cases different structures have been woven into the volume to fuse structure and building.

Museum Het Valkhof has a glass façade creating an illusion of depth like that of the IJsselstein municipal office. → 17 The blue insulation material shimmers through the glass, sometimes offering a vague glimpse of the enormous installations, and allows daylight to enter showcases containing silverware through a glass sheet inside. Strong lines are conferred on the façade by the positioning of the sheets of glass like scales, while the horizontal lines are accentuated by the narrow aluminium profiles that hold the glass in place. → 18 The continuous horizontal lines are unbroken on the south wall too, although this is actually called for by the need for ventilation. The ventilation openings have been placed in the façade by placing the sheets of glass at more of an angle than elsewhere, creating ventilation ducts between the two sheets of glass placed one on top of the other. → 19

The north and a part of the east walls are different from the other, closed façades of the museum. The outside corridor here has a fully glass façade, with the glass continuing in the roof surface. The detail orientation of the east wall is different too. While the aluminium profiles in the rest of the building accentuate the horizontal lines, the enormous trusses in this wall give it a strongly vertical orientation. → 20 In spite of the different characters of the separate parts, they nevertheless clearly form a single whole; the only difference is that in this part of the building the 'flesh beneath the skin' has been left out. The structure (the rib-cage) has been left behind, and the paring away of the glass, opaque, scaly green skin offers a view of the interior of the body. To create the image of an opened body, it was important to place the trusses in the long east façade outside the volume and to continue them as

genuine ribs over the glass roof before seamlessly rejoining the intact body of the building. Their scale – two UNP-80 profiles with tall steel plates welded in between – emphasises their presence. This detail is like the detailing of the façade of the municipal office in IJsselstein, where the suspected rear construction is also briefly visible in the shape of the concrete discs. The scale of the ribs, incidentally, also has a more pragmatic reason: the trusses also keep out a part of the heat of the sun. At the same time this transparent – and thus absent – façade offers visitors a wonderful view of the park and the river Waal.

On the side facing the square, the glass façade of the museum has been rotated through an angle. In four stages the façade faces the river Waal. According to the designers, the angular rotations are derived from the changing directions of the pieces of land jutting out into the Waal. The façade thus illustrates the third detail principle: the imaginary continuation in the building of the lines in its surroundings. This detail principle was also applied in the REMU building, where the plinth follows the direction of the brick city hall. Although the lines are probably aligned with the attractive surroundings, and in the case of the REMU building have probably been derived from the city hall, details of this kind seem above all to be architects' details, which outsiders can hardly fathom, if at all.

After the first overhanging, only the façade of the museum moves, acquiring only more depth with each change of scale. This is visible to some extent because the deeper cavity makes the glass darker. In the eyes of Van Berkel and Bos, the façade is the first Big Detail, and the staircase is the second. The yellow woodwork of the oversized handrail and balustrades is an orientation point in the grey concrete environment. The wooden surround is practically without detail; the planks are simply set one above another and meet abruptly in the corners. → **21** The high spot of these details consists of the handrails, which are made of almost banal but highly effective wooden planks. They are attached to the wooden surround with very simple pegs. The absence of smaller details places emphasis on the staircase as a whole, as the Big Detail. The concrete stairway itself, which helps to ensure the stability of the building, is characterised by different slopes, and the steps have different widths. This determines the speed of going up or down it. While the very wide steps serve as landings as

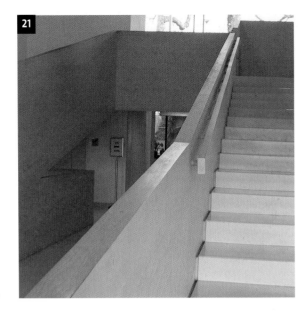

thus as meeting places, the narrow ones encourage you to pass on quickly.

The staircase carries visitors from the entrance to the corridor with the wonderful view of the park and the river Waal. The aluminium ceiling, on the other hand, guides them from the stairs to and through the exhibition halls. This is the third Big Detail. Gracefully rippling in two directions, it moves through the rooms. The installations and lighting are fitted above the ceiling. In principle the aluminium strips hang fairly traditionally from the ceiling, but the strips themselves and the system into which they click have been sawn and bent to measure by the computer. By the way, Van Berkel had to make some concessions in the implementation of this ceiling. The first idea was to make it in wood, but in order to achieve the movements in two directions it would have been necessary to bend the strips to measure one by one. This proved to be too much for the budget. Aluminium strips were much more flexible, but even with this material the curves still had to be tempered. Tests eventually determined the maximal length of curvature of the strips.

Detail as indirect object

Unlike the museum, the Möbius House was not affected by budgetary limitations on the implementation of the concept. In this case, the familiar Möbius strip served as the basis for a home with two studios allowing both shared and individual working and home life. The loop suggests endlessness, continuity, and when applied to a building it means a seamless transition from indoors to outdoors. → **22** The continuity is primarily visual. When a route ends with the studio and bedroom jutting out incredibly above the entrance, the enormous areas of glass and the floating character of these rooms allow their emotional absorption in the surroundings. Inside the house too, sheets of glass ensure that practically every room is connected with the rest. There is no obstacle to the eye, by which the Möbius strip, which is

practically impossible to make, can still be 'experienced'.
→ 23

The concrete strip holding the storey-high glass in place is continuous and can be regarded as the main structure. It therefore resembles the aluminium profiles of the façade of Museum Het Valkhof, for example. Of course, the concrete strip is virtually without detail – because it has to reinforce the image of a continuum – and has a limited number of – minimal – seams. This has been achieved by spraying concrete onto the insulation material and then spreading it out in a flat surface. The glass is held in place on the inside by standard steel profiles. The Möbius House contains hardly any 'normal window frames'. Other modern architects have also used steel angles to keep glass in place, but this villa achieves particularly sharp details and joints.

While the concrete strip forms the main structure of the façade, in this fascinating house the seams between the concrete are the smallest details, and they form the structure. Unlike the exterior, where the concrete details have been eliminated, the interior consists of concrete cast in situ, with every formwork panel made to measure. This gives the concrete a velvety sheen. The seams and the form spacer holes confer a certain rhythm on the rooms, and the seams also serve to accentuate the movements in the interior.

So the use of details is close to Marco Frascari's claim: 'Details are the indirect or direct expressions of the structure and use of buildings.'[6] It is the details that structure the casings and volumes. The details are not a Leitmotiv, as in the work of Scarpa, nor does Van Berkel play around as this Italian master does with a large number of different materials in order to create fully composed and complicated details. Van Berkel's details are bigger and simpler. This is possible because the details are not subject but indirect object, to emphasise both the sculptural quality of the casing as well as the spatiality in and around the buildings. This is done so cleverly and consistently that what Van Berkel once wrote about Scarpa's details – details offer the architect an unprecedented vitality and poetic force through their thematic authenticity – applies just as well to Van Berkel's own buildings and details.

1. B. van Berkel and C. Bos, 'Het ideale detail: thema en motief', *Forum*, 1987, no. 4.
2. B. van Berkel and C. Bos, 'Storing the detail', *Mobile Forces*, Berlin 1994.
3. See note 2.
4. B. van Berkel, *Crossing Points*, Berlin 1993.
5. See note 2.
6. M. Frascari, *The Tell-the-Tale Detail*, Philadelphia 1982.

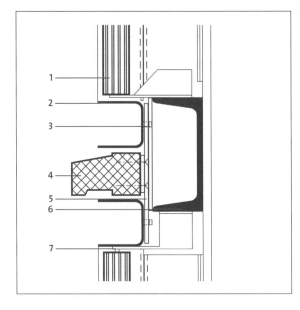

Detail of stone façade
1 basalt lava cladding
2 stainless steel U-section
50 x 50 x 3 mm
3 socket-head screw
4 untreated iroko
5 aluminium sheeting
6 steel structure
7 fixing clamp for façade
cladding

**Roof edge of aluminium
façade**
1 30 x 50 x 3 mm aluminium
U-section, clear anodized
2 3 mm pre-formed
aluminium sheeting
3 10 mm metal façade
cladding
4 iroko lath, untreated
5 steel structure
6 50 x 50 x 3 mm stainless
steel U-section
7 socket-head screw
8 untreated iroko

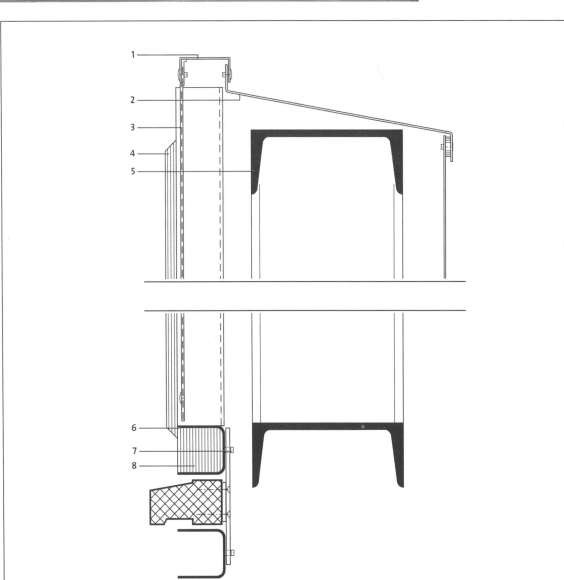

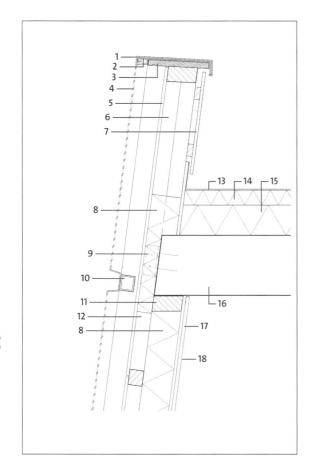

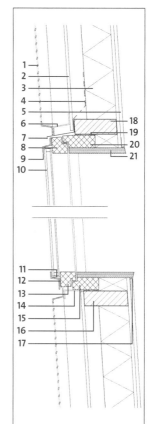

Roof edge
1 pre-formed hot-galvanized steel section
2 pre-formed tingle
3 18 mm water-resistant board
4 perforated steel façade cladding
5 10.5 mm thick cement-bonded board
6 50 x 50 x 5 mm box section
7 cement-bonded board
8 insulation
9 anchor for fixing box section
10 box section for securing façade cladding
11 wooden cleat
12 cavity
13 two-ply bituminous roofing
14 insulation laid to falls
15 insulation
16 precast concrete slab
17 10.5 mm thick cement-bonded board
18 plaster coat

Detail of window
1 perforated steel façade cladding
2 cement-bonded board
3 insulation
4 plastic flashing
5 cement-bonded board
6 50 mm wide steel section
7 pre-formed steel section
8 54 x 54 mm wood
9 pre-formed stainless steel section
10 insulating glass
11 pre-formed glass mounting
12 neoprene
13 50 x 54 mm wood
14 pre-formed steel section
15 40 x 90 mm wood
16 50 x 100 mm wooden cleat
17 plaster stop
18 50 x 150 wooden cleat
19 Compriband
20 40 x 114 mm wood
21 18 mm plywood, painted

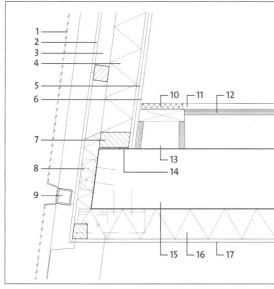
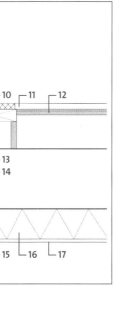

Detail at insulated intermediate floor
1 perforated steel façade cladding
2 cement-bonded board
3 box section
4 insulation
5 cement-bonded board
6 plaster coat
7 wooden cleat
8 anchor
9 box section for securing façade cladding
10 20 mm jatoba board (removable)
11 jatoba parquet
12 underlay
13 cableway
14 PVC foam tape
15 concrete floor slab
16 100 mm insulation
17 6 mm Eterplan boards on wooden battens

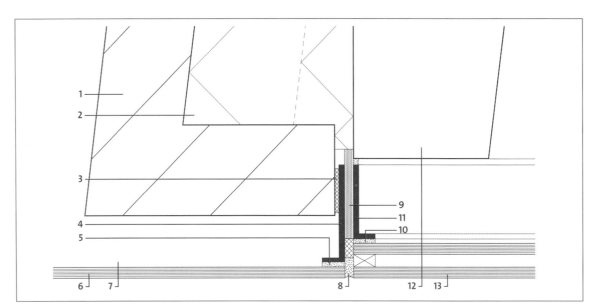

Horizontal façade detail
1 80 mm precast concrete
2 insulation
3 PVC foam tape
4 20 x 85 x 5 mm angle
5 sealant
6 single glazing
7 ventilated cavity
8 sealant on backup strip
9 neoprene
10 sealant
11 20 x 65 x 5 mm angle
12 in situ concrete
13 insulating glass

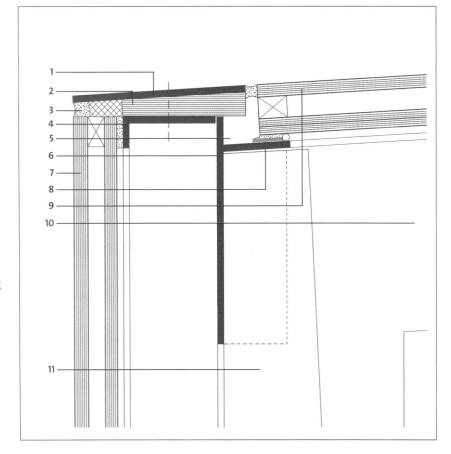

Junction glazed façade and glass sun room roof
1 120 x 5 mm steel plate
2 neoprene
3 sealant on backup strip
4 20 x 65 x 5 mm angle
5 drainage
6 edge profile: 150 x 5 mm plate + 45 x 5 mm strip
7 insulating glass
8 soft and hard neoprene
9 aminated and toughened insulating glass
10 glass roof structure
11 steel profiles for absorbing wind load

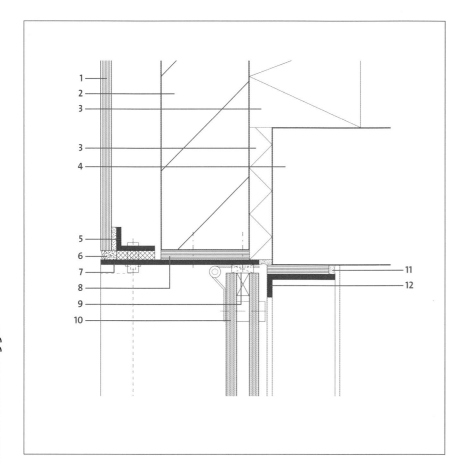

1 single laminated glass
2 precast concrete
3 insulation
4 in situ concrete
5 20 x 35 x 5 mm angle
6 sealant on backup strip
7 5 mm stainless steel plate
8 neoprene
9 sealing profile
10 laminated and toughened
insulating glass
11 sealant and neoprene
12 20 x 65 x 5 mm angle

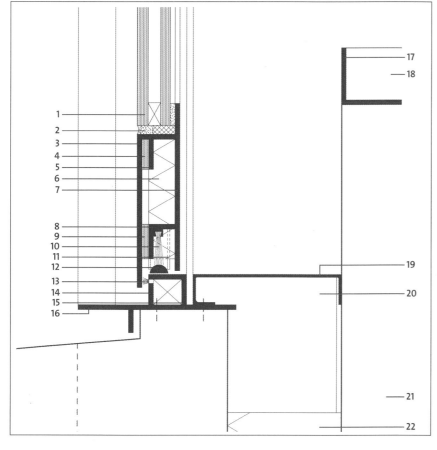

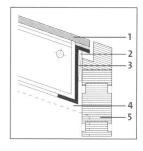

**Horizontal connection
wooden door and glazed
façade**
1 single laminated glass,
mechanically bonded to
stainless steel section
2 stop profile
3 5 mm stainless steel section
4 side of timber ceiling
5 door of plywood planks,
short end-face exposed

**Detail of bottom of glazed
sliding door**
1 toughened and laminated
insulating glass
2 black sealant
3 135 x 5 mm steel plate
4 neoprene
5 24 x 30 x 5 mm angle
6 insulation in steel tube
7 145 x 5 mm steel plate
8 24 x 30 x 5 mm angle

9 neoprene
10 brush
11 110 mm dia runner
12 16 mm dia runner
13 brush
14 steel strip
15 28 x 34 x 5 mm angle
16 25 x 135 x 5 mm T-section
17 50 x 50 x 4 mm angle
18 finish layer
19 pre-formed 3 mm stainless

steel cable duct cover
20 cable duct
21 in situ concrete
22 insulation

Roof edge of south façade, glass panes allow for ventilation
1 aluminium profiled coping
2 aluminium profile
3 box section
4 insulation
5 single laminated glass with opaque film
6 view of welded steel plate
7 box section
8 ventilation openings
9 18 mm underlay
10 two-ply roofing
11 insulation
12 compression layer
13 concrete floor
14 insulation

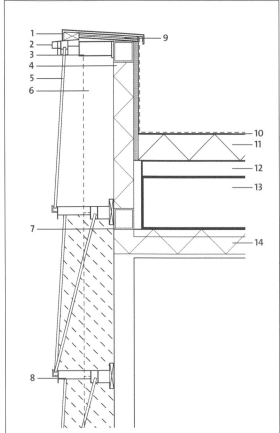

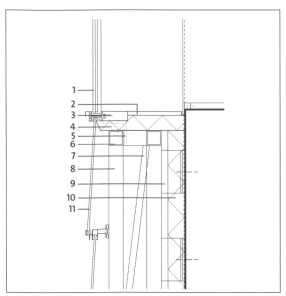

Scaly glass façade (west elevation)
1 transparent insulating glass
2 burglar-proof steel plate
3 aluminium section
4 insulation
5 angle
6 80 x 80 x 5 mm steel tube
7 angle
8 tubular steel façade structure
9 fixing of façade structure to concrete
10 insulation, outer side painted blue
11 single laminated glass with opaque film

Detail of roof edge at aluminium panels

1 aluminium edging strip
2 water-resistant plywood
3 neoprene cleat
4 aluminium upper profile
5 insulation
6 suspension bracket for louvred panel
7 clear anodized louvres
8 edge beam
9 cement fibreboard
10 DPC membrane
11 solar shading
12 high-E insulating glass
13 view of aluminium profile
14 concrete tile on tile supports
15 roofing
16 insulating board
17 sloping screed
18 compression layer
19 hollow-core slab floor
20 sealing
21 spray-on plaster

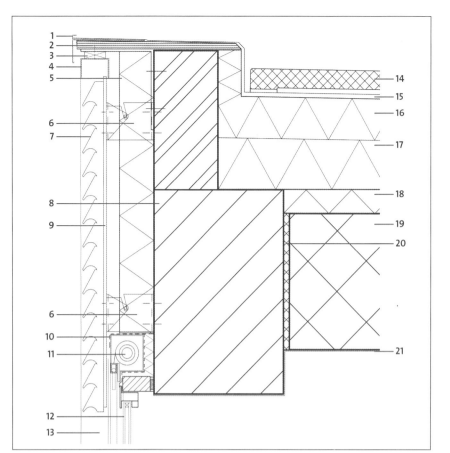

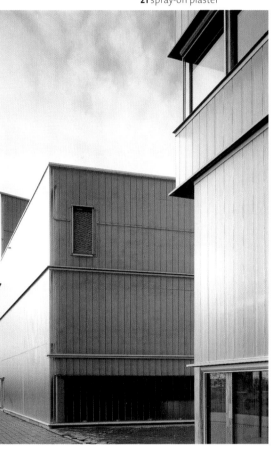

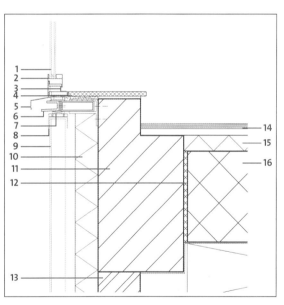

Detail at intermediate floor

1 high-E insulating glass
2 aluminium frame
3 pre-formed aluminium finishing
4 cast stone window ledge
5 aluminium drip
6 composite profile with nylon for thermal break
7 neoprene cleat
8 thermally broken aluminium top profile
9 glass plank
10 insulation
11 edge beam
12 sealing
13 gas concrete
14 floor finish
15 compression layer
16 hollow-core slab floor

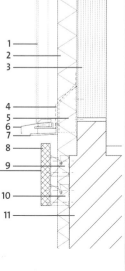

Detail of junction with ground plane

1 glass plank
2 insulation, outer side colour spray-painted
3 precast inner wall
4 DPC membrane
5 fixing of profile to concrete
6 drip
7 composite profile, continuous
8 precast concrete panel
9 suspension bracket for concrete panel
10 compression-resistant insulation
11 concrete structure

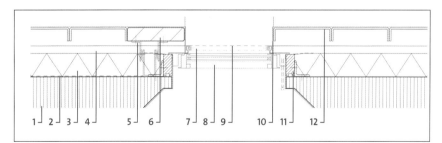

Horizontal façade detail at frame

1 precast concrete inner leaf
2 film
3 insulation, outer side colour spray-painted
4 lightly ventilated cavity
5 stainless steel fixing for façade panel
6 precast concrete façade panel

7 solar shading
8 aluminium tilt-turn window
9 aluminium drip
10 aluminium stop profile
11 sub-frame
12 glass plank

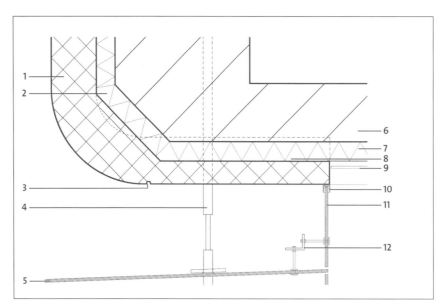

Detail of connection curved concrete façade and glazed lower front
1 in situ concrete
2 insulation
3 throat
4 turnbuckle
5 single strength toughened glass
6 in situ concrete
7 insulation
8 timber framing
9 cement fibreboard
10 30 x 30 mm aluminium U-section
11 single strength toughened glass
12 80 x 80 mm aluminium angle

UN Studio NMR laboratory Utrecht 2001

156

Glazed roof edge
1 stainless steel fixing
2 glass
3 neoprene
4 plywood
5 single glazing, screen-printed
6 timber framing
7 cement fibreboard on background structure
8 stainless steel fixing
9 80 x 80 x 8 mm steel angle
10 moisture-tight seal
11 30 x 30 x 3 mm powder-coated aluminium section
12 aluminium frame
13 aluminium ventilation grille
14 pre-formed powder-coated aluminium sheet
15 insulating glass
16 aluminium profile
17 gravel
18 bituminous roofing
19 plywood
20 insulation laid to falls
21 steel duct
22 Gaboon plywood
23 stucco
24 precast concrete lintel
25 plaster stop

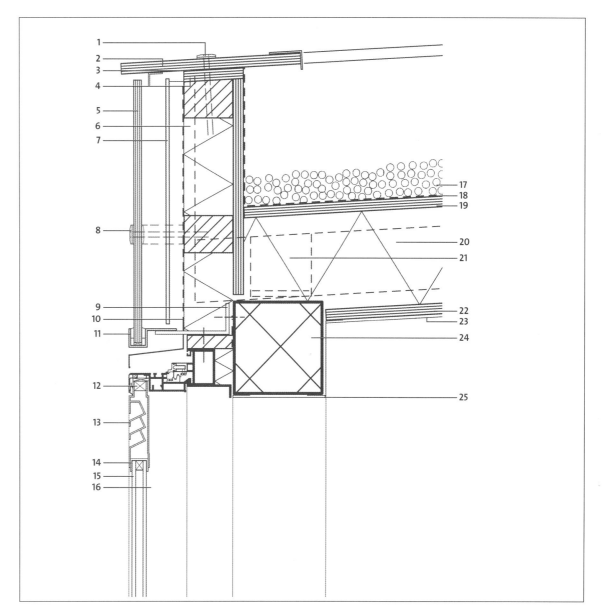

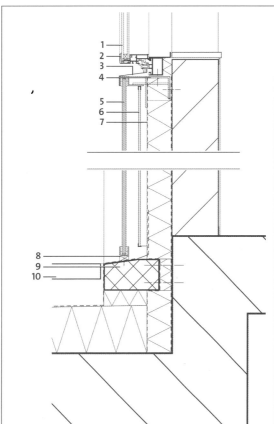

Junction glazed front and aluminium louvres
1 insulating glass
2 aluminium frame
3 pre-formed coloured aluminium sheet
4 80 x 80 mm steel angle
5 screen-printed single strength glass
6 cement fibreboard on background structure
7 moisture-proof membrane
8 30 x 30 mm coloured aluminium profile
9 precast concrete edge
10 Luxalon aluminium louvres

Rudy Uytenhaak
The nap of the surface

With the possible exception of an early glass penthouse with a generously overhanging roof (Amsterdam, 1989) → **1**, the work of Rudy Uytenhaak has little in common with that of Mies van der Rohe (1887-1969). While Mies concentrated on the abstraction of his buildings, composing the façades in such a way that perfect objects were the result, Uytenhaak designs Expressionist buildings in which the different surfaces have an expression of their own. While for Mies 'God was in the detail', Uytenhaak talks about the nap of the surface and uses this concept to investigate the potential depths of a façade, often involving series of manipulated material and complicated details to arrive at different textures. And while Mies filled in his façades with nothing but steel and glass, irrespective of the location, Uytenhaak designs plastic façades of concrete, glass, brick and other materials, in which the choice of material is largely derived from the context.

And yet Rudy Uytenhaak's research on three-dimensional façades still derives from Mies' façades with I-profiles (corner detail, Commonwealth Promenade Apartments, Chicago, 1956). → **2** Uytenhaak even wanted to profile the façades of the housing project in the Weesperstraat (Amsterdam, 1992) in the first instance with Mies-like I-profiles. Uncertainty – the housing in the Weesperstraat was his first real large-scale commission – and the setting led him to switch to concrete prefab elements. Split jambs now provide the necessary relief and vertical alignment like Mies' profiles. → **3** The concrete transverse jambs have even been sheared to accentuate the vertical lines; this enlarges their physical surface while reducing their contribution to the play of lines. The transverse jambs catch more light, and at the same time the dark strip of shadow underneath them is reduced because of the specific form of the jambs. The filling that has been set slightly recessed between the jambs consists of light aluminium window frames and concrete with a textile pattern. In this respect the façade in the Weesperstraat is based not only on Mies, but also on the architect Gottfried Semper (1803-1873). In his *Bekleidungstheorie*, Semper distinguished between the wall that forms a permanent part of a building, and the partition or membrane that can be seen as a filling between the permanent one. While the construction has to be firm and solid, the membrane is more temporary. Although neither the vertical nor the transverse jambs are construction, Uytenhaak illustrates this theory at the far end and the balconies of the low volume in the Weesperstraat, where the filling between the jambs has been left out. The textile has disappeared; the permanent structure is left. The end walls also extend slightly beyond the side walls of the other volumes of the complex in the Weesperstraat, but it is much less manifest there, and has a different significance. While Uytenhaak seems to be using the façades in the Weesperstraat to accentuate the difference between structure and filling, in the rest of the building he is primarily out to make the building legible by showing which components the construction of the block consists of, in which the street walls dominate the side walls. Although he thus plays with both filling and structure, the façade covered with these prefab elements still works as a whole. The fact that it is actually constructed of prefab elements the size of a housing unit is cleverly camouflaged in the detailing. The vertical joints between the elements form the heart of the jambs, and thus form an essential part of the profiling of these jambs. The sheared protruding transverse jambs hide the horizontal joints from sight. The effect of this façade is thus completely different from the canal-side façades in this complex. → **4** Here the concrete vertical and horizontal members function much more as a free-standing frame to bring about a transition between the small-scale environment of the canals and this large housing project. The effect of a loose structure with the slightly protruding lower façades and balconies apparently hanging freely in it is achieved by applying relatively wide joints between the balconies and the concrete. Not only is the independence of the concrete screen accentuated on the side of the volume of the building by making the actual façade bend inwards, but on the upper side the frame is detached from the roof edge of the 'real' façade. → **5** Steel tubing holds the concrete structure at a discrete distance. By the way, at the same time the concrete structure ensures that the building does not break down into separate elements, but remains a whole in spite of the detailing.

Screens and frames

The later concrete façades, of which the best known are those in the Ministry of Housing, Spatial Planning and Environment (VROM) offices in Haarlem (1997) and in De Balk ('Hoop, Liefde en Fortuin', Amsterdam, 2002), are clearly derived from the two Weesperstraat façades. The main difference is that they now really are constructed from independent concrete brackets, which Uytenhaak has arranged like the tiles of a roof. → **6** The distinction between structure and content is even stronger than in the Weesperstraat. In Haarlem, that difference is primarily accentuated by the choice of materials. Western red cedar window frames have been set in the deep recesses of the concrete elements. The wood, as well

as the polished pieces of green glass that have been incorporated in the faces of the concrete, temper the hardness of the concrete. The wood has been left untreated so that it will turn grey and slowly but surely take on the colour of the concrete. This process will reduce the distinction between structure and filling in time.

The same brackets seem to have been used on the north, south and west façades, but this is not the case; the depth of the ribs varies considerably, although the forms are congruent. In the south and west walls the transverse jambs are deep to keep sunlight out of the offices as much as possible. They are much less deep in the north wall to allow a maximum of daylight to enter. The concrete elements themselves already create depth, but they are given a special expression by putting the façades on the run. The system explodes, or rather implodes, at the entrance from the clash of the concrete brackets coming from two directions. → **7** The real façades seem to have been removed here, leaving the concrete brackets hanging from the thermal zinc-coated steel construction. No matter how strange this façade may look, it is a completely logical continuation of the ground plan. Uytenhaak had arranged light courtyards in a certain pattern to bring enough daylight into the 25-metre deep building. This system also called for a light courtyard on the corner and thus at the entrance. The two systems (façade brackets and light courtyard) intersect here. In his urge to make the systems clear, however, Uytenhaak goes too far at the entrance. The white wooden frames, for instance, are abruptly sawn off immediately around the corner. → **8** Although this detail makes it clear that the light courtyard coming outside here is actually a closed space, it increases the chaos – in an area where there is an awful lot to see anyway – and certainly does not make anything clear. Even more complex are the joints where Uytenhaak's rigid directions demand not only that a light courtyard cuts the concrete façade, but also that the wooden façade has

to be shown. This results in a series of far too complex horizontal details that are only detrimental to the system. → **9** The level of information is too diffuse to indicate to outsiders how the different systems interact. Uytenhaak has applied the concrete elements in De Balk, the enormous building on the Oostelijke Handelskade in Amsterdam, in a more controlled way. → **10** Here he primarily uses them on the one hand to achieve the three-dimensionality that he is after and to give the gigantic façade an unusual texture. On the other hand, this prevents the block from disintegrating into a lot of separate balconies. The screen has been kept detached from the side walls, and in this way complex and puzzling clashes of materials are avoided.

Accentuating materiality

The Haarlem VROM office was also the first building in which Uytenhaak made use of wavy bricks. In making these bricks Uytenhaak attempts to use present-day techniques to imitate the rich masonry of buildings from the seventeenth and eighteenth century. By breaking the material open, as it were, and giving it depth, he accentuates both the texture and the materiality of the stone. To achieve this effect Uytenhaak manipulates the manufacturing process of the bricks. The wire-cut bricks are sheared in Nieuw-Sloten so that a saw-tooth effect could be obtained in parts of the façades. For the Zandstra villa (1992) in Amersfoort Uytenhaak simply had polystyrene blocks placed in the moulds to produce bracket-shaped bricks. → **11** The result is a rich, three-dimensional façade. Uytenhaak went on to cooperate with the manufacturer in developing a special nozzle to produce wavy bricks. More than the other shapes of bricks, the wavy brick poses a number of problems with regard to the details. Ideally he would like to use them in a stretcher bond and to rotate them through 180° per course, so that the round shape comes above the hollow (wicker basket bond). This would yield the strongest relief, but in this case the colouring would have to be done right through the bricks (and that is expensive), and water may be left on the protruding pieces, which could result in damage (formation of algae), so the bricks have to have a very high density.

In Haarlem the wicker basket bond is only applied where the bricks are protected from rain. The rest of the brickwork passage is in normal stretcher bond, resulting in smooth, horizontal waves. A wicker basket bond is also applied in the Cascade building of the Eindhoven Technical University (1999), but there the bricks are placed vertically. → **12** The effect of the relief of vertically placed bricks proved to be even stronger than when they are horizontal. This is probably connected with the reduced effect of shadow, because when a horizontal wicker basket bond is applied some of the stones are in shadow, which tones down the relief. Besides, both

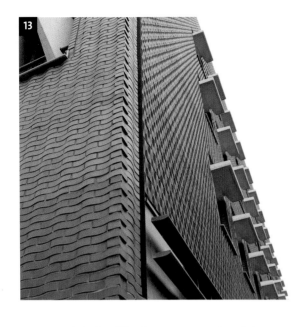

rainwater (which will lead to an even ageing of the façade) and light turn out to pass very beautifully along the masonry.

As in Haarlem, in Eindhoven Uytenhaak set two façades next to one another which are covered with the same materials but nevertheless look completely different from one another. He achieves this by applying the same wavy bricks in the west façade, but placed horizontally to produce a maximal effect with what is actually a minimal adaptation. → **13** Moreover, he applies different, ornamental brise soleils on both façades to keep out the sunlight or to allow (some of) it to enter. In the south façade the white concrete elements for which marble is used as an additive are placed horizontally, while they are vertical in the west façade. → **14** In both cases they are placed slightly off centre to keep out direct sunlight as much as possible while still allowing indirect sunlight to enter. By hanging from tubing, the brise soleils in the west façade retain their character as independent elements in the beautifully and consistently made reveals. The masonry has been allowed to continue on one side, which creates an extra accent by bringing the ends of the bricks into sight, while very smooth hardstone has been used for the sill and the other side of the reveal. Uytenhaak uses the metaphor of the hand to indicate subtle differences in the use of material, such as in the reveals but also, of course, in the two masonry façades. After all, the palm of the hand is not the same as the back of the hand, but the material is the same. This is how Uytenhaak expresses the specific (architectural and engineering) criteria imposed on the different façades. These façades are not the last in the development of masonry façades. Uytenhaak investigates new forms. For instance, trapezium-shaped bricks were applied in De Balk in an unusual stretcher bond. → **15** These highly coloured bricks form a kind of little stairway in these façades, creating a special play of light as well as harmonising well with the stepped shape created by the concrete brackets.

Uytenhaak also investigates new manufacturing processes. Actually, he wants to apply prefabricated ceramic façades instead of masonry ones. He considers masonry to belong to the nineteenth century. Besides the practical advantages, façades constructed in this manner can be lighter too. In addition, it is no longer necessary to use complete and thus heavy bricks. For the Zaaneiland apartment block (Zaandam, 1996) he had the bricks sawn asymmetrically in two lengthwise and then presented both the smooth and the rough side. The bricks have different depths, so that the ribbed sides come to lie in the shadow and thereby provide an extra texture. The extremely narrow cross joints combined with the striking blue bed joints accentuate the depth of the surface. Moreover, other ceramic materials can be used as well. In the patio homes/shops in Zeewolde (1992), for example, he made a prefabricated ceramic façade with tiles for the blind. → **16**

With these kinds of manipulated bricks too Uytenhaak manages to accentuate the materiality of the bricks. He is not always out to emphasise the weight of the façade. This is what happens with the patio homes in Sloten (1992), Villa Zandstra in Amersfoort, the waterfront homes in Zaanstad (1996) and the brick façades of the Cascade building. This impression is primarily created by the header details of these façades. These façades extend beyond the side walls, and the bricks here have been applied to both the head and the rear of the surface. They thus look like massive brick walls.

In the House of the Arts in Apeldoorn (1995), on the other hand, Uytenhaak counters the weight of the masonry façades directly by showing how they are constructed. → **17** A kind of phased shift in the holes that are made allows the concrete construction to come into view. In this way he makes it obvious that the brickwork façades are thin, weak membranes that need concrete to remain upright.

Rietveld versus Van Tijen

Besides heavy concrete and brickwork walls, Uytenhaak also designs curtain walls. He uses the opposition between the two types to accentuate the differences between the surfaces. In this connection he makes the comparison with the inside and the outside of an apple; they are completely different, but they combine to form a whole. It is interesting in this respect that the types of façade enable Uytenhaak to express the inside, the construction of the building, in its casing, especially in housing, where the construction is achieved by means of tunnel shuttering. The closed, supporting parts of the building are covered with closed masonry or concrete elements, while the open parts are allowed to remain as transparent as possible.

Uytenhaak gives his curtain walls a wooden base. Thermal bridges can be avoided more cheaply with wood

19

20

21

22

23

Rudy Uytenhaak The nap of the surface

than with steel transverse beams, and the use of wood gives these façades more of the pavilion-like character that Uytenhaak is trying to find. The hard glass curtain walls, which are often regarded as inaccessible, are softened by the wooden jambs. Uytenhaak's first genuine curtain wall can be found in the houses on the Koningin Wilhelminaplein (Amsterdam, 1991). → **18** There was no money for a façade of this kind, so Uytenhaak constructed a glass-like façade out of different components from different factories. The butted frame has been attached to the concrete, and aluminium sliding glass walls have been fitted. For the concrete floors and partition walls he applied strips of coloured glass with the help of the simplest double window profiles. → **19** The joints between the different components of the curtain façade on the Koningin Wilhelminaplein are covered with Western red cedar panels, which serve not only to hide the joints and to create a whole, but also to camouflage the inevitable differences of size between the various components. This façade now looks very flat, in strong contrast to the brickwork façades with very deep reveals.

It is as if Uytenhaak found this façade too mono, too flat and lacking in nap, as well as being unnecessarily complicated because it is made up of many different elements. In the next buildings, then, he is searching for a simpler system and at the same time for a more layered composition. He appears to have had in mind a cross between Gerrit Rietveld's curtain wall for the Amsterdam Academy (1967) → **20** and that of the architect Van Tijen in the Bergpolder flats (Rotterdam, 1934). → **21** Rietveld fixed the glass as it were to the protruding window-sills that rested on the spandrels. In this way he both created a space for the radiators and optimised the amount of daylight that entered. Van Tijen, on the other hand, designed what is above all a very simple façade. He made holes in the I-profile, inserted tubes into them that had been cut in half, and placed the glass on top of this in the tubes. Both systems

161

are ruled out by the current regulations (fire spread, sound gaps and thermal bridges), but their study has led Uytenhaak to the highly expressive curtain wall of the Cascade building, which represents a cross between the two systems.

The urge to simplify the curtain wall led in the first instance to an improved and efficient use of the wooden panels. While they served primarily as a finishing layer on the Koningin Wilhelminaplein, in the housing on the Zaaneiland the simple sheets of glass have been hung in them by means of equally simple hooks. This system renders the double window profiles redundant. The strips have become more a part of the façade, and at the same time they retain the same function as the concrete jambs in the housing in the Weesperstraat and the I-profiles of Mies: they accentuate the vertical lines of the building.

At the same time Uytenhaak, like Rietveld, was looking for ways to make the curtain wall more plastic. He does not want to make sterile curtain walls. The first step in this direction was made in the student flats on the Plantage Muidergracht (Amsterdam, 1993), where Uytenhaak used standard wooden window frames for the curtain wall. → **22** Placing two jambs side by side is almost inevitable on a façade like this because these elements require two jambs for their production and transportation – this is what gives them their stability. To reduce the thickness of this packet, Uytenhaak placed the jambs of the individual elements not side by side, as is usual, but behind one another. This removes one jamb from sight and at the same time gives the façade an extra depth. The effect is further enhanced by coating the sides of the topmost jambs with red lead. → **23** This detail is particularly strong as you pass by the flats. The vermilion gradually disappears from sight and the wall becomes flatter. The curtain façade of the Tourmaline tower block in Almere (2001), where tin plates were used instead of glass to cut expenses, is really a cross between the Plantage Muidergracht and Zaaneiland versions. This effect is obtained because the wooden frames in which the plates hang have been sheared on the side that is in view. Light and the reflection cause their appearance to change as one walks by.

To handle rain water and from the point of view of implementation, however, it is more logical to place not the vertical but the transverse jambs of this sort of façade element behind one another. This is the case in Uytenhaak's best curtain wall so far, that of the Cascade building. → **24** This time the overhang is no less than 60 cm per floor. Of course, this form, that is a perfectly logical continuation of the Rietveld façade in which the incorporation of the jump in dimensions in the wall itself solves the technical problems of the Academy façade, made it impossible to make a single continuous

curtain wall. Uytenhaak has chopped up the façade per storey, while still allowing the glass to continue generously beneath the overhang. → **25** The façade, which consists of Western red cedar panels with stainless steel brackets in which the patterned glass with bevel siding is hung, thereby acquires a dynamism of its own that is more or less independent of the arrangement of the building. This façade has many constructional advantages. Firstly, the continuation of the glass makes it possible to hang the awnings out of sight. Moreover, the glass that hangs beneath the overhang and thus partly in front of the window already filters the direct sunlight that enters the building to a large extent; according to Uytenhaak, the façade functions like a modern version of traditional stained-glass windows. The view, on the other hand, is not blocked by the hanging curtain wall. In addition, by chopping the building up by means of overhangs, Uytenhaak devised a simple solution for the risk of fire spread and sound gaps. The facilities for this are situated beneath the protruding floor.

Detaching the surfaces

Although it is not really necessary in the light of the big differences between the materials used, Uytenhaak accentuates the difference between the various façades by making them self-contained surfaces that seem to have been put in place independently of one another. That is why the wavy masonry of the Cascade building extends beyond the curtain wall. In Uytenhaak's other, older buildings the composition is built up from surfaces too. The thin wedge of masonry on the Koningin Wilhelminaplein is detached from the curtain wall by means of the bracket-like balconies, the roof edge hangs far out over the curtain walls, and – on a lower level of scale – the entrance is slightly detached from the front. → **26, 27**

The separation of the different surfaces is carried to extremes in the House of the Arts in Apeldoorn. → **28** Every surface is independent here; even the different

layers of masonry are brought into sight through the application of a sort of phased shift in the large openings. The brickwork façade is in turn kept at a distance from the Eternit-coated façades by means of steel tubes, and in the detailing the two end walls are detached from the side wall. In the detailing of the lower volume, including the bar, the glass volume seems to have been extracted from the concrete wedge, and the steel roof is not completely in line with the rest of this volume.

In terms of detail, this makes the joints of the different surfaces somewhat easier to handle. Stacking materials on top of one another, pushing them together, or creating a 'remote' link is simpler than creating logical and architecturally interesting points at which all those different materials meet at different angles. In addition, the details are now partly hidden from sight. The use of overhanging or continuous surfaces casts a shadow over the details. Finally, in architectural terms it enables Uytenhaak to break open the massive character of the volumes of the building. They acquire an exciting layered and spatial aspect. This is particularly true of the housing on the Koningin Wilhelminaplein, where no less than five units per storey had to be created. There was a danger that the building would be too prominent in the park-like surroundings. The building has been exploded, as it were, to create space in the volume.

The last resource that Uytenhaak uses to enrich the façades and to give them more depth is to give the balconies and railings a special treatment. The balconies often have remarkable forms and protrude considerably from the mass of the building. They sometimes seem to lead a life of their own. At the rear of the Droogbak (Amsterdam, 1989), for instance, they execute an exciting dance, at the same time as they detract attention from the not always equally consistent details. → **29** In the Weesperstraat the balconies have different depths and are bevelled with different corners.

The railings also play an important part in this case. As in the choice of the materials for the façades, Uytenhaak aims to strike a balance between open and closed, in which the experience of the user and the passer-by determines the final implementation. Uytenhaak has used railings of different thickness (Sloten), glass (Tilburg) → **30** or perforated steel sheets (Weesperstraat) → **31**, and he is now looking into the possibility of mechanically twisted steel strips. The strips of the housing in the Slotlaan in Zeist (1999) → **32** are so concealed that it is almost impossible to look into them from the street. This guarantees the privacy of the occupants, as well as hiding obtrusive objects like rubbish bins, crates of beer and chairs from sight. The seated residents still have a clear view through the open upper part of the fence.

Rudy Uytenhaak has developed a wide range of elements for the composition of façades. Which resources he deploys and in which combination depend on the

setting. The Weesperstraat has a concrete look because of the highly urban surroundings; the combination of terracotta-coloured bricks and a green curtain wall is very suitable in the park-like surroundings of the Koningin Wilhelminaplein; the wavy brickwork façades of the Technical University Eindhoven are orientated towards the urban setting, while the more open and friendly curtain walls with their wooden panelling seek more contact with the surrounding greenery. In addition, the façade must effect a transition from city to intimacy.[1] '[Uytenhaak] strips the volumes of his buildings down to surfaces of different textures that meet and overlap one another. The layered nature of the surfaces and volumes and surfaces placed behind one another is a means of introducing scale and rhythm at every level and of connecting different levels of scale with one another.'[2] Finally, façades, like his buildings, must be three-dimensional; the surfaces must be tactile and variegated. They must have a nap. The strength of deploying the different methods to achieve this effect lies above all in control of the resources. Uytenhaak sometimes made mistakes in this. The House of the Arts is the clearest example, where too many different materials have been used and too many details have been deployed to reveal the construction of the building and the different surfaces. The VROM building in Haarlem is overwhelmed by a plethora of complicated details too. These buildings have (in places) too many surfaces with too much nap. It is in the buildings with a more reticent use of material that he shows how rich the buildings can be. The Droogbak in Amsterdam, the apartments on the Koningin Wilhelminaplein, the Cascade building in Eindhoven, the urban villas in Tilburg (1996) → **32** and De Balk are examples of this. Instead of the materials and the details doing one another to death, the different textures of these buildings are mutually reinforcing. The surfaces and their details are alive, and that is exactly what Uytenhaak is out to achieve.

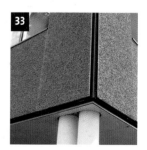

1. Inaugural lecture by Rudy Uytenhaak to the Technical University Eindhoven, 1993.
2. Leo Versteijlen, 'Vlakkenbarok. Woningbouw van Rudy Uytenhaak', *de Architect*, 1993, no. 6.

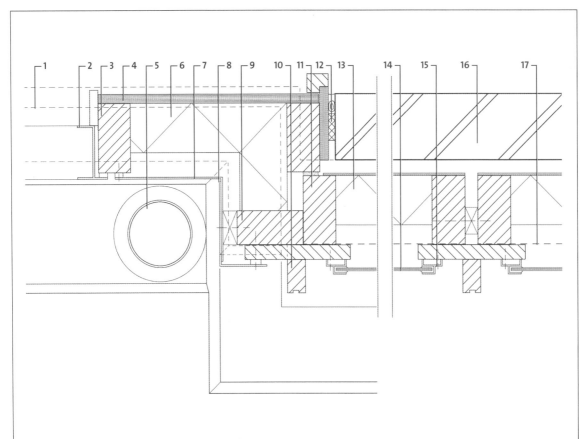

Horizontal detail of composite curtain wall
1 edge of concrete floor
2 aluminium sub-frame
3 52 x 105 mm beam
4 plywood
5 rainwater drain
6 insulation
7 powder-coated aluminium
8 anodized aluminium
9 52 x 105 mm beam
10 28 x 50 mm western red cedar batten
11 52 x 105 mm beam
12 sealant on backup strip
13 insulation
14 Colorbel (coloured glass)
15 aluminium double window profile
16 calcium silicate brick
17 vapour resistant film

164

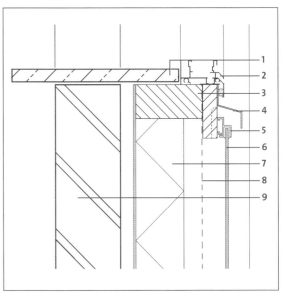

Junction of window and glazed spandrel of curtain wall
1 black window ledge
2 aluminium frame
3 52 x 105 mm beam
4 drip
5 aluminium double window profile
6 Colorbel (coloured glass)
7 insulation
8 vapour resistant film
9 calcium silicate brick

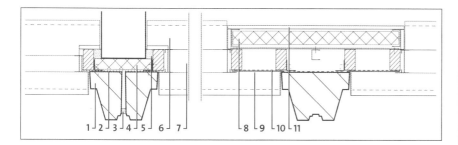

Junction precast concrete panels and 'cleft' mullions on aluminium façade unit
1 precast concrete mullion
2 DPC membrane
3 sealant on backup strip
4 insulation
5 PUR foam
6 window ledge
7 aluminium frame
8 insulation
9 2 mm powder-coated aluminium
10 DPC membrane
11 plasterboard

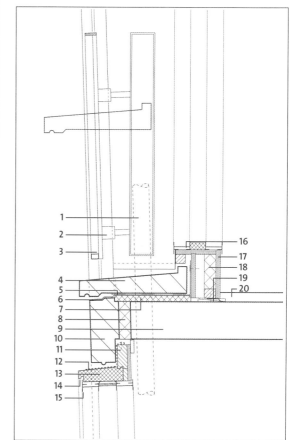

Roof edge
1 precast concrete unit
2 roofing
3 insulation
4 Roofmate insulation
5 film
6 fixing precast unit
7 concrete roof slab
8 PUR foam
9 section
10 timber sub-frame
11 aluminium frame

Junction French balcony and aluminium façade unit along canal
1 rainwater drain
2 fixing of balustrade to column
3 balustrade
4 precast concrete sill
5 5 mm granulated rubber
6 film
7 Roofmate insulation
8 isokorf thermal break
9 concrete floor
10 precast concrete unit
11 50 x 114 mm wood
12 lead
13 67 x 114 mm framing timber
14 timber 'nose'
15 aluminium sub-frame
16 aluminium sub-frame
17 plywood
18 insulation
19 spandrel panel fixing
20 covering floor

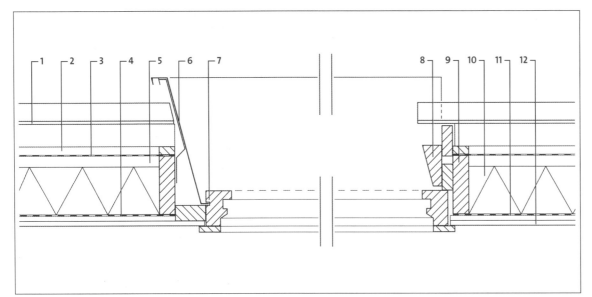

Horizontal detail of frame in Eternit façade
1 Eternit panel
2 rails
3 mullions
4 vapour resistant film
5 cavity
6 aluminium pre-formed sheet
7 wooden frame
8 wooden moulding
9 wooden beam
10 insulation
11 moisture barrier
12 plasterboard

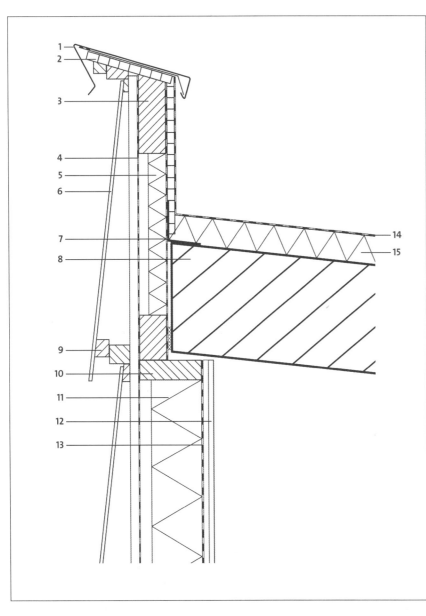

166

Roof edge Eternit façade
1 galvanized steel coping
2 water-resistant plywood
3 wooden beam
4 vapour resistant film
5 insulation
6 Eternit panel
7 fixing of construction to roof structure
8 concrete roof slab
9 rails
10 timber structure
11 insulation
12 plasterboard
13 moisture repellent film
14 roofing
15 insulation

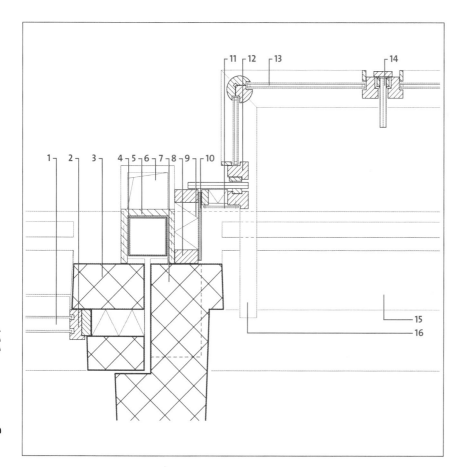

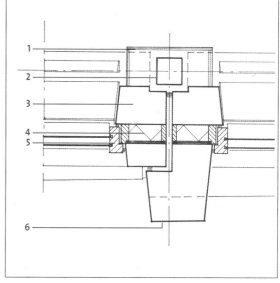

Horizontal junction of timber light well and façade with concrete L-shapes

1 insulating glass
2 sliding patio door
3 precast concrete element
4 150 mm box section
5 fire-resistant cladding for box section
6 pipes
7 L-shaped precast concrete unit
8 wooden cleats
9 insulation
10 panel
11 Colorbel (coloured glass)
12 timber frame, white
13 insulating glass
14 white fin
15 view of L-shaped precast façade unit
16 protruding sill

Horizontal junction of façade with concrete L-shapes and frame (north elevation)

1 fire-resistant casing
2 150 mm steel tube
3 precast L-shaped concrete façade unit
4 sub-frame with insulation
5 western red cedar frame with fixed light
6 polished sloping surface of hook shape

Roof edge of façade with concrete L-shapes (south elevation)

1 EPDM roofing
2 insulation
3 vapour resistant film
4 compression layer laid to falls
5 hollow-core slab floor
6 MDF finishing
7 zinc cap
8 zinc on tingles
9 precast L-shaped concrete façade unit
10 sub-frame with insulation
11 western red cedar frame fixed light
12 EPDM membrane
13 precast L-shaped concrete façade unit
14 western red cedar frame with sliding window

Rudy Uytenhaak Cascade building Eindhoven Technical University 1999

Junction horizontal corrugated brickwork and frame
1 horizontal course of corrugated bricks
2 insulation
3 concrete floor
4 masonry construction
5 steel tube supporting solar shading unit
6 precast solar shading unit
7 wooden window frames
8 reveals and sill finished in blue Belgian limestone
9 seamless recessed jointing

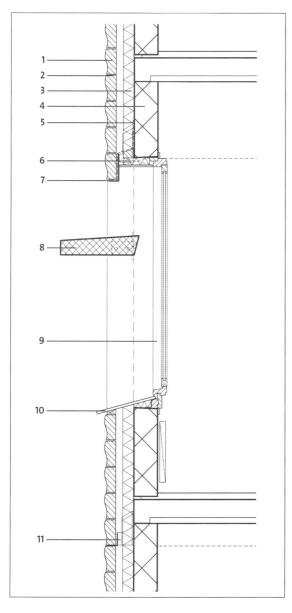

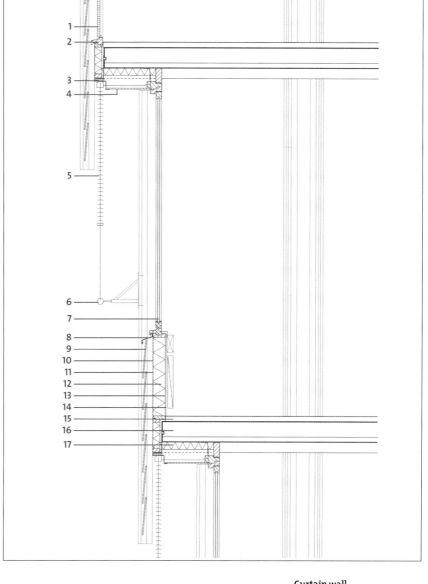

169

Junction vertical corrugated brickwork and frame
1 vertical course of corrugated bricks in stack bond
2 pointing in black mortar
3 insulation
4 precast inner leaves
5 vapour resistant film
6 cleat
7 masonry structure
8 precast solar shading unit
9 wooden window frames
10 reveals and sill finished in blue Belgian limestone
11 brickwork support

Curtain wall
1 double-walled polycarbonate sheet
2 wooden window frames
3 pre-formed aluminium section
4 cement fibreboard
5 aluminium solar shading
6 continuous aluminium pipe on spacers
7 insulating glass
8 drip
9 clear toughened patterned glass between timber mullions
10 black fabric
11 3 mm Menuiserite cement fibreboard
12 insulation
13 vapour resistant film
14 rear panel
15 compression layer
16 concrete floor
17 insulation

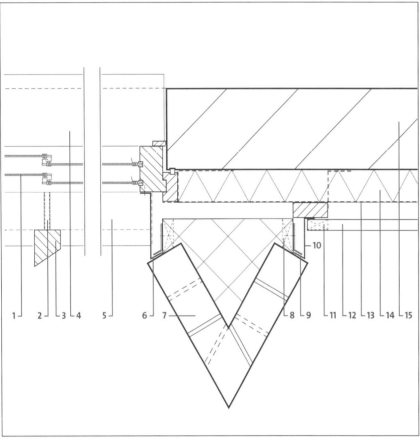

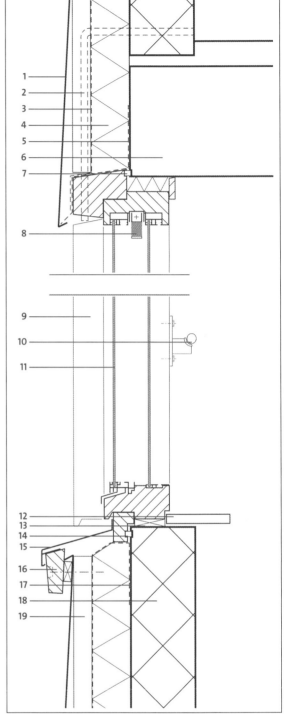

Horizontal detail of façade at 'brick point' that 'sticks out' of steel curtain wall
1 sliding window
2 tube fixing on sills
3 western red cedar lath
4 window ledge
5 steel drip
6 pre-formed aluminium profile
7 precast concrete unit faced with bricks
8 wooden cleats
9 sealed joint
10 pre-formed profile with tingles
11 sealing tape
12 steel façade cladding
13 moisture repellent breather membrane
14 insulation
15 concrete wall

Junction of steel façade and frame
1 steel façade cladding
2 PE water spout at verandas
3 moisture repellent breather membrane
4 insulation
5 waxed tape
6 concrete floor
7 PVC foam tape
8 solar shading
9 western red cedar
10 tubular steel safety barrier at veranda
11 sliding window
12 window ledge
13 PUR
14 PVC foam tape
15 steel drip
16 continuous rail
17 wax ribbon
18 precast concrete
19 38 x 89 mm rails

Detail of façade at balcony
1 green railings
2 precast concrete slab
3 western red cedar frame
4 pinewood plank
5 façade cladding
6 battening
7 moisture repellant membrane
8 insulation
9 PUR foam
10 fixing of spandrel
11 compression layer
12 concrete floor
13 draught barrier and sealed joint

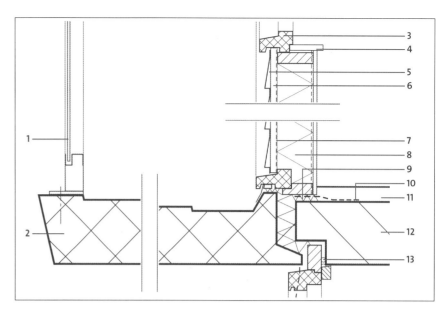

Junction precast concrete unit and frame
1 insulating glass
2 wooden frame
3 pinewood lath
4 aluminium drip
5 precast concrete unit
6 sealant on backup strip
7 cement fibreboard
8 insulation
9 vapour check
10 plasterboard
11 Fermacel
12 precast façade panel
13 angle for fixing façade panel
14 PUR foam
15 insulation
16 DPC membrane
17 plywood
18 acoustic baffle

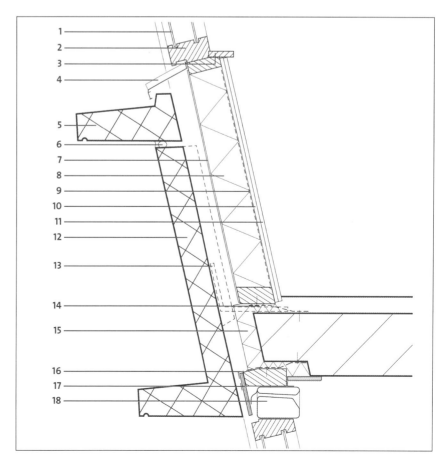

Koen van Velsen
From compelling elements to whispering objects

In close proximity in the Spoorstraat in Hilversum are an unobtrusive dark-brown brickwork box and an almost deconstructivist volume consisting of shear independent elements. → **1, 2** The former, an office, is almost nothing. It is a borderline case: architecture or just an 'ordinary building'? The architect himself is more outspoken: 'This is nothing more than bricks that rise from the ground. It is primarily intended to be inconspicuous.' The other building, a shop/office/apartment on the other hand, seems to have been designed to attract attention. With the yellow brick walls sticking out of the building, the steel construction placed outside the volume, and the strangely shaped roof elements, it is completely different from the other buildings in this rather sober street. At first sight there is nothing in these two buildings that betrays the fact that they were designed by the same architect. Yet they are both the work of Koen van Velsen. Van Velsen finds it easy to explain why the differences are so great. He does not want to have a signature. Each building must be unique, because the programme of demands, the client and the locations are always unique too. His plans are developed in the first instance with this in mind; the choice of materials does not play any role at this stage, when the spaces and the transitions between the spaces are at issue. By the way, it is a matter not just of the internal spaces, but also of the urban space, how the building fits into the environment, and the transitions between the building and the immediate surroundings. Thinking about the choice of materials for these spaces only starts when the plan has been drawn up, although by this time the mood that the materials and colours are supposed to evoke has already been decided on. This design procedure means that Van Velsen's façades and walls are for a long time non-material lines on paper; they only take on shape once he is completely convinced that the choice of materials is the closest to 'the dream of the space'.

The difference between the striking apartment cum office and the unobtrusive brick building can also be explained in terms of the years of experience. The first was completed in 1982, the second in 1998. Over the years, Van Velsen has become better and more economical at making his spatial dreams, and thus his ideas about architecture and its significance, come true. In his text 'Over architectuur is niets te zeggen' [There is nothing to say about architecture], Van Velsen writes: 'Architects are increasingly asked to supply images, and architecture seems to be increasingly evaluated in terms of the image. This tendency, as I see it, is a reduction of the profession of architect; architecture as spatial art is reduced to décor architecture (...). Modern architecture is the attempt to control the space in a certain way. To this end the architect describes "things" and lays down in sketches and specifications how those "things" will determine the space. The architect is successful if "the things" express the architect's spatial intentions. So architecture does not produce "things", but above all space.'[1]

In terms of urban development, this citation indicates that at any rate buildings may not function as décor (any longer), but must be the walls of the city. A décor is ephemeral; a city wall is much more permanent. To this end the façades must be less 'functionalist'. An authentic urban building, after all, will most probably outlive its present users and thus its present function. This calls for a special relation between building, function and use of materials. The choice of materials can become much freer by detaching it from the present function. Van Velsen uses the façade composition in combination with the materials to prise the building loose from existing associations with regard to its function.

In the Hilversum office cum apartment Van Velsen creates a spatial façade by building it up from different more or less transparent surfaces that lie on top of one another or make contact with one another abruptly. Its layered quality makes it difficult to see exactly where the façade begins. The outermost layer is the construction for stability. The HE-profiles are placed transversely, with the body in view, to make the construction more manifest. → **3** The shop front lies behind them, so that you have to look around or past the construction to see what is inside. This tones down the openness suggested by the large glass shop window consisting of two parts, of which the lower one slopes inwards. The grill wall panels above look like Japanese Shoji screens, but prove to be much less transparent. The roof construction, finally, consists to a large extent of glass. → **4** As in the case of the other apparently transparent surfaces, you cannot see inside through this glass, because the surfaces are at an angle, you look straight through the roof structure and see nothing but sky. Through the way it is placed, and of course through the use of material, the roof, like the protruding building walls, does not really mark where the volume ends. They illustrate the passage from inside to outside and the individualisation of the surfaces and elements. → **5**

Inside the building too the spaces are continuous where possible, so that many architectural elements can be regarded as 'free-standing'. The frames of the sliding doors, for example, are clamped sheer between the brick walls, the ceiling and the floors. This makes the elements independent of one another; after all, the walls, ceiling

and floors seem to continue without any interruption, and the frame is a clearly finite element.

The interior does not allay the confusion created by the exterior. 'It is not an apartment or office in the traditional sense,' writes critic Janny Rodermond.[2] The building may contain anything. That it is nevertheless not as timeless as Van Velsen wants his buildings to be nowadays is due to a large extent to its wildness. Real city façades are less compelling, less trendy, more neutral. The buildings he designs now are thus much less clamorous. Moreover, the flat detailing and the choice of materials, especially the panels, make the building rather difficult to maintain.

The public library in Zeewolde (1989) → **6** is in many respects a logical follow-up to the Hilversum apartment. The library is built up from independent elements too, but this time they are related to one another in a more convincing way, producing more of the impression of a single building. Besides, the concrete façades in particular are more abstract and thus less showy – if one can speak of façades at all, because these façades are not completely closed surfaces. First of all, they consist almost exclusively of holes. The basis for this façade design was the question: how far can you open up a concrete façade without losing the function of a closed wall? The many holes are holes, not windows. At least, that is how their detailing is applied. The double glass has been set in the concrete without any visible frame. → **7** In the library itself narrow strips of Western red cedar press the glass against the concrete. This detail is a good example of the different moods that Van Velsen wants to evoke with this façade. Relatively hard and silent on the outside; a good deal friendlier on the inside. The seemingly construction-free suspension of the concrete façade reinforces doubts about the functioning of the sturdy concrete wall as a façade. By making use of supporting sandwich panels and attaching them to the floors of the storeys, it was possible to apply a narrow strip of glass underneath with only here and there a steel

column. As a result, the façade, which despite the large number of holes still looks heavy, seems to float. Like that floating, opening the joints at the corners – almost a standard detail in Van Velsen's buildings – has a double meaning. → **8** First of all, it creates the impression of four detached surfaces, while at the same time this detail reveals the thinness and with it the relative lightness of the façade. The latter is accentuated because the plates have been cut off at an angle of 45°, which makes them look thinner than they really are. The concrete façade of the library is very abstract, seeming to anticipate in this the later façades of his buildings. Against and on top of this volume, however, Van Velsen placed other, more or less independent elements, which reduce the abstraction of the whole. The colonnade at the front with a volume covered with the polycarbonate plates on top in wooden frames, the closed black steel box at the side, the staircase packaged in corrugated sheets, but above all the unusual roof construction which protrudes at various points over the façade, temper the severity of the building. The muteness of these elements, by the way, is as great as that of the main volume. The functions remain hidden until a tour of the building reveals what their purpose is. If the Hilversum apartment was too fragmented into different elements, in Zeewolde Van Velsen has found a better balance between making the components independent and then reuniting them again. The pavilion on struts, for example, is separated from the concrete box by a corridor with a floor of glass bricks. Tempered light from the sky lights filters into the entrance area beneath the pavilion. In the details as well, the front building, corridor and main building are the different elements that are detached from one another by means of the subtle staggering of the steel profiles on which the concrete corridor floor is supported. → **9** In addition, the pavilion sticks out of the building on one side, while it is slightly recessed on the other to make room for the entrance. Still, the comprehensive overhanging roof links the two volumes tightly together and leaves no room for any misunderstanding of their coherence. → **10** The interior of the library contains a large number of different atmospheres, in which the construction plays an important part. The intermediate floor rests on systems of three sloping columns with a narrow steel tube in the middle that end in concrete plates to absorb the punching force. → **11** The circular base plate, although it is embedded in concrete, is clearly recognisable. The effect of the construction can be read off. This construction is important spatially too. The bookcases designed by Van Velsen, for example, cannot be placed against the sloping columns, so both the bookcases and the systems of columns are left standing alone in the space. On the intermediate storey wooden beams are wedged between narrow steel columns. It is

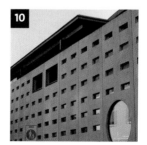

fascinating to see how much the construction contributes to the mood in the areas. Downstairs strange and down to earth; upstairs strange but friendlier. Some of the upstairs mood is also conveyed below because of the application of wooden beams there too which poke through the concrete ceiling. Here the construction certainly is 'merely a means of creating the envisaged spatiality and effects'.[3]

Far–near

After the library in Zeewolde and the renovation and extension of the Rijksakademie (1992) in Amsterdam, the buildings grow quieter. They recede in order to be able to function as more timeless city walls and objects. At the same time attention is drawn by the exciting, though sometimes minuscule details. In the buildings that lend themselves for it – buildings that can be 'touched' – Van Velsen handles materials and details in such a way that the perception of the building changes as you approach it.

From a distance the Pathé multi-screen cinema in Rotterdam (1996) looks like a severe but curiously shaped, floating more or less white box. → 12, 13 When you get closer, however, the façade turns out to be less severe and less closed. This makes the building less remote, less forbidding than it looked at first sight. At close quarters you can see that the white plastic plates are not placed everywhere exactly around the functional volumes. Various niches have been introduced between the building and its covering to complete the sculpturality of the body and to break that body open. → 14 Air is created in the solid body. Then you notice that the plates are not smooth; they are moulded, and are fastened to the steel construction with particularly heavy bolts, making the façade more sensitive and vulnerable.

Finally, the boundary between the square of landscape architects West 8 and the interior of the cinema becomes visible. Van Velsen made this out of a glass screen that lacks almost any detail. It was intended to be as unobtrusive at possible at close quarters too in order to allow the square to continue into the cinema. → 15 That is why the glass fins have been fixed moment-tight to the upper side with sturdy steel corner profiles and bolts. → 16 This enables the fins, that absorb the horizontal forces of the façade, to disappear three metres above the ground.

The surfaces change as you get closer to them in the interior as well. When you enter the 1,000 m^2 foyer it looks sober and serene, but every surface is layered except the surfaces of the auditoria. The stainless steel plates on the floor have a light structure and the walls are covered with paper with a dot pattern to suggest holes. Finally, the stainless steel plates covering the few columns that support the auditoria turn out to be held together by hollow rivets– one of the most sensitive steel connections–, and moreover the plates are slightly turned at top and bottom. → 17 The tight organisation of the space is not disturbed by sloping lines except those of the many stairs. Stability bonds are nowhere to be seen. The very complicated steel construction, which was necessary because the cinema is built on top of a car park and the auditoria overhang it, is hidden behind the white plastered walls of the auditoria, all of which are stable in themselves.

So not only is this cinema exemplary of the way in which Van Velsen neutralises his façades – even though he takes this further each time, a process in which the forms of the buildings are simplified too – but this withdrawal of the construction is an important theme in his later buildings too. As can be seen from the construction of the cinema, this does not mean that they become simpler, and besides their architectural effect seems to be enhanced as a result. A spectacular example of this can be seen in the crazily overhanging balconies which stick out from the block of flats in Borneo Sporenburg (Amsterdam, 1999) without any visible construction. → 18 Their effect is made all the more powerful because the other, much shallower balconies are supported by asymmetrically placed consoles.

If columns and beams remain in sight, Van Velsen often packages them in such a way that, just like the other spatial objects, they become abstract volumes. This makes the interiors quieter, but more exciting at the same time. The concealing of the construction and the less prominent presentation of what has been made are connected with Van Velsen's development. 'I used to be a carpenter with ideas,' Van Velsen says, referring to his education via the Lower Technical School, Intermediate Technical School and ending after the Academy of Architecture. 'Now I am much more a person with ideas, and the way it is made becomes less important.'

In terms of looks, the Dutch Film and Television Academy (1999) in Amsterdam is somewhat comparable to the

Koen van Velsen From compelling elements to whispering objects

13

14

15

16

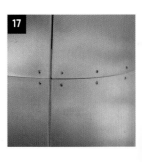

17

18

Pathé cinema, although the form of the academy is much more minimal. → **19** The academy has a ground plan like a parallelogram, without bulges. The only break in the façade is on the fourth floor at the roof terrace. → **20** The encircling concrete border that helps to frame this hole and the continuous façade ribs ensure that the hole barely disrupts the look of the façade. From the Waterlooplein it is mainly framed glass that can be seen, but the association of glass with transparency does not apply to this building. This is logical in terms of its function: after all, a film academy needs relatively little daylight. The glass in this façade is primarily used to create an attractive city wall that fits in with its surroundings. Genuine windows were only used where that was functionally necessary, in the offices. These windows too have minimal detail. → **21** They are glued, so that they could be made without frames. As a result, they look very like the simple glass plates of the rest of the façade that are held in place by aluminium profiles in front of closed wooden boarding.

The fascinating thing about this façade is that, on the one hand, Van Velsen has not made a façade pattern with windows. The openings are not introduced to make the building, its arrangement and function, comprehensible to the outside world, but only to introduce daylight where necessary. On the other hand, the (future) user of the building can open up the façade relatively easily – and replace the wooden panels by double glued windows – for more daylight and view. The look of the façade – the façade as part of the city wall – will barely change, if at all, if such changes are made in the future. The building has become an object that can accommodate any adaptation easily from inside, also because the silver-coloured ventilation grilles look rather temporary.

Quieter and quieter

The materials and details of the façade of the Film Academy are such that the function of the façade of the

building has been subordinated to the function of a city wall. This also applies to Van Velsen's office in Hilversum. The small brick building is primarily intended to form an urban space as unobtrusively as possible. Ordinary wooden frames have been used – though with glued glass – which match the other buildings in the area. → **22** And yet the building has a number of small details which give it enough of a sparkle to counteract any suggestion of ordinariness. For example, blind niches have been applied at the side. Ordinary windows were not allowed here. This meant that the rhythm of the façade was continued around the corner. In addition, strips of bricks set on their side have been introduced in the masonry to give the building a further layer. Attention is also drawn to the protruding roof edging, the bizarre steel beam placed on the roof – which has now been removed – and the completely flat porches above the various entrances. They are minuscule, aesthetic extras that have a powerful effect, although few architects will be satisfied with so little.

Van Velsen went a step further with the extension of the town hall in Terneuzen (1996). → **23** This façade is so completely absorbed by its surroundings that it does not seem to want to be there. The town hall has been covered with light-blue glazed bricks in two gradations of shininess. Thanks to the colour, the building is almost absorbed in the grey sky above the Westerschelde; the bricks glisten and reflect the sunlight. Even then, though, it still puts on a modest front. The use of two kinds of bricks means that one part of the façade glistens in a slightly different way from the other. This was enough for Van Velsen. The façade is completely flat in order not to disturb its severe look. The glued windows lie exactly in the surface of the bricks. → **24** The aluminium roof edging ensures an even more perfect transition from building to sky.

The exceptions are to be found at the front and rear of the building. On the side of the square, the building has a large overhang though it is not meant to show off → **25**, unlike that of the old town hall by Van den Broek and Bakema (1972), or that of Van Velsen's ING building (1999) on the other side of the square. This overhang appears to have been introduced merely to prevent the new building from blocking the view of the monumental building of Van den Broek and Bakema from the shopping street as little as possible. The ceiling of the overhang is in white plaster, and the apparent thinness of the façade is visible, negating the solidity and weight and thus the monumentality of the overhang. → **26** Moreover, this façade is made completely of glass that is framed in a concrete border that continues to the offices below the car park and finally links the new building to the Van den Broek and Bakema building. The glass façade at the back affords the office workers a fantastic view of the Westerschelde, but this glass it not intended

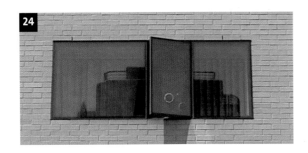

to bring about a visual link between the building and the square, because behind the glass can be seen the closed volumes of the magistrates' court. From the square this façade allows little or nothing to be seen. This is the opposite of the glass façade of the University Museum (1996) in Utrecht, for example, where Van Velsen placed a wooden box behind the glass, and where the complete transparency is intended precisely to arouse the curiosity of the passers-by. → **27**

In Terneuzen the glass has not been used to make a façade. No façade, no material – even less striking than the chameleonic façade of the rest of this building. That is why Van Velsen made no attempt to turn the glass façade into something spectacular. While in Utrecht horizontally placed glass fins absorb the wind forces, in Terneuzen simple box sections link the glass façade with the concrete construction behind it.

The extension of the town hall is as unobtrusive as possible, and a part of the programme has even been carried out underground beneath the car park. These spaces receive daylight on the one hand through the corridor framed by a concrete border. The offices and conference rooms situated more deeply beneath the car park receive daylight from three patios. The patio façades have much more relief than the new building. The largest is built of concrete sandwich elements which stick out above ground level and function as a balustrade too, thereby linking the square with the underground offices.

Van Velsen's design, choice of materials and handling of detail of the new building for the Media Commissioner's Office (Dutch Media Authority, 2001) in Hilversum are similar. → **28** The form of the building follows that of its surroundings closely, even leaving large holes for the trees. → **29** The façades are made of glass and slightly shiny aluminium plates – which Van Velsen chose after the roofing fitted with stainless steel wafers failed to provide the flatness required of the façades. Both materials reflect the surroundings, thereby reducing the presence of the building. In order to achieve this effect, it was necessary to attach the façade materials to the rear construction without any detail. → **30**

The ING building diagonally opposite the extension of the Terneuzen town hall is a completely different building. It is much more of an eloquent object. → **31** The oval shape of the intermediate storey rests on the sharp corner of the ground floor. → **32** On top of this is a

copper roof – or at least, what looks like one. In fact the storey is purely architectural, without a function. Much more volume is suggested than the building actually contains – volume that was necessary to make a real square. All that can be seen through the holes in the structure is air. It is tempting to make a comparison with the two buildings in Hilversum. There too an Expressionist and a mute volume, both by Van Velsen, stand side by side. But the differences are enormous. While Van Velsen constructed his Hilversum shop/apartment/office from independent and very compelling elements, he kneads the ING bank from two quiet materials that retain their beauty for a long time: glued masonry with a copper fascia board. The windows have no frames, and deep joints which function almost as negative window frames have been introduced between the different windows. The presence of this building is a consequence of its form and its site on the square; the materials and details 'merely' confirm its character as an object. Van Velsen: 'The library in Zeewolde consists of many elements, which in turn are made from different materials. Often this is somewhat exaggerated. That something is different has to come from within, has to be intrinsic. It does not necessarily have to be realised in a different material. If you do that, there is a risk that the building will fall apart. I want to achieve as much as possible with as few materials and as little construction as possible.' This attitude results in less and less details. While Zeewolde, the renovation of Total Design (Amsterdam, 1987) and the Rijksakademie were characterised by an overabundance of details that primarily revealed the secret of the construction and contributed to the rich mood of these buildings, with the striving for a more reticent use of material the detail has also become more introverted. They are often visually absent details or details that draw attention in a very subtle way. The details of the glass walls and doors in the Media Commissioner's Office, where thermal zinc-coated profiles were used, in some cases with only the 'nose' visible, are a typical example of details that are only dimly present. 'The detail itself is nothing, it has no meaning for me,' says Van Velsen. 'The details only have to evoke an atmosphere. We want to stop the detail from working as an ornament or as a separate thing that is too prominently present instead of working spatially.' In this process, Van Velsen does not try to attain authenticity in terms of material technique. Many buildings, it is true, still show how the different materials are linked together, but at least as many details are hidden. 'I am interested in using details to make a dream come true, not to create a reality.'

1. K. van Velsen, 'Over Architectuur is niets te zeggen', *Archis*, 1991, no. 9.
2. J. Rodermond, 'Koen van Velsen ontwerpt lichtend voorbeeld in stadsvernieuw-ingsbuurt', *de Architect*, 1982, no. 9.
3. P. Vollaard, P. Groenendijk, '"Constructie is een hulp-middel". Koen van Velsen over materialen en geknutsel', *Architectuur en Bouwen*, 1990, no. 10.

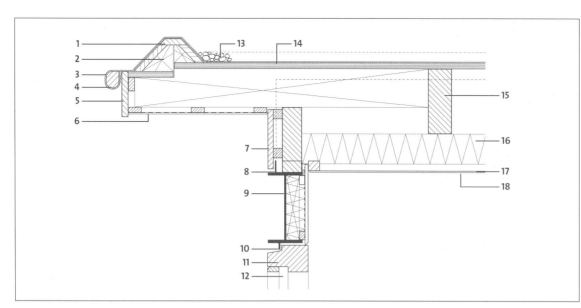

Junction projecting roof and raised pavilion
1 water-resistant plywood
2 angle fillet
3 zinc
4 beaded batten
5 unpainted western red cedar
6 5 mm wire gauze perforated Masonite
7 unpainted western red cedar
8 welded strip
9 IPE 240
10 welded strip
11 frame
12 polycarbonate
13 gravel
14 roofing
15 timber floor joists
16 insulation
17 damp-proof membrane
18 5 mm Masonite

Koen van Velsen Public library Zeewolde 1989

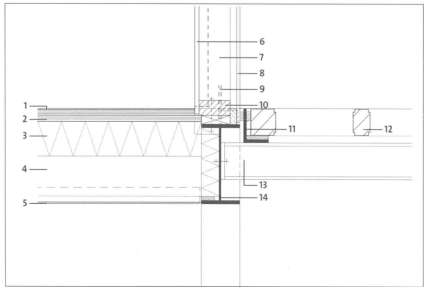

Detail of junction between raised pavilion and glass brick walkway
1 2 mm linoleum
2 2 x 18 mm underlay
3 semi-rigid mineral wool (100 mm)
4 75 x 225 mm timber joists
5 5 mm Masonite
6 plasterboard
7 insulation
8 plasterboard
9 starter bars for fixing wall
10 wooden cleats
11 100 x 75 x 8 mm angle iron
12 concrete floor with glass bricks
13 HE 120A
14 IPE 240

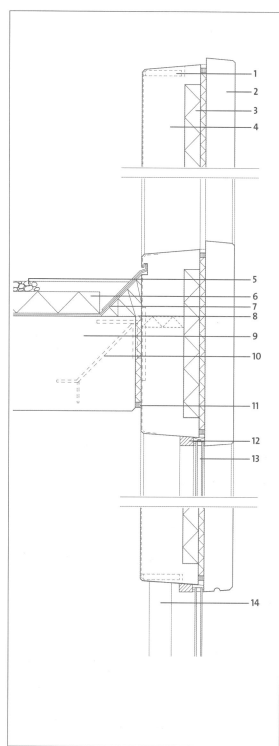

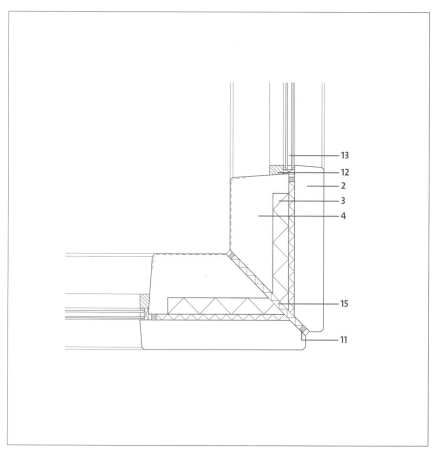

Sectional elevation of concrete main volume
1 95 x 320 x 10 mm stainless steel end plate
2 outer leaf precast concrete sandwich panel
3 insulation (part of sandwich panel)
4 inner leaf precast concrete sandwich panel
5 gravel
6 insulation
7 roofing
8 insulated angle fillet
9 concrete floor slab
10 cast-in-place anchors for fixing façade
11 sealant on backup strip
12 western red cedar glazing bead
13 insulating glass
14 steel column
15 insulation

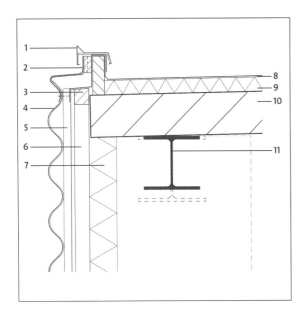

Roof edge
1 aluminium edging strip
2 coping
3 wooden cleat
4 corrugated plastic sheeting
5 construction for fixing corrugated sheeting
6 3 x 12.5 mm plasterboard
7 100 mm mineral wool; 100 kg/m²
8 roofing
9 50 mm PS
10 150 mm gas concrete with gradient
11 construction

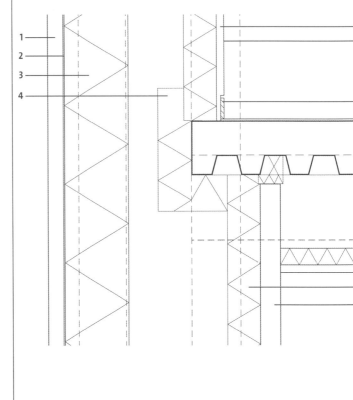

Typical make-up of cinema wall
1 3 x 12.5 mm plasterboard
2 damp-proof membrane
3 200 mm mineral wool; 50 kg/m²
4 100 mm mineral wool; 100 kg/m²
5 2 x 12.5 mm plasterboard
6 Protector 1313 wall finishing
7 wooden skirting board
8 2.5 mm linoleum
9 composite decking
10 50 mm mineral wool; 35 kg/m²
11 2 x 12.5 mm plasterboard
12 100 mm mineral wool; 100 kg/m²
13 4 x 12.5 mm plasterboard

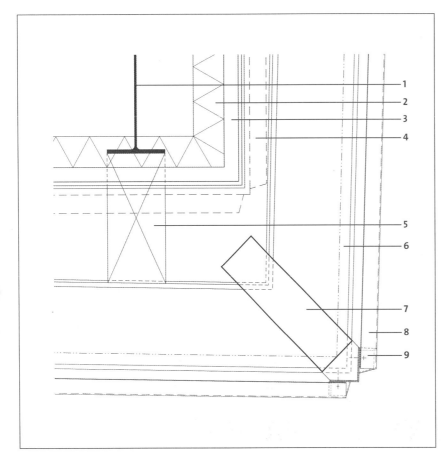

Horizontal detail corrugated sheet façade at set-back corner
1 construction
2 100 mm mineral wool; 100 kg/m²
3 3 x 12 mm plasterboard
4 upper and underlying synthetic façade cladding
5 bracket
6 aluminium edging strip
7 construction
8 corrugated plastic sheeting
9 wooden cleat

Roof edge
1 pre-formed aluminium roof
2 water-resistant plywood
3 open perpends
4 insulation
5 Foamglas®
6 vitrified brick
7 plastic flashing
8 auxiliary structure for roof edge
9 roofing
10 insulation
11 wide-slab floor

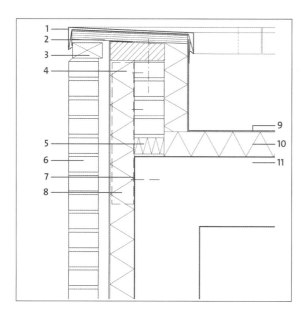

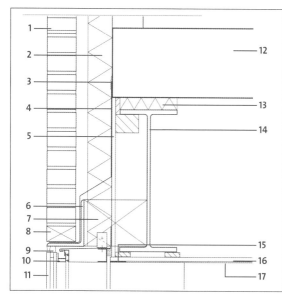

Façade/frame junction
1 vitrified brick
2 insulation
3 aluminium clamp profile
4 plastic flashing
5 cement bonded particle board
6 angle
7 fixing of angle to IPE beam
8 open perpends
9 coloured sealant on backup strip
10 glass fixing
11 double glass
12 wide-slab floor
13 PUR
14 IPE beam
15 plaster stop
16 plasterboard
17 wall paint

Details of cantilever on side facing square
1 vitrified brick
2 pigmented/coloured pointing mortar
3 insulation
4 aluminium clamp profile
5 plastic flashing
6 support structure for brickwork
7 weepholes
8 stainless steel lintel
9 wall paint
10 plaster stop
11 skirting flush with wall finishing
12 floor finish
13 sand cement floor
14 wide-slab floor
15 PS foam
16 mirror laminate on wood backing

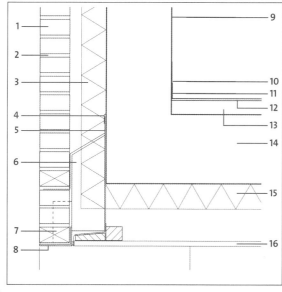

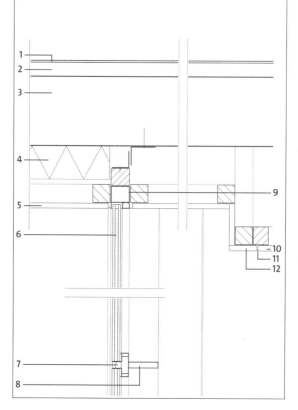

Side elevation with view of patio

Junction of cantilever and glass façade (front)
1 floor finish
2 sand cement floor
3 wide-slab floor
4 PS foam
5 mirror laminate on wood backing
6 insulating glass
7 steel section
8 steel strip
9 thermally insulated glazing profile
10 ceiling
11 plaster stop
12 colour painted MDF

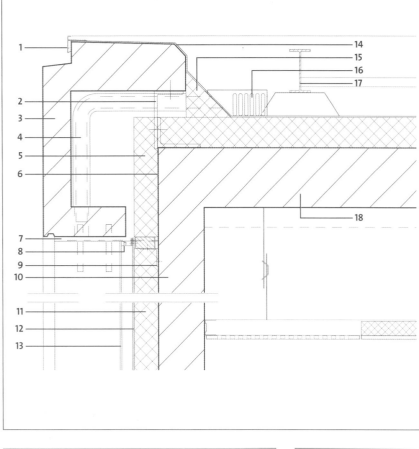

Roof edge
1 Compri colour powder-coated roof trim
2 angle for fixing precast roof edge
3 precast roof edge
4 overflow with damp-proof insulation
5 insulation
6 waterproof membrane
7 steel bracket
8 Bostic profile
9 anchor
10 precast concrete unit
11 insulation
12 cladding
13 single glazing
14 two-ply roof covering
15 PS angle fillet
16 gravel stop
17 window cleaners' rail
18 wide-slab floor

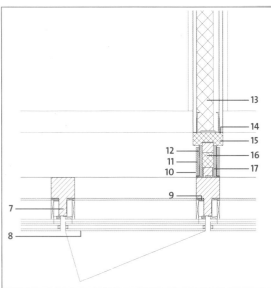

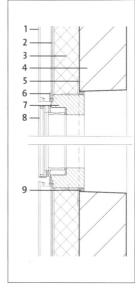

Typical façade details: horizontal (left), vertical (right)
1 single glazing
2 cladding panel
3 insulation
4 precast concrete
5 angle
6 Bostic profile
7 frame
8 insulating glass
9 draught strip
10 Abet 880 Lucida HPL
11 8 mm plywood
12 24 kg/m² lead
13 metal stud wall
14 plaster stop
15 hardwood
17 8 mm plywood
16 mineral wool

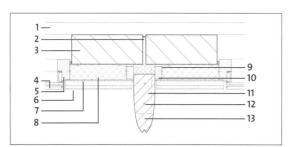

Horizontal façade detail at mullions
1 cable duct seen from above
2 sealant on backup strip
3 precast concrete
4 insulating glass
5 frame
6 single glazing
7 cladding panel
8 insulation
9 angle
10 cleat
11 steel bracket at mullion
12 dowels
13 precast concrete façade unit

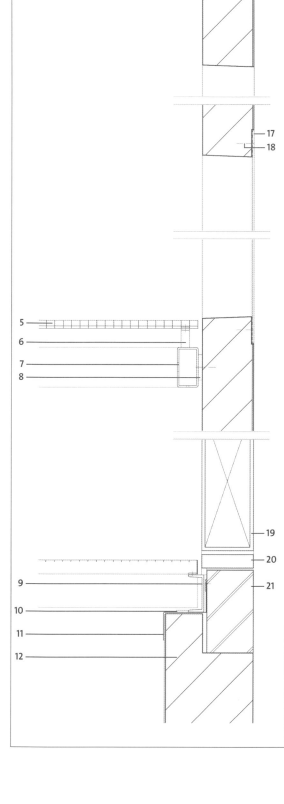

Section through façade (not climate-proof)
1 wooden framework, concealed anchorage to concrete
2 bitumen
3 pre-formed stainless steel section
4 precast concrete panel, blue on inside, black on outside
5 grid floor
6 60 x 60 mm T-section
7 150 x 75 x 8 mm box section
8 bar connector coupling
9 UNP section
10 steel plate
11 DPC membrane
12 foundation beam
13 rigid, trafficable insulating panel
14 anchoring elements
15 Keim concretal lasur, semi-transparent, black
16 sealed joint
17 laminated safety glass
18 flat countersunk head screw fixing
19 tilt and fold door, finished in light blue (inside) and black (outside) to match concrete
20 blue Belgian limestone sill
21 brickwork

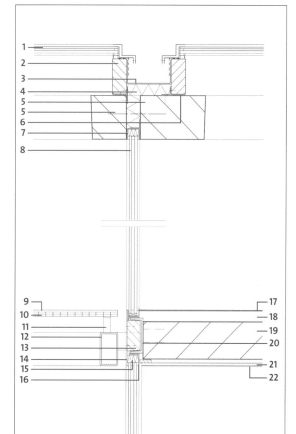

Section through climate-proof 'inner' wall at 2nd floor
1 insulating glass, toughened outer pane
2 wooden framework, concealed anchorage to concrete
3 bitumen
4 trafficable insulation
5 precast concrete panel, black on outside, blue on inside
6 foam strip
7 100 x 40 x 4 mm cold-rolled U-section
8 laminated insulating glass
9 6 mm clear glass
10 grid floor
11 60 x 60 mm T-section
12 150 x 75 x 8 mm box section
13 guide rail for fixing
14 stainless steel plate
15 foam strip
16 angle
17 aluminium flooring
18 compression layer
19 hollow-core slab floor
20 UNP 160
21 timber battens
22 aluminium sheeting

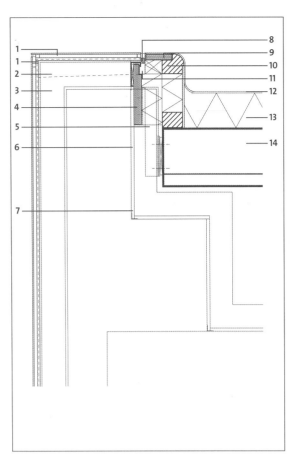

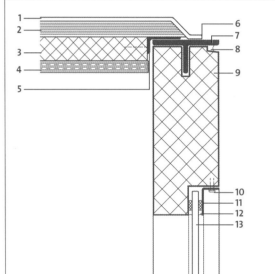

Glass door
1 Dorma coupling for floor-mounted door spring
2 10 mm toughened glass door
3 door strip bonded to toughened glass door
4 toughened glass
5 iroko batten, clear-painted
6 80 x 40 x 7 mm welded frame of T-sections, mitre-welded at corners
7 welded-on brackets for fixing frame
8 8 mm float glass
9 stainless steel raised head screw
10 sealant on backup strip
11 electricity cable for 'out' sign
12 2 mm stainless steel L-section
13 laminated iroko jamb, clear-painted

Junction roof/wooden frame
1 Soprema Inox roofing
2 18 mm plywood, glued on wood core
3 28 mm wood core
4 15 mm thick iroko planks, blind nailed
5 40 x 20 x 3 mm L-section, hot-galvanized
6 straight-cut roofing
7 80 x 40 x 7 mm T-section, hot-galvanized
8 sealed joint
9 80 x 200 mm iroko frame
10 stainless steel raised-head screw
11 2 mm stainless steel L-section
12 sealant on backup strip
13 8 mm float glass

Roof edge of glass façade with glass continuing into roof plane
1 structural glazing; laminated inner pane
2 slope in case of runoff
3 aluminium frame, colour enamelled
4 30 mm plywood
5 background structure
6 plasterboard
7 angle bead
8 sealant on backup strip
9 waterproof plywood
10 beaded batten
11 pre-formed stainless steel section
12 Soprema stainless steel roofing
13 insulation
14 wide-slab concrete floor

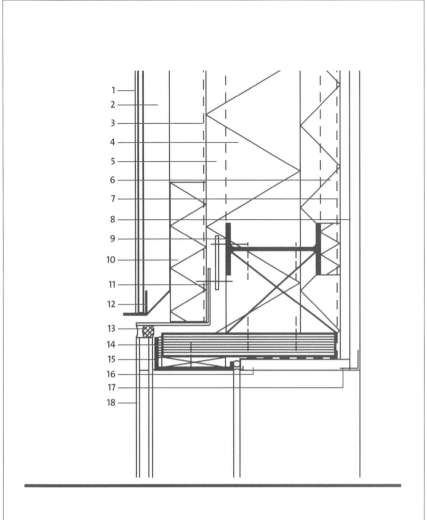

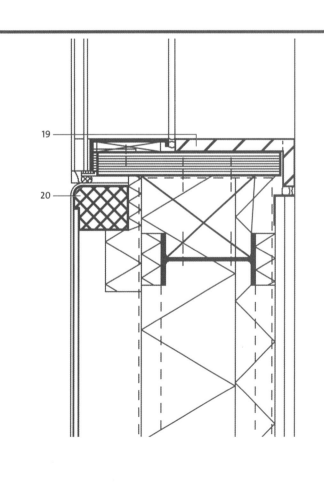

Junction of aluminium façade and structural glass front

1 aluminium façade panels
2 timber battens
3 waterproof breather membrane
4 insulation
5 steel structure
6 background structure
7 waterproof membrane
8 2 x 12.5 mm plasterboard
9 IPE section
10 rigid rot-proof insulating panel
11 70 x 95 x 3 mm stainless steel L-section
12 30 x 30 x 3 mm stainless steel L-section
13 aerated sealed joint
14 30 mm plywood
15 40 x 90 mm aluminium frame
16 plasterboard
17 angle bead
18 structural glazing
19 white marble window ledge
20 hardwood rail

Prof. Ir. Wiel Arets Architects & Associates bv

Academy of Arts and Architecture
Herdenkingsplein 12
Maastricht
project architects: Wiel Arets, Jo Janssen
project team: Lars van Es, Anita Morandini, René Holten, Maurice Paulussen; Paulus Egers (model); Kim Zwarts, Hélène Binet (photography)
client: Rijkshogeschool Maastricht
contractor: Laudy Bouw & Planontwikkeling bv
structural consultant: Grabowsky & Poort Consulting Engineers
building services consultant: F.M.J.L. van de Wetering (light)
design-completion: 1989–1993
floor area: 4,000 m² GFA

AZL insurance company head office
Akerstraat 92
Heerlen
project architects: Wiel Arets, Dominic Papa, Ani Velez
project team: Lars van Es, Jo Janssen, Malin Johanson, Maurice Paulussen, Joanna Tang, René Thijssen, Richard Welten; Hein Urlings (site supervisor); Wiel Arets, Pieter Kromwijk (Eerenbeemt & Kromwijk), Dominic Papa (landscaping); Paul Eegers, Joanna Tang (models); Hélène Binet, Kim Zwarts (photography)
client: Pensioenfonds AZL Beheer Heerlen
contractor: Laudy Bouw & Planontwikkeling bv
management consultant: Veldhoen Facility Consultants bv
structural consultant: Ingenieursbureau Grabowsky & Poort bv
building services consultant: Tema Ingenieurs bv
building physics consultant: Cauberg-Huygen Raadgevende Ingenieurs bv
design-completion: 1991–1995
floor area: 3,600 m² GFA

Police station
Maastrichterlaan/Randweg
Vaals
project architects: Wiel Arets, Rhea Harbers
project team: Delphine Clavien, Michel Melenhorst; VFC bv (site supervisor) Paulus Egers (models); Hélène Binet, Kim Zwarts (photography)
client: South Limburg Regional Police Force, Cadier & Keer

contractor: Van Zandvoort bv
management consultant: Veldhoen Facility Consultants bv
structural consultant: Ingenieursburo Palte bv
building services consultant: TEMA Ingenieurs bv (mechanical); Huygen bv (electrical)
building physics consultant: Cauberg-Huygen Raadgevende Ingenieurs bv
design-completion: 1993–1995

Police station
Beerselaan/
Heeswijksestraat
Cuijk
project architects: Wiel Arets, Dorte Jensen, Ralph van Mameren, René Thijssen
project team: Paul van Dongen, Harold Hermans, Michel Melenhorst; Hein Urlings (site supervisor); Doris Annen, Wiel Arets, René Thijssen (furniture design); Kim Zwarts (photography)
client: North Brabant Police Unit
contractor: Giesbers Bouw bv
building services consultant: TEMA Ingenieurs bv
design-completion: 1994–1997

Lensvelt company premises
Industrieterrein Hoogeind
Breda
project architects: Wiel Arets, Ivo Daniëls, René Thijssen
landscape architect: West 8
project team: Paul van Dongen; Hélène Binet, Kim Zwarts (photography)
client: Lensvelt bv
contractor: Korteweg Bouw bv; Holthuis bouwbegeleiding
management consultant: Traject Vastgoed & Adviesgroep bv
structural consultant: Ingenieursbureau A. Palte bv
building physics consultant: Cauberg-Huygen Raadgevende Ingenieurs bv
design-completion: 1995–1999
floor area: 5,710 m² GFA

Hedge House
Kasteel Wijlre Park
Wijlre
project architects: Wiel Arets, Bettina Kraus
project team: Lars Dreessen, Frederik Vaes; Hein Urlings (site supervisor); Jeremy Bryan, Frederik Vaes (models); Hélène Binet (photography)
client: Marlies and Jo Eyck
contractor: Contractorsbedrijf Xhonneux bv
structural consultant: Ingenieursbureau Palte bv

building services consultant: Huygen installatieadviseurs bv
building physics consultant: Cauberg-Huygen Raadgevende Ingenieurs bv
design-completion: 1999–2001
floor area: 280 m² GFA

University Library
'De Uithof' university campus
Utrecht
project architects: Wiel Arets, Pauline Bremmer, Dominic Papa, René Thijssen, Henrik Vuust, Richard Welten
landscape architect: West 8
project team: Pedro Anão, Harold Aspers, Lars Dreessen, Eva Gjessing, Franziska Herb, Harold Hermans, Petra Jacquet, Peter Kaufmann, Guido Neijnens, Michael Pedersen, Frederik Vaes, Michiel Vrehen; Pedro Anão, Mai Henriksen, Kees Lemmens (models); Hélène Binet, Kim Zwarts (photography)
client: Utrecht University
contractor: IBC-Heymans; Gardner bv, Vogt bv (façade); GTI (services)
structural consultant: ABT adviesbureau voor bouwtechniek bv
building services consultant: Huygen installatieadviseurs bv; Adviesbureau Peutz & Associates bv (acoustics)
building physics consultant: Cauberg-Huygen Raadgevende Ingenieurs bv
design-completion: 1997–2001; 2001–2004

Benthem Crouwel Architekten bv bna

Benthem House
De Fantasie 10
Almere
project architect: Jan Benthem
client: Jan Benthem
contractor: Jan Benthem
structural consultant: Jan Benthem
building services consultant: Jan Benthem
building physics consultant: Jan Benthem
completion: 1984
floor area: 65 m² GFA

Terminal West
Amsterdam Airport
Schiphol
project architects: Jan Benthem, Hans Smit, Thijs Veldman
client: NV Luchthaven Schiphol
contractor: KLS 2000
structural consultant: ABT-DHV Advies- en Ingenieursbureau
building services consultant: Ketel-Deerns raadgevende ingenieurs vof
building physics consultant: Adviesbureau Peutz & Associes bv
completion: 1993
floor area: 120,000 m² GFA

World Trade Centre
Amsterdam Airport
Schiphol
project architects: Jan Benthem, Mels Crouwel, Guus Brockmeier, Roelof Gortemaker, Pieter van Rooij, Vignelli Associates (interior)
client: Kantorenfonds Nederland bv with Amsterdam Airport Schiphol; now: Schiphol Real Estate
contractor: Projectcombinatie P4 consisting of: Nelissen van Egteren, DURA, Dirk Verstoep
structural consultant: Bureau de Weger Rotterdam; now: Royal Haskoning
building services consultant: Raadgevend Technies Buro Van Heugten bv
building physics consultant: Raadgevend Technies Buro Van Heugten bv
design-completion: 1991–1996
floor area: 34,000 m² GFA, with 3,000 parking spaces
  second phase:
client: Schiphol Real Estate
contractor: Combinatie: Volker Wessels Stevin Bouw and IBC Utiliteitsbouw
completion: 2003
floor area: a further 34,000 m² GFA, with 2,700 parking spaces

Provincial hall
Martinikerkhof 12
Groningen
project architects: Jan Benthem, Mels Crouwel, Stan Rietbroek
client: Groningen Provincial Executive
contractor: Lodewijk Geveke Bouw
structural consultant: Ingenieursbureau Wassenaar bv
building services consultant: Deerns Raadgevende Ingenieurs bv
completion: 1996
floor area: 13,500 m² GFA

Malietoren office building
Utrechtsebaan
The Hague
project architects: Jan Benthem, Mels Crouwel, André Staalenhoef
client: Multi Vastgoed bv
contractor: Wilma Bouw bv
structural consultant: Ove Arup & Partners International Ltd., Corsmit Raadgevend Ingenieursburo
building services consultant: TM Verhoeven
building physics consultant: D.G.M.R.
completion: 1996
floor area: 25,000 m² GFA

013 pop music centre
Veemarktstraat 44
Tilburg
project architects: Jan Benthem, Mels Crouwel, Pieter van Rooij
client: Tilburg Public Works department
contractor: M & M bouw
structural consultant: Adviesburo F. Tielemans

building services consultant: Technisch Adviesburo W. Schlappi bv
building physics consultant: Adviesbureau Peutz & Associes bv
completion: 1998
floor area: 6,400 m² GFA

Villa Arena
De entree 1
Amsterdam-Zuidoost
project architects: Jan Benthem, Mels Crouwel, Stan Rietbroek, Florentijn Vleugels
client: Ontwikkelingsmaatschappij Centrumgebied Zuid Oost: ING Vastgoed Ontwikkeling bv
contractor: Bouwcombinatie Zuid Oost: vof BAM Bredero, Ballast Nedam Utiliteitsbouw bv
structural consultant: Ingenieursgroep Van Rossum
building services consultant: Hiensch Engineering bv
building physics consultant: Adviesbureau Peutz & Associes bv
completion: 2001
floor area: 180,000 m² GFA

CEPEZED bv

Two without a roof house
Straat van Ormoes 145-147
Delft
project architects: Architectenbureau Cepezed bv, Delft
client: J.H. Pesman and A.J. van Seijen families
project coordination: Bouwteam General Contractors bv, Delft
structural consultant: P. de Jong
building services consultant: dhr. F. Boonstoppel
design-completion: design (competition): 1989; construction 1989
floor area: 196 m² GFA

Woeste Willem Crèche
Ben Goerionstraat 6
Rotterdam
project architects: Architectenbureau Cepezed bv, Delft
client: Stichting de Oosterprins
project coordination: Bouwteam General Contractors bv, Delft
structural consultant: IDCS bv, Hoofddorp
building services consultant: Raadgevend Ingenieursbureau Boonstoppel, Nijmegen
building physics consultant: idem RIB
design-completion: 1993–1994
floor area: 486 m² GFA

Centre for Human Drug Research
Zernikedreef 10
Leiden
project architects: Architectenbureau Cepezed bv, Delft
client: Stichting C.H.G.

Onroerend Goed
project coordination:
Bouwteam General
Contractors bv, Delft
structural consultant: IDCS bv,
Hoofddorp
building services consultant:
Raadgevend
Ingenieursbureau
Boonstoppel, Nijmegen
building physics consultant:
idem RIB
design-completion: 1993–1995
floor area: 1,200 m² GFA

CEPEZED offices
Phoenixstraat 60
Delft
project architects:
ir. J.H. Pesman; M.E. Cohen
client: Architectenbureau
CEPEZED bv
project coordination:
Bouwteam General
Contractors bv
structural consultant: ECCS,
Hoofddorp
building services consultant:
Elders Rust bv, Giessenburg
design-completion: 1998–1999
floor area: 1,290 m² GFA

Bullewijk thermal
transmission station
Schepenbergweg
Amsterdam-Zuidoost
project architects:
Architectenbureau Cepezed
bv, Delft
client: NV Energiebedrijf UNA,
Amsterdam
contractor: Bouwbedrijf
Buitenhuis, Landsmeer
structural consultant: Bekker
& Stroband bv, Amsterdam
building services consultant:
Merkx Installatietechniek bv,
Beverwijk
design-completion:
1997–2000
floor area: 392 m² GFA

Porsche works
Porschestraße
Leipzig
Germany
project architects:
Architectenbureau Cepezed
bv, Delft
client: dr. Ing. H.c.f. Porsche
Aktiengesellschaft
project coordination: Agiplan
structural consultant: Baum &
Weiher
building physics consultant:
Bartenbach Lichtlabor
design-completion:
2000–2001
floor area: 15,000 m² GFA for
factory and office

ÖAW Forschungsgebäude
Graz
Schmiedlstraße 6
Graz
Austria
project architects:
Architectenbureau Cepezed
bv; Architekturbüro DI Peyker
client: Austrian Academy of
Sciences
contractor: Rapatz und Jahn
structural consultant:
Ingenieursbüro Wendl
building services consultant:
TB Pickl

building physics consultant:
Gerhard Tomberger
design-completion:
1999–2000
floor area: 5,068 m² GFA

Erick van Egeraat associated architects (EEA)

Haus 13 IGA Stuttgart
Störzbachstraße
Stuttgart
Germany
project architects: Erick van
Egeraat, Francine Houben,
Birgit Jürgenhake, Marjolijn
Adriaansche, Dick van
Gameren, Luis Pires, Jana
Schulz
client: Landenshauptstadt
Stuttgart; Entwicklungs-
gesellschaft Baden-
Württemberg GmbH,
Stuttgart
structural consultant: ABT
Adviesburo voor Bouw-
techniek bv, Delft; Dipl.-Ing.
Klaus Wilhelm, Stuttgart
adviseur installatie: Ketel
raadgevende ingenieurs bv,
Delft; Fritz Baumgärtner,
Stuttgart (mechanical); Hans
Henning Schindler, Stuttgart
(electrical)
building physics consultant:
Forschungsgemeinschaft
Bauphysik, Stuttgart
completion: 1993
floor area: 1,175 m² GFA
note: Erick van Egeraat in
collaboration with Mecanoo
architects

Stuivesantplein apartment
complex
Geefhuishof 1 t/m 35
Tilburg
project architects: Erick van
Egeraat, Monica Adams,
Gerben Vos, Ard Buijsen, Joep
van Etten, Kerstin Hahn, Birgit
Jürgenhake, Colette Niemeijer,
Stefanie Schleich
client: Wonen Midden
Brabant, Tilburg
contractor: Remmers
Bouwbedrijf, Tilburg
structural consultant:
ABT Adviesburo voor
Bouwtechniek bv, Delft
building services consultant:
Sweegers en de Bruijn,
's-Hertogenbosch
design-completion: 1999
floor area: 3,920 m² GFA

ING Bank & Nationale
Nederlanden head office
Andrássy út
Budapest
Hungary
project architects: Erick van
Egeraat, Tibor Gáll, Atilla
Komjáthy, Maartje Lammers,
Astrid Huwald, Gábor Kruppa,
János Tiba, Stephen Moylan,
William Richards, Dianne
Anyika, Paul-Martin Lied,
Emmett Scanlon, Ineke
Dubbeldam, Ard Buijsen,
Miranda Nieboer, Harry
Boxelaar, Axel Koschany,
Tamara Klassen
client: ING Real Estate
International and Nationale
Nederlanden Real Estate

Hungary Ltd.
contractor: C.F.E. Hungary Kft.
structural consultant:
ABT Adviesburo voor Bouw-
techniek bv, Delft; Mérték
Épitészeti Stúdió Kft,
Budapest
building services consultant:
Ketel raadgevende ingenieurs
bv, Delft; Ove Arup & Partners,
London (mechanical); Mérték
Épitészeti Stúdió Kft,
Budapest (electrical)
*building physics and acoustic
consultant:* Adviesburo Peutz
& Associes bv, Mook
completion: 1994
floor area: 7,830 m² GFA

Ichthus College
Posthumalaan 90
Rotterdam
project architects: Erick van
Egeraat, Monica Adams,
Maartje Lammers, Luc Reyn,
Cock Peterse, Jeroen ter Haar,
Kerstin Hahn, Paul Blonk,
Colette Niemeijer, Nienke
Booy, Aude de Broissia, Ezra
Buenrostro-Hoogwater, Ard
Buijsen, Joep van Etten, Pavel
Fomenko, Matthias Frei, Bas
de Haan, Folkert van Hagen,
Sara Hampe, Julia Hausmann,
Sabrina Kers, Perry Klootwijk,
Ramon Knoester, Harry
Kurzhals, Paul-Martin Lied,
Mika Lundberg, Lisette Magis,
Jos Overmars, Karolien de
Pauw, Claudia Radinger,
Stefanie Schleich, Ole
Schmidt, Ronald Ubels, Rowan
van Wely, Boris Zeisser
client: Ichthus Hogeschool
Rotterdam
contractor: Giesbers bouw bv,
Wijchen
structural consultant: ABT
Adviesburo voor Bouw-
techniek bv, Delft
building services consultant:
ABT Adviesburo voor
Bouwtechniek bv, Velp
building physics consultant:
Adviesburo Peutz & Associees
bv , Mook (acoustics)
completion: 2000
floor area: 20,000 m² GFA

Crawford Municipal Art
Gallery
Emmet Place
Cork
Ireland
project architects: Erick van
Egeraat, Maartje Lammers,
Michael Rushe, Marylse van
Bijleveld, Astrid Huwald, Claire
Booth, Patrick Creedon, Aylin
Jorgensen-Dahl, Gerwen van
der Linden, Stefan Frommer,
Folkert van Hagen, Perry
Klootwijk
client: City of Cork Vocational
Education Committee, Cork
contractor: John F. Supple Ltd.
structural consultant: Horgan
Lynch & Partners, Cork
building services consultant:
Ove Arup & Partners, Cork
(mechanical and electrical)
completion: 2000
floor area: 830 m² GFA

Mezz Poppodium
Keizerstraat 69
Breda
project architects: Erick van
Egeraat, Maartje Lammers,
Boris Zeisser, Gerben Vos, Bas
de Haan, Anja Blumert, Mark
Brouwers, Ilse Castermans,
Folkert van Hagen, Ramon
Karges, Ruben Kuipers, Paul-
Martin Lied, Gerwen van der
Linden, Nils van Merrienboer,
florent Rougemont, Dirk
Schonkeren, Steven Simons,
Maureen Slattery, Alexander
Tauber, János Tiba, Jesse
Treurniet, Jerry van
Veldhuizen, Daniël Vlasveld
client: City of Breda
contractor: M&M Bouw
Brabant, Eindhoven
structural consultant: Ove
Arup & Partners, London; PBT,
Delft
building services consultant:
Ove Arup & Partners, London;
Ingenieurburo Linssen,
Amsterdam (mechanical and
electrical)
building physics consultant:
Ove Arup & Partners,
Cambridge; Ingenieurburo
Linssen, Amsterdam
(acoustics)
design-completion:
1996–2002
floor area: 1,550 m² GFA

Town hall
Castellumstraat
Alphen aan den Rijn
project architects: Erick van
Egeraat, Monica Adams,
Massimo Bertolani, Ralph van
Mameren, Harry Pasterkamp,
Rowan van Wely, Ronald Ubels,
Ilse Castermans, Jerry van
Veldhuizen, Matthieu
Brutsaert, Jeroen ter Haar,
Ezra Buenrostro Hoogwater,
Jasper Jägers, Colette
Niemeijer, Sonja Gallo,
Gerwen van der Linden, Katrin
Grubert, Steven Simons, Oliver
von Spreckelsen, Gerben Vos,
Aude de Broissia, Sabrina
Friedl, Frank Huibers, Bora
Ilhan, Ramon Karges, Sabrina
Kers, Perry Klootwijk, Paul-
Martin Lied, Christian Nicolas,
Jos Overmars, Nuno Pais, Cock
Peterse, Claudia Radinger, Luc
Reyn, Anke Schiemann, Filipa
Tomaz
client: City of Alphen aan den
Rijn
contractor: HBG
Utiliteitsbouw, Rotterdam
structural consultant: ABT
Adviesburo voor Bouw-
techniek bv, Delft
building services consultant:
Sweegers en de Bruijn,
's-Hertogenbosch
building physics consultant:
Adviesburo Peutz & Associes
bv, Mook
completion: 2002
floor area: 25,000 m² GFA

Architectuurstudio Herman Hertzberger

Centraal Beheer insurance
company offices
Willem Alexanderlaan 651
Apeldoorn
project architect: Herman
Hertzberger with Architecten-
bureau Lucas en Niemeyer
project team: Rob Blom van
Assendelft, Hans Schotman,
Boudewijn Delmee, Ellen
Mensingh-v.d Meiden, Marijke
Teijsse, Henk de Weijer, Wim
Oxenaar
client: Centraal Beheer,
Apeldoorn
contractor: Ballast Nedam
Utiliteitsbouw, Amstelveen
structural consultant:
Adviesburo D3BN Civiel
Ingenieurs, Amsterdam; Dicke
& v.d. Boogaard, Rotterdam
building services consultant:
Raadgevend Technisch Buro
Van Heugten bv, Nijmegen;
Raadgevend bureau Twijnstra
en Gudde
design-completion: 1967–1972
floor area: 30,536 m² GFA

Extension of Centraal
Beheer insurance company
offices
Willem Alexanderlaan 651
Apeldoorn
project architect: Herman
Hertzberger
project team: Dolf Floors, Jan
van den Berg, Dickens van der
Werff, Ariënne Matser, Cor
Kruter
client: Centraal Beheer,
Apeldoorn
contractor: Ballast Nedam
Utiliteitsbouw, Amstelveen
structural consultants: ABT,
Velp
building services consultant:
Raadgevend Technisch Buro
Van Heugten, Nijmegen
building physics consultant:
DGMR Raadgevende
Ingenieurs bv, The Hague
design-completion: 1990–1995
floor area: 7,000 m² GFA,
including car park

Ministry of Social Affairs
A. van Hannoverstraat 4-6
The Hague
project architect: Herman
Hertzberger
project team: Wim Oxener,
Henk de Weijer, Jan Rietvink,
Folkert Stropsma, Heleen
Reedijk
client: Government Buildings
Agency, The Hague
contractor: Aannemersbedrijf
Boele & Van Eesteren, The
Hague
structural consultants:
Adviesburo D3BN Civiel
Ingenieurs, Amsterdam
building services consultant:
Deerns, Rijswijk
building physics consultant:
DGMR Raadgevend
Adviesburo, The Hague
design-completion: 1979–1990
floor area: 56,000 m² GFA

Chassé Theatre
Claudius Prinsenlaan 8
Breda
project architect: Herman Hertzberger
project team: Willem van Winsen, Cor Kruter, Folkert Stropsma, Ariënne Matser, Patrick Fransen, Marijke Teijsse, Heleen Reedijk, Laurens Jan ten Kate, Henk de Weijer, Geert Mol, Akelei Hertzberger
client: City of Breda
contractor: Albouw BBM bv, Breda
structural consultant: Adviesbureau voor Bouwtechniek ABT, Velp
building services consultant: Ingenieursbureau A. Bervoets bv, Breda
consultant on theatre technology, acoustics and building physics: Prinssen en Bus Raadgevende Ingenieurs bv, Uden
design-completion: 1992–1995
floor area: 16,000 m² GFA

Montessori College Oost
Polderweg 3
Amsterdam
project architect: Herman Hertzberger
project team: Willem van Winsen, Geert Mol, Ariënne Matser, Henk de Weijer, Folkert Stropsma, Roos Eichhorn, Heleen Reedijk, Marijke Teijsse, Cor Kruter
client: Stichting Montessori scholengemeenschap Amsterdam
project management: Bureau Project coordination Nederland, Houten engineering
contractor: Ballast Nedam Utiliteitsbouw, Utrecht
structural consultants: Ingenieursgroep van Rossum, Amsterdam
building services: Burgers Ergon Contractors, Amsterdam; Verstappen van Amelsvoort bv, Nuland
art: Akelei Hertzberger, Amsterdam
design-completion: 1993–2000
floor area: 17,016 m² GFA

Extension of Vanderveen department store
Koopmansplein
Assen
project architect: Herman Hertzberger
project team: Willem van Winsen, Laurens Jan ten Kate, Folkert Stropsma, Ariënne Matser, Andrew Dawes, Cor Kruter
client: Warenhuis Vanderveen, Assen
contractor: Vosbouw bv, Assen
structural consultants: Ingenieursburo Wassenaar, Haren
building services consultant: IHN Groningen, Groningen
design-completion: 1993–1998
floor area: 600 m² GFA

Mecanoo architects

Hillekop housing project
Hillelaan and Hillekopplein
Rotterdam-Zuid
project architects: Francine Houben, Erick van Egeraat, Chris de Weijer, Henk Döll, Aart Fransen, Cock Peterse, Holger Wirthwein, Sjaak Jansen, Sylvie Beugels, Hans van der Heijden
client: Stichting Tuinstad Zuidwijk (now: Estrade)
contractor: Van der Vorm Bouw bv, Papendrecht
structural consultant: ABT adviesbureau voor bouwtechniek, Delft/Velp
design-completion: 1987–1989
floor area: 600 m² GFA hotel, restaurant & café space; 186 public sector houses

Private house and studio
Rotterdam
project architects: Francine Houben, Erick van Egeraat, Theo Kupers, Bjarne Mastenbroek, Cock Peterse, Inma Fernandez-Puig, Birgit Jürgenhake, Marjolijn Adriaansche
client: private
contractor: Van Omme & de Groot bv, Rotterdam
structural consultant: ABT Adviesbureau voor bouwtechniek bv, Delft
design-completion: 1989–1991
floor area: approx. 300 m² GFA

Public library
Het Baken 3
Almelo
project architects: Henk Döll, Maartje Lammers, Aart Fransen, Jan Bekkering, Joanna Cleary, Renske Groenewoldt, Leen Kooman, Alexandre Lamboley, Anne-Marie van der Meer, Miranda Nieboer, William Richards, Gerrit Schilder jr., Toon de Wilde
client: Stichting Openbare Bibliotheek Almelo
contractor: Aannemersbedrijf Goossen, Almelo
structural consultant: Adviesbureau de Bondt bv, Rijssen
building services consultant: Raadgevend ingenieursbureau Schreuder bv, Apeldoorn
design-completion: 1991–1994
floor area: 4,780 m² GFA

Faculty of Economics and Management, University of Professional Education Utrecht
Padualaan 101
Utrecht
project architects: Francine Houben, Chris de Weijer, Erick van Egeraat, Henk Döll, Monica Adams, Aart Fransen, Marjolijn Adriaansche, Carlo Bevers, Giuseppina Borri, Henk Bouwer, Gerrit Bras, Birgit de Bruin, Ard Buijsen, Katja van Dalen, Annemieke Diekman, Harry Kurzhals, Miranda Nieboer, William Richards, Mechthild Stuhlmacher,

Nathalie de Vries, Wim van Zijl
client: Stichting financiering Exploitatie Huisvesting Uithof, Utrecht
contractor: Hollandsche Beton Maatschappij bv, Utrecht
structural consultant: ABT Adviesbureau voor Bouwtechniek bv, Delft/Velp
building services consultant: Technical Management bv, Amersfoort
design-completion: 1991–1995
floor area: 23,500 m² GFA

Library Delft Technical University
Prometheusplein 1
Delft
project architects: Francine Houben, Chris de Weijer, Aart Fransen, Carlo Bevers, Erick van Egeraat, Monica Adams, Marjolijn Adriaansche, Henk Bouwer, Gerrit Bras, Ard Buijsen, Katja van Dalen, Annemiek Diekman, Alfa Hügelmann, Axel Koschany, Theo Kupers, Maartje Lammers, Paul Martin Lied, Bas Streppel, Astrid van Vliet
client: ING Vastgoed Ontwikkeling bv, The Hague
contractor: Van Oorschot Versloot Bouw bv; Boele van Eesteren V.O.F., Rotterdam
structural consultant: ABT adviesbureau voor bouwtechniek bv, Delft/Velp
building services consultant: Ketel raadgevende ingenieurs bv, Delft
building physics consultant: Peutz Associes bv, Molenhoek
design-completion: 1993–1997
floor area: approx. 15,600 m² GFA

Entrance National Heritage Museum
Schelmseweg 89
Arnhem
project architects: Francine Houben, Aart Fransen, Michel Tombal, Chris de Weijer, Alfa Hügelmann, Joke Klumper, Pascal Tetteroo, Patrick Eichhorn, Rick Splinter, Michael Dax, Saskia Hebert, Theo Kupers
client: Nederlands Openluchtmuseum, Arnhem; Rijksgebouwendienst Directie-oost, Arnhem
contractor: Strukton Bouwprojekten bv, Maarssen
structural consultant: Goudstikker-de Vries/ACN bv, Capelle a/d IJssel
building services consultant: Technical Management bv, Amersfoort
design-completion: 1995–2000
floor area: 3,185 m² GFA

St Mary of the Angels Chapel
Nieuwe Crooswijkseweg 123
Rotterdam
project architects: Francine Houben, Francesco Veenstra, Ana Rocha, Huib de Jong, Martin Stoop, Natascha Arala Chaves, Judith Egberink, Henk Bouwer
client: R.K. begraafplaats

St. Laurentius, Rotterdam
contractor: H&B Bouw bv, Sassenheim
structural consultant: ABT adviesbureau voor bouwtechniek bv, Delft
design-completion: 1998–2001
floor area: 120 m² GFA

MVRDV

Porters' Lodges Hoge Veluwe National Park
Otterloo, Hoenderloo, Arnhem/Rijzenburg
project architects: MVRDV: Winy Maas, Jacob van Rijs and Nathalie de Vries with Joost Glissenaar, Elaine Didyk, Jaap van Dijk
client: Stichting Nationaal Park De Hoge Veluwe
contractor: Wolfswinkel bv, Hoenderloo
structural consultant: ABT, Velp
building physics consultant: DGMR, Arnhem
design-completion: 1994–1996
floor area: 3 x 30 m² net

WoZoCo
Ookmeerweg
Amsterdam-Osdorp
project architects: MVRDV: Winy Maas, Jacob van Rijs and Nathalie de Vries with Willem Timmer, Arjan Mulder, Frans de Witte
client: Woningbouwvereniging Het Oosten, Amsterdam
contractor: Intervam, Regio West
structural consultant: Pieters Bouwtechniek, Haarlem/Delft
building physics consultant: DGMR, Arnhem
architectural engineering: Bureau Bouwkunde, Rotterdam
design-completion: 1994–1997
floor area: 7,500 m² net

Villa VPRO
Media Park
Sumatralaan 45
Hilversum
project architects: MVRDV: Winy Maas, Jacob van Rijs and Nathalie de Vries with Stefan Witteman, Alex Brouwer, Joost Glissenaar, Arjan Mulder, Eline Strijkers, Willem Timmer, Jaap van Dijk, Fokke Moerel, Joost Kok
client: VPRO, Hilversum
contractor: Voormolen Bouw bv, Rotterdam
structural consultant: Pieters Bouwtechniek, Haarlem; Ove Arup & Partners, London
building services consultant: Ketel Raadgevende ingenieurs, Delftand and OAP, London
building physics consultant: DGMR, Arnhem
architectural engineering: Bureau Bouwkunde, Rotterdam
design-completion: 1993–1997
floor area: 10,000 m² GFA

Dutch Pavilion Expo 2000
Expo site –
Europa Boulevard 3
Hanover
Germany
project architects: MVRDV: Winy Maas, Jacob van Rijs and Nathalie de Vries with Stefan Witteman, Jaap van Dijk, Christoph Schindler, Kristina Adsersen, Rüdiger Kreiselmayer
client: Stichting Nederland Wereldtentoonstellingen, The Hague
contractor: HBG Bouw bv, Rijswijk
structural consultant: ABT, Velp
building services consultant: Technical Management, Amersfoort
architectural engineering: ABT Bouwkunde, Velp; Bureau Bouwkunde, Rotterdam
building physics consultant: DGMR, Arnhem
design-completion: 1997–2000
floor area: 8,000 m² GFA

Thonik Studio
Weesperzijde 79
Amsterdam
project architects: MVRDV: Winy Maas, Jacob van Rijs and Nathalie de Vries with Bart Spee and Eline Strijkers
client: Studio Thonik, graphic designers
contractor: Konstand Van Polen bouwbedrijf
structural consultant: Pieters Bouwtechniek, Haarlem/Delft
building physics consultant: DGMR, Arnhem
design-completion: 1998–2001
floor area: 290 m² net

Silodam apartment block
Amsterdam
project architects: MVRDV: Winy Maas Jacob van Rijs and Nathalie de Vries with Frans de Witte, Eline Strijkers, Duzan Doepel, Bernd Felsinger; competition entry with Tom Mossel, Joost Glissenaar, Alex Brouwer, Ruby van den Munckhof, Joost Kok
client: Rabo Vastgoed, De Principaal bv
contractor: Bouwcombinatie Graansilo's V.O.F. (Bouwbedrijf M.J. de Nijs en Zonen bv and Kondor Wessels Noord)
structural consultant: Pieters Bouwtechniek, Delft
building physics consultant: Cauberg Huygen, Rotterdam
architectural engineering: Bureau Bouwkunde, Rotterdam
design-completion: 1995–2002
floor area: 19,500 m² GFA

Office for Metropolitan Architecture

Kunsthal
Westzeedijk
Rotterdam
project architects: Rem Koolhaas, Fuminori Hoshino
project team/consultants: Petra Blaisse, Kyoko Ohashi, Hans Werlemann (interior); Gunter Förg (contributing artist: light installation in restaurant)
client: City of Rotterdam
contractor: Dura Bouw, Rotterdam
structural consultant: Cecil Balmond, Ove Arup; City of Rotterdam
completion: 1992
floor area: 7,000 m² GFA

Grand Palais
Bd des Cités Unies 1
Lille
France
project architects: Rem Koolhaas/OMA; co-architect: François Delhay, F.M. Delhay-Caille
client: City of Lille (Pierre Mauroy, mayor); SAEM Euralille (Jean-Paul Baietto, general manager); Association Lille Grand Palais (Jean Delannoy, vice-chairman)
structural consultant: Cecil Balmond/Ove Arup & Partners
completion: 1994
floor area: 45,000 m² GFA, incl. 1,230 parking spaces

Educatorium
De Uithof university campus
Utrecht
project architects: Rem Koolhaas, Christophe Cornubert; preliminary design: Koolhaas, Cornubert, Gary Bates, Luc Veeger, Clement Gillet
project team: Richard Eelman, Michel Melenhorst, Jacques Vink, Gaudi Houdaya, Enno Stemerding, Frans Blok, Henrik Valeur, Boukje Trenning; contributing artists: Joep van Lieshout (Rotterdam), Andreas Gurski (Dusseldorf); technical support: Christian Müller, Eric Schotte
client: Utrecht University, Marianne Gloudi
contractors: BAM Bredero, Bunnik/A.de Jong airconditioning bv, Schiedam; Ergon Electric bv, Utrecht; GTI Rotterdam-Capelle bv, Rotterdam; Lichtindustrie Wolter & Drost-Evli bv, Veenendaal
structural consultant: ABT Adviesbureau voor Bouwtechniek bv; Rob Nijsse, Frans van Herwijnen, Velp-Delft; Robert-Jan van Santen, Lille (façades); Ingenieursburo Linssen, Henk Knipscheer, Amsterdam (services engineer)
building services consultant: FBU, Utrecht; W/E adviseurs

duurzaam bouwen, Gouda (ecology); TNO-TUE, Rens van Luxemburg, Eindhoven (acoustics); Curve, Hellevoet-sluis (projection box)
budget: Berenschot Osborne bv, Utrecht
design-completion: 1993–1997
floor area: 11,000 m² GFA

Dutch embassy
Kloosterstraße/Roland Ufer
Berlin-Mitte
Germany
project architects: Rem Koolhaas, Erik Schotte, Gro Bonesmo
client: Dutch Ministry of Foreign Affairs
consultants: De Weger Architecten en Ingenieurs; Huygen Elwako Raadgevende Ingenieurs bv (building services); Ove Arup & Partners Berlin
design-completion: 1999–2001
cubic content: total 25,340 m³ (embassy, car park, living areas)

Maison à Bordeaux
Bordeaux
France
project architects: Rem Koolhaas with Maarten van Severen
project team: Julien Monfort, Jeanne Gang, Bill Price, Jeroen Thomas, Yo Yamagata, Chris Dondorp, Erik Schotte, Vincent Costes; Maarten van Severen, Raf de Preter (built-in furniture and moveable platform); Petra Blaisse (interior consultant); Vincent de Rijk (bookcase)
client: private
structural consultant: Ove Arup & Partners: Cecil Balmond, Robert Pugh; Michel Régaud, Bordeaux (coordination and technical assistance); Robert-Jan van Santen (façade consultant); Gerard Couillandeau (hydraulics)
completion: 1998
floor area: 600 m² net (house and guesthouse)

Casa da Música
Rotunda da Boavista
Porto
Portugal
project architects/team: Rem Koolhaas, Fernando Romero, Isabel da Silva, Barbara Wolff, Matthias Hollwich, Uwe Herlyn, Adam Kurdahl, Moritz von Voss, Shohei Shigematsu, Jens Hommert, Erik Schotte, Donald van Dansik
client: Porto 2001
consultants: Ove Arup + Partners, Cecil Balmond, Rory McGowan, Patrick Teuffel (structural); TNO – TUE Centre for Building Research, J. van Luxemburg, M. Hak, M. Prinsen (acoustics)
design-completion: 1999–2003
floor area: 23,000 m² GFA; 28,000 m² parking spaces; 7,500 m² plaza

Prof. Ir. Hans Ruijssenaars – de architectengroep

Public Library
Vosselmanstraat
Apeldoorn
project architect: Hans Ruijssenaars
client: Stichting Gemeenschappelijk Openbare bibliotheek
contractor: Ufkes aannemingsmaatschappij bv
structural consultant: Raadgevend Ingenieursbureau Witteveen & Bos
design-completion: 1980–1984
floor area: 7,160 m² GFA

ATO laboratory
Bornsesteeg 59
Wageningen
project architect: Hans Ruijssenaars
client: Ministry of Agriculture, Nature Management and Fisheries
contractor: IBC Bouwgroep bv, Best
structural consultant: Adviesbureau Heijkman, Huissen
design-completion: 1990–1993
floor area: 11,486 m² GFA

Town hall
Markt 1
Apeldoorn
project architect: Hans Ruijssenaars
client: City of Apeldoorn
contractor: Bouwcombinatie van den Belt IGB, Twello
structural consultant: ABT, Arnhem
building services consultant: Adviesburo Treffers & Partners
building physics consultant: Peutz & Associes
design-completion: 1998–1992
floor area: 32,600 m² GFA

Stadserf: Town hall, theatre, library and archives
Stadserf
Schiedam
project architect: Hans Ruijssenaars
client: Dienst Gemeentewerken, Schiedam
contractor: Abouw BBm
structural consultant: ABT Adviesburo voor Bouwtechniek, Velp
building services consultant: Adviesbureau Treffers & Partners
building physics consultant: Adviesbureau Peutz & Associes
design-completion: 1991–1997
floor area: 22,500 m² GFA

Apartment and retail complex
Kerkbrink
Hilversum
project architect: Hans Ruijssenaars
client: Wilma Vastgoed
contractor: Muwi, Amersfoort
structural consultant: Constructie & Adviesbureau Steens
building services consultant: Ingenieursbureau Linssen

building physics consultant: Adviesburo Peutz & Associes
design-completion: 1993–1998
floor area: 8,400 m² retail space; 47 apartments

Apartment and retail complex
Kerkbrink
Hilversum
project architect: Hans Ruijssenaars
client: Wilma Vastgoed bv
contractor: Dura Bouw bv
structural consultant: D3BN
building services consultant: Ingenieursbureau Linssen
design-completion: 1994–1998
floor area: total 19,500 m² GFA; 3,930 m² retail, 28 houses, 410 parking spaces

Public library and art library
Stadshart
Amstelveen
project architect: Hans Ruijssenaars
client: Stadshart Amstelveen Ontwikkelingsmij.
contractor: Bouwbedrijf M.J. de Nijs & Smit's Bouwbedrijf
structural consultant: D3BN
building services consultant: Lingestreek bv, Gorinchem
design-completion: 1993–2001
floor area: 6,500 m² GFA

UN Studio

REMU electricity substation
Smalle Pad
Amersfoort
project architect: Ben van Berkel, UN Studio
project team: Harrie Pappot (project coordinator), Pieter Koster, Hugo Beschoor Plug, Jaap Punt, Rik van Dolderen
client: Regionale Energie Maatschappij Utrecht (REMU), Utrecht
technical consultant: Hollandsche Beton Maatschappij, Rijswijk
design-completion: 1989–1993

Bascule bridge and bridgemaster's house
Purmerend
project architects: Ben van Berkel, Freek Loos (project coordinator), Ger Gijzen
client: City of Purmerend
consultants: Ingenieursbureau Amsterdam
design-completion: 1995–1998
floor area: 36 m² GFA; bridgemaster's house approx. 12 m high

Möbius House
Het Gooi
project team: Ben van Berkel, Aad Krom, Jen Alkema, Matthias Blass, Caroline Bos, Remco Bruggink, Marc Dijkman, Casper le Fèvre, Rob Hootsmans, Tycho Soffree, Giovanni Tedesco, Harm Wassink
interior design: Ben van Berkel, Jen Alkema, Matthias Blass
client: private
contractor: Kemmeren Bouw, Aalsmeer
technical consultants: ABT,

Velp; Heijckmann Bouwadviesbureau, Huissen
design-completion: 1993–1998

Museum Het Valkhof
Kelfkensbos
Nijmegen
project team: Ben van Berkel (architect), Henri SnelandRob Hootsmans (coordination), Remco Bruggink (interieur), Hugo Beschoor Plug, Walther Kloet, Marc Dijkman, Jacco van Wengerden, Luc Veeger, Florian Fischer, Carsten Kiselowsky
landscaping: Bureau B&B, Stedebouw en landschapsarchitectuur, Michael van Gessel; City of Nijmegen, town planning department, Mark van Gils
client: Stichting Museum Het Valkhof
contractor: Nelissen van Egteren Bouw Zuid bv, Venray
structural consultant: Adviesbureau voor Bouwtechniek bv, Arnhem
building services consultant: Ketel Raadgevende Ingenieurs, Delft
design-completion: 1995–1998
floor area/volume: approx. 6,100 m² GFA/39,382 m³

Municipal office and theatre
Overtoom
IJsselstein
project team: Ben van Berkel (architect) Harm Wassink (project coordinator), Henri Borduin, Jeroen Steur, Oliver Heckmann, Luc Veeger, Casper Le Fèvre, Marion Regitko, Kiri Heiner, Jacco van Wengerden, Aad Krom, Niek Jan van Dam, Karst Duêrmeyer
landscape architect: Lodewijk Baljon, Amsterdam
client: City of IJsselstein (T.E.M. Wijte); 't Fulco Cultural Centre (E.H.M.F. Caris)
contractor: Aan de Stegge bv, Goor
consultants: Huisman en van Muijen bv., 's-Hertogenbosch; Peutz & Associes bv, Molenhoek; Adviesbureau D3BN, Amsterdam; PKB Bouwadviseurs, Diemen
design-completion: 1996–2000
floor area/volume: 9,066 m² plus 7,000 m² parking/5,500m³ building site: 3,400 m²

NMR laboratory
Leuvenlaan
De Uithof university campus
Utrecht
project team: Ben van Berkel (architect), Harm Wassink and Walther Kloet (project coordinator), Marion Regitko, Jacco van Wengerden, Ludo Grooteman, Laura Negrini, Paul Vriend, Mark Westerhuis, Jeroen Kreijnen, Henri Snel, Marc Prins, Aad Krom
client: Utrecht University
contractor: Nelissen van Egteren, Utrecht and Hoofddorp

structural consultant:
ABT, Velp
design-completion: 1997–2001
floor area: 10,000 m² GFA

Rudy Uytenhaak Architectenbureau bv

Koningin Wilhelminaplein
housing project
Koningin Wilhelminaplein
Amsterdam
project architect: Rudy
Uytenhaak
client: BPF Bouw
contractor: Bouwbedrijf
Teerenstra bv
structural consultant:
Grabowski en Poort
ingenieursbureau
building services consultant:
De Winder
building physics consultant:
Adviesburo Peutz &
Associes bv
design-completion: 1989–1991
floor area: 32,000 m² GFA

Weesperstraat housing
project
Weesperstraat
Amsterdam
project architect: Rudy
Uytenhaak
client: Stichting Onze Woning
contractor: Smit's Bouw-
bedrijf bv
structural consultant:
Heijckmann, adviesbureau
voor bouw constructie
building physics consultant:
M + P raadgevende
ingenieurs bv
design-completion: 1985–1992
floor area: 21,000 m² GFA

House of the Arts
Nieuwstraat 377
Apeldoorn
project architect: Rudy
Uytenhaak
client: City of Apeldoorn
contractor: Koopmans bv,
Aannemingsbedrijf Ribberink
structural consultant:
De Bondt bv, Rijssen
building services consultant:
Adviesburo Peutz &
Associes bv
building physics consultant:
Fuchs Consultants
design-completion: 1991–1995
floor area: 5,548 m² GFA

VROM office building
Kennemerplein
Haarlem
project architect: Rudy
Uytenhaak
client: Nemeog bv, Utrecht
contractor: Van Wijnen West,
Dordrecht
structural consultant:
Heijckmann, adviesbureau
voor bouw constructie
building services consultant:
Sweegers, P. de Bruyn
building physics consultant:
Sweegers, P. de Bruyn
design-completion: 1994–1997
floor area: 8,840 m² GFA

Cascade building,
Eindhoven Technical
University
De Rondom university
campus
Eindhoven
project architects: Rudy
Uytenhaak, Hugo Boogaard
client: Eindhoven Technical
University
contractor: Heijmans Bouw
structural consultant:
Aronsohn Raadgevende
Ingenieurs bv
building services consultant:
Deerns Raadgevende
Ingenieurs bv
building physics consultant:
Nelissen
design-completion: 1997–1999
floor area: 5,660 m² GFA

Tourmaline
Weerwater
Almere
project architects: Rudy
Uytenhaak, Marco Romano
client: Hopman
Projectrealisatie bv
contractor: Bouwbedrijf
M.J. de Nijs & Zn. bv
structural consultant:
Ingenieursgroep
van Rossum bv
building services consultant:
bv adviesbureau
Installatietechniek T & H
building physics consultant:
Santberger Advies &
Ingenieursbureau
design-completion: 1997–2001
floor area: 5,600 m² GFA

Hoop, Liefde en Fortuin
('De Balk')
Oostelijk Havengebied:
Borneolaan/C. van
Eesterenlaan/Rietlandpark
Amsterdam
project architects: Rudy
Uytenhaak, Engbert van der
Zaag
project team: André
Hillebrand, Jos Rijs, Jasper
Molenaar, Charles Hueber,
Martin Dalenberg, Jaap Hikke,
Bas Cuppen, Peter Rutten,
Niek Beran
client: Woningbedrijf
Amsterdam, Bouwfonds
Wonen; Stadsdeel Zeeburg:
health care centre and crèche
client art: Amsterdams Fonds
voor de Kunst
artist: Willem Oorebeek
contractor: ERA Bouw bv;
Oosthoek/Kemper (precast
façade units)
cost consultant: Moerkerken
en Broekzitter bv
structural consultant: Pieters
Bouwtechniek
building services consultant:
Temid Raadgevende Inge-
nieurs BV
structural drawings: Zegelaar
& Partners BV
design-completion:
1996–2002
floor area: 167 owner-occupied
units; 202 rental units –
average UFA 96 m²/unit;
223 parking spaces; crèche:
1,600 m²

Architectenbureau Koen van Velsen bv

Public library
Kerkstraat 2
Zeewolde
project architect: Koen van
Velsen
project team: Gero Rutten,
Okko van der Kam, Toon de
Leeuw
client: IJsselmeerpolders
Development Authority
contractor: Bouwbedrijf
H. Koopmans bv, Apeldoorn
structural consultant: Strackee
bv, Amsterdam
building services consultant:
Treffers en Partners, Baarn
design-completion: 1988–1989
floor area: 1,250 m² GFA

Multi-screen cinema
complex
Schouwburgplein 101
Rotterdam
project architect: Koen van
Velsen
project team: Gero Rutten,
Lars Zwart, Marcel Steeghs,
Okko van der Kam
client: Pathé Cinemas
Amsterdam
contractor: Van Hoorn bv,
Capelle a/d IJssel
structural consultant: D3BN
The Hague
building services consultant:
TM Amersfoort
building physics consultant:
Van Dorsser, The Hague
design-completion: 1994–1996
floor area: 8,463 m² GFA

Town hall
Oostelijk Bolwerk 4
Terneuzen
project architect: Koen van
Velsen
project team: Gideon de Jong,
Lars Zwart, Okko van der Kam,
Marcel Steeghs
client: City of Terneuzen
contractor: Bouwcombinatie
Stenen Beer Terneuzen
structural consultant: Van
Rossum, Almere
building services consultant:
Jonker Engineering Techniek,
IJmuiden
building physics consultant:
LBP, Utrecht
design-completion: 1993–1996
floor area: 6,000 m² net

Dutch Film and Television
Academy
Markenplein 1
Amsterdam
project architect: Koen van
Velsen
project team: Gero Rutten,
Gideon de Jong, Lars Zwart,
Marcel Steeghs, Bureau
Bouwkunde
client: Amsterdam School of
Arts
contractor: Friso Aanne-
mingsmij., Sneek
structural consultant: D3BN
The Hague
building services consultant:
TM Amersfoort
building physics consultant:
LBP, Utrecht

design-completion: 1997–1999
floor area: 8,035 m² GFA

Vos House
Borneo-eiland
Amsterdam
project architect: Koen van
Velsen
project team: Gideon de Jong,
Lars Zwart, Marcel Steeghs
client: B. Vos, Eemnes
contractor: Visser & Mol,
Hoogkarspel
structural consultant: Strackee
bv, Amsterdam
building physics consultant:
LBP, Utrecht
completion: 1999
floor area: 140 m² net

Media Commission Office
(Dutch Media Authority)
Hoge Naarderweg 78
Hilversum
project architect: Koen van
Velsen
project team: Chris Arts,
Gideon de Jong, Gero Rutten,
Marcel Steeghs, Merijn de
Jong, Tom Bergevoet
client: Dutch Media Authority,
Hilversum
contractor: E.A. van den
Hengel bv, Soest
structural consultant: D3BN
The Hague
building services consultant:
Huisman en van Muijen,
's-Hertogenbosch
building services contractor:
Lingestreek bv, Gorinchem
building physics consultant:
LBP, Utrecht
design-completion: 1998–2001
floor area: 3,372 m² GFA

Photo credits

Introduction (pp. 7 to 16)
Chinese characters: # 24,
'body', 'book' (taken from: Van
Berkel & Bos, *Effects; radiant
synthetic*, Amsterdam,
1999, p. 88)
Miller Hare: # 10
Francine Houben/Mecanoo
architects: # 26
Benoit Mandelbrot: # 9
(see for example:
http://alepho.clarku.edu/~djo
yce/julia)
Antonio Martinelli: # 20, 21, 25
Grant Mudford: # 17
Giorgio Pezzato: # 13
Hans Werlemann: # 7, 37, 38

Wiel Arets (pp. 18 to 31)
Prof. Ir. Wiel Arets Architects &
Associates bv, renderings,
photo: # 1, 24, 25, 26;
project p. 30
Christian Richters:
project p. 28
Kim Zwarts:
projects pp. 23 to 27, 29

**Benthem Crouwel
(pp. 32 to 45)**
Gert von Bassewitz: # 16
Benthem Crouwel Architekten
BV bna: # 15, 18
Pieter Boersma: # 14
Yukio Futagawa: # 19
Jannes Linders: # 3, 17; projects
pp. 38 to 44

CEPEZED (pp. 46 to 59)
CEPEZED BV, drawings,
renderings: # 5, 6, 33;
project p. 52
Hedrig-Blessing: # 18
Yukio Futagawa: # 9
Fas Keuzekamp: # 1, 2, 4, 16, 17,
31, 32; projects pp. 52 to 59
John Linden: # 10, 11
Franz Schulze: # 14

**Erick van Egeraat
(pp. 60 to 75)**
Erick van Egeraat associated
architects: (logo) # 2;
renderings # 3, 8, 24; projects
pp. 73, 74
Mecanoo architects (logo): # 1
Christian Richters: # 9, 10, 19;
projects pp. 66 to 72
Lebbeus Woods: # 5
(illustration taken from
http://members.tripod.com/~
septimus7/ibea/gall10.html)

**Herman Hertzberger
(pp. 76 to 87)**
Architectuurstudio Herman
Hertzberger: # 20b
Architectuurstudio Herman
Hertzberger: project pp. 86, 87
(previously published in
Tectónica no. 10; 1999/2000)
John Cava (Keith Eayres after
Herman Hertzberger): # 13
Herman van Doorn: projects
pp. 83, 84, 85

Herman Hertzberger:
projects pp. 82, 86
George
Meguerditchian/Centre
George Pompidou: # 12
Le Corbusier: # 21

Mecanoo (pp. 88 to 101)
Francine Houben/Mecanoo
architects: # 9, 10
Christian Richters: projects
pp. 94 to 101

MVRDV (pp. 102 to 115)
Jan Derwig: project pp. 114, 115
Rob 't Hart: project p. 108
Ed Melet: project p. 113
MVRDV, drawings, renderings:
13; 23, 26a, 26b
Rob Nijsse (ABT-Consult),
photos, sketch: # 21, 22, 27
Hans Werlemann: # 4, 20;
projects pp. 109 to 112

OMA (pp. 116 to 129)
Reinhard Friedrich: # 8
Rob Nijsse (ABT-Consult): # 6
OMA, drawings, renderings: #
24 to 27; projects pp. 125, 128
Christian Richters: projects
pp. 122, 124
Hans Werlemann: # 12 to 15,
20 to 23; projects pp. 123, 126,
127

**Hans Ruijssenaars
(pp. 130 to 143)**
Jan Derwig: # 6, 7, 26; projects
pp. 136 to 142
Grant Mudford: # 2
Netherlands Architecture
Institute, Rotterdam: # 1

UN Studio (pp. 144 to 157)
Jan Derwig: # 2 (taken from:
Ben van Berkel, *Crossing
Points*, Berlin 1993)
Christian Richters: # 22, 23;
projects pp. 151 to 156
Kim Zwarts: project p. 150

**Rudy Uytenhaak
(pp. 158 to 171)**
Werner Blaser: # 2
Luuk Kramer: projects pp. 164
to 168; 170
Rudy Uytenhaak
Architectenbureau: # 11, 20, 21,
31; project p. 171

**Koen van Velsen
(pp. 172 to 185)**
Arthur Blonk/Caroline
Koolschijn/arcasa:
project pp. 184, 185
Gerhard Jaeger:
project pp. 178, 179
Christian Richters:
projects pp. 180 to 183

All other photos
accompanying the texts:
Ed Melet

Colophon

The publication of this book was made possible by a contribution from the Netherlands Architecture Fund.

The author thanks Piet Vollaard for his comment and advice.

Translation: Robyn de Jong-Dalziel, Peter Mason
Editing: Els Brinkman, Paula Vaandrager
Design: Arlette Brouwers and Koos van der Meer, Emst
Adaptation of drawings: Rob Reitsma, Dordrecht
PrePress Studio Groenendaal, Nieuwegein
Print and lithography: Die Keure, Bruges, Belgium
Production: Caroline Gautier (NAi Uitgevers)
Gepke Bouma (handel in woorden en daden)
Publisher: Simon Franke

NAi Publishers is an internationally orientated publisher specialized in developing, producing and distributing books on architecture, visual arts and related disciplines.
www.naipublishers.nl info@naipublishers.nl

Available in North, South and Central America through D.A.P./Distributed Art Publishers Inc, 155 Sixth Avenue 2nd Floor, New York, NY 10013-1507, Tel 212 627 1999, Fax 212 627 9484.

Available in the United Kingdom and Ireland through Art Data, 12 Bell Industrial Estate, 50 Cunnington Street, London W4 5HB, Tel 208 747 1061, Fax 208 742 2319.

ISBN 90-5662-185-X
Printed and bound in the Netherlands